A Grand Madness

Also by Dianne Ebertt Beeaff

HOMECOMING
A Book of Poetry

A GRAND MADNESS,
TEN YEARS ON THE ROAD WITH U2

POWER'S GARDEN
A Novel

SPIRIT STONES,
Unravelling the Megalithic Mysteries of
Western Europe's Prehistoric Monuments

ON TRAIGH LAR BEACH
A Short Story Collection

Dianne Ebertt Beeaff

A Grand Madness
U2 Twenty Years After

Hawkmoon Publications
Tucson, Arizona

A Grand Madness
U2 Twenty Years After
Copyright ©2019 by Dianne Ebertt Beeaff

Hawkmoon Publications
7502 E. Calle Cabo
Tucson, Arizona
USA 85750
Grimspound@aol.com

All photographs by Dianne Ebertt Beeaff unless otherwise noted.

Front cover photos: Bono (Debbi Voisey); The Edge (Sue Fell); Adam (John Harris); Larry Mullen Jr. (Dianne Beeaff)
Back cover photo: Design Photography, Tucson, Arizona, USA

Cover Concept: Jane Hobson Bouflale and Sharon Nicks
Cover Design: Kris Taft-Miller
Interior Design: Sharon Nicks, Types, Tucson, Arizona USA

The quote from Margaret Silf's *Sacred Spaces, Stations on a Celtic Way* (2014) on page 111 is reproduced with permission from Lion Hudson plc through PLSclear.

ISBN: 978-09656188-7-8
Library of Congress Control Number: 2018915097
ISBN: 978-0-9656188-9-2 (ebook)
Printed in the United States of America

FOR DAN

Table of Contents

Acknowledgements

My sincere thanks to all those who in some way assisted in the production of this book. First and foremost to my husband, Dan, for his unwavering love and encouragement. To Sharon Harton for expert editorial assistance. To Sharon Nicks of *Types* for interior design. To Sharon Nicks and Jane Hobson Bouflale for cover concept. To Kris Taft-Miller for cover design. To Sue Fell, Sharon Harton, John Harris, Michelle Perez, and Debbi Voisey for photographs. To Declan Cormack for website research. To all of the above for their valued friendship. And to U2's ardent and devoted fan base.

Last, but certainly not least, my enduring gratitude to Adam, Larry, Bono, and Edge for their splendid music, their empowering vision, and their matchless class.

A Grand Madness
U2 Twenty Years After

PREFACE

"If you've opened this book, you're a U2 fan. Or maybe you're just curious." With these words I began my memoir, *A Grand Madness, Ten Years on the Road with U2*, first published in 2000. That preface stands true today.

A Grand Madness covered thirty-eight concerts in twenty cities over ten years, from January of 1987 through September of 1998, and followed the band's *Joshua Tree*, *Zoo*, and *Popmart* tours.

With only five concerts, including the opening show in Phoenix and the band's two legendary December 1987 performances at Sun Devil Stadium in Tempe, Arizona, my *Joshua Tree* experiences opened my heart, mind, and soul to U2's vision, impressive back catalog, philosophy, and musicianship.

With *Zoo TV*, I considered both *Achtung Baby*, the toured album, and what became known as *The Berlin Bootlegs*—U2's stolen rehearsal tapes. I attended the tour opener in Lakeland, Florida, and first met Bono in Charlotte, North Carolina. I presented him with a copy of Native American Joy Harjo's book of poetry, *In Mad Love and War*, at Arizona State University's Activity Center in Tempe, and got taken by scalpers in Atlanta, Georgia.

The *Zoo Tour's Outside Broadcast* took me to America's West Coast for pre-US-election stadium shows that included Larry's Halloween birthday in Los Angeles, and Bono and Larry at the Mirage in Las Vegas.

Zooropa, the album, coincided with the European *Zoo Tour* concerts and featured surreal moments from the war in Bosnia, the Dadist theatre troupe MacNas, Salman Rushdie and Roger Daltry in London, Edge's birthday in Glasgow, and Naomi Campbell strutting her stuff for Adam at the RDS in Dublin. A creepily distraught MacPhisto rang up Princess Diana, the Archbishop of Canterbury, Margaret Thatcher, and the United Nations. Also notable from those days—the implausible Mr. Pussy's Café Deluxe in Dublin City, with Bono and his entourage in the "Royal Box", and, in 1995, *A Conversation with Bono*, part of the *Swansea Festival of Literature and Writing* in Wales.

The *Popmart Tour* became identified with "diehard" fans. On a road trip with three friends, we caught the Las Vegas opener and subsequent concerts in San Diego, Salt Lake City, and Phoenix. Old World concerts in London, Leeds, and Dublin followed, the last incorporating the tragic death of Princess Diana. Tampa, Miami, and Jacksonville, Florida, rounded out my *Popmart* experiences.

And then, in the fall of 1998, by great good fortune I caught the making of U2's The Sweetest Thing video on the streets of Dublin, and Bono, Adam, Larry, and Edge each signed my journal outside their Hanover Quay studio. "I'll catch you later," Bono said, before rushing off to catch a plane. "Yes," I thought then, "I will."

And I have.

The dictionary defines "fan" as "an enthusiastic follower or admirer," the more pejorative "fanatic" being "excessively enthusiastic." Over the years I've been both. With now ninety-one concerts in thirty-three cities over thirty years, how could it be otherwise?

This *Grand Madness* follow-up, as recorded in my journals, advances my U2 story from that fortuitous Hanover Quay meeting. I look at *The Elevation Tour, The Vertigo Tour, The 360 Tour, The iNNOCENCE + eXPERIENCE Tour* (*The i/e Tour* Part 1), *The Joshua Tree 2017 Tour*, and *The eXPERIENCE + iNNOCENCE Tour* (*The i/e Tour* Part 2).

This account reflects one individual's experience. If you're not a U2 fan, this book will give you insight into and some appreciation and understanding of a fan's mind-set. But if you *are* a fan, especially a U2 fan, you'll know exactly what I mean.

The preface to *A Grand Madness, Ten Years on the Road with U2* closed with a Charlotte Joko Beck quote from her excellent book, *Nothing Special* (HarperOne, 1993). In discussing our responses to emotional events, "It's wise," Joko Beck says, "to wait until the mud clears."

For me the mud has cleared again, and I'd like to tell you what else I've seen. "In order to live right up to the end, one has to travel right up to the end." And what a long, strange trip it's been.

Some of you out there are no doubt shaking your heads and muttering "enough already." Fair enough. Here's the place then, where, if you've opened this book, you close it again and move on. But if you're game, let's head off together for more *Grand Madness*.

1.

The Elevation Tour

"Live easy, live calm and the storm cannot hurt you."
– Eurypides

Monday, October 12, 1998

I've been back home from Dublin for over two weeks already. An extraordinary adventure, from Mary and Declan's quintessential Irish wedding to the filming of U2's The Sweetest Thing video in Fitzwilliam Square. Last week, I finally saw the end result, which was much the same as we'd witnessed last month.

Visibly upset—Bono having forgotten her birthday—Ali climbs into a buggy mounted on a flat-bed truck. Bono follows and off they go. He offers her the Artane Boys Band, Irish step-dancers, male strippers gyrating on a fire engine, the other three U2 band members, Boyzone, and Rani, the poor stressed-out elephant. In the end, Bono just mouths "I'm sorry." I do like the added strings on this new version. The release is rumored to precede a November *Best of U2* album, and Ali has been given all rights to the song.

Monday, October 19, 1998

A new U2 album to be out in July of next year.

Friday, October 23, 1998

I'm outside for lunch on a perfect, calm, and quiet day. The sky, filled with lazy black-bottomed clouds, has intermittent patches of blue. It even rained a bit yesterday. Last night, I watched a bootleg of the first Dublin *Popmart* show, our little group all lined up at the barrier.

Tuesday, October 27, 1998

Spent some time with another U2 video this afternoon.

Santiago, Chile. So emotional. One of the best shows I've ever seen and I wasn't even there. I would have preferred this one as an official release to the Mexico City one. The Abuelas (Grandmothers) filed onstage for One, carrying placards of their missing grandchildren. Bono recited all of their names. [The Grandmothers of Plaza de Mayo, a human rights group, believe four to five-hundred children were stolen at birth from women who had been kidnapped and murdered as part of Argentina's recent military dictatorship.]

Wednesday, October 28, 1998

The band will be giving an interview in conjunction with their *Best of U2* album due out next week. They'll pick and choose from questions emailed in yesterday and then call selected fans. The interview will air November 10.

Friday, October 29, 1998

Last night, we saw Eugene O'Neill's *Long Day's Journey Into Night* at the ATC [the Arizona Theatre Company]. Edmund quotes from Baudelaire. "Be drunk," he says. "Be drunk with wine, with poetry, or with virtue. But be drunk." Only a select and fortunate few of us have the talent, capacity, and genius to live like that. I suspect Bono is one of them. Perhaps so, too, Leonard Bernstein. When he was about ten years old, he put one finger on a piano key and knew he had "touched the hand of God."

Wednesday, November 4, 1998

Picked up the *Best of U2* album this morning.

Sunday, December 6, 1998

A gorgeous winter day. Snow has blanketed the front range. Black clouds sweep across, trailing snow behind them in long black veils.

The website *Interference.com* posted a *Late Late Show* where U2 performed All I Want Is You as a tribute to Omagh [Omagh, County Tyrone, Northern Ireland. On August 15, 1998, terrorists—the Real Irish Republican Army—detonated a car bomb in the town center, killing twenty-nine people—fourteen women (one pregnant with twins), nine children, and six men]. They opened with a stunning North and South of the River, the lyrics of which focus on conflict, always too prevalent in the world. As if to demonstrate this, the Israeli Knesset just voted against the removal of the words "holy" and "martyr" from the grave of a Jewish man shot after murdering twenty-seven Muslim worshippers.

Sunday, January 18, 1999

Sue and Jane had another fab sojourn in Dublin. Only there two days and they still managed to see the entire band. All but Adam stopped for a chat. Larry—uncharacteristically—signed autographs and even asked Sue if she wanted a photo, a generosity she strongly felt had been prompted by a remark by Bono about Larry's new-found Christmas spirit. I'm still hoping my new book, *A Grand Madness, Ten Years on the Road with U2*, will be printed by May and I'll have a chance to give each of them a copy—whether they want one or not!

Tuesday, February 2, 1999

Desmond Tutu passed on a powerful notion to Bono in the Ngunu Bantu word "ubuntu," which means "I am, because we are."

Earlier today, I picked up a Las Vegas ramp shot for *A Grand Madness*—Bono in his Mirror Ball Man suit. Danielle [my daughter] said he looked like a baked potato.

Then this afternoon I went out to have a publicity shot taken for the new book's back cover. What an attractive woman I was, the photographer gushed. Well, of course! Who's going to tell a paying customer—"My God, you look like hell. I don't think there's anything I can do!"

Sunday, March 7, 1999

Desperately short of rain. Not a single African daisy has blossomed yet, though aloe vera and honeysuckle are wildly in bloom.

Just watched a *Rattle and Hum* outtake tape this morning. An outstanding Stand By Me duet with Bruce Springsteen and Bono, who will be inducting Springsteen into the *Rock and Roll Hall of Fame* next week.

Tuesday, March 16, 1999

A chilly winter's night. A storm rolled through from California yesterday, dropping buckets of rain after nearly four months of drought.

I'll sort four photo galleries for *A Grand Madness* while we're in New Orleans, so the book may be ready by May after all. I leave for Dublin on May 29.

Friday, March 19, 1999

Here we are in Nawlins! Just had a wander through the French Quarter. Bourbon Street still has its strip joints and peep shows, but they're a little less blatant than they used to be. Lots of Cajun music and great blues in town. I love the floor-to-ceiling doors and shutters, all thrown wide open, music streaming out.

Bono inducted Bruce Springsteen into the *Rock and Roll Hall of Fame* Wednesday night. Sporting a new look—the slicked-back black hair and Elvis Costello glasses of Dublin's The Sweetest Thing video shoot last year—Bono sang a rather rough line from Curtis Mayfield's People Get Ready. We've heard he underwent a throat operation a few months back.

Sunday, March 21, 1999

Rounded the corner to Decatur Street, New Orleans, this morning and picked up the fleeting strains of I Still Haven't Found What I'm Looking For. So I loitered outside a camera shop studying engraved cigarette lighters until it finished.

Thursday, April 1, 1999

Yesterday, on a gorgeous desert spring day, subtle perfumes of primrose, pyracantha, and aloe in the air, I picked up tickets for my UK and Ireland flights.

It's been raining all day, soft and gentle, the mountains obscured—pale-blue reflections from an overcast evening sky. Winter's crispness slides in with each opening of the patio door for fireplace wood.

The Kosovo situation continues to decline. After the Bosnian fiasco, the Serbs overran a large section of the country, and then Albanians moved into the province and demanded independence. En masse, the Serbs began slaughtering them. Entire families were crammed into their homes and burned alive! Countless throats slashed. Russia has ordered warships into the Gulf.

Monday, April 5, 1999

Today's Gemini horoscope in the newspaper reads, "Puzzle pieces fall into place. Everything is being prepared for your grand entrance. Maintain emotional equilibrium. Sprinkle anecdotes with humor. Taurus, Leo, Scorpio figure in the scenario." I don't anticipate any grand entrance, but Bono is a Taurus, Edge is a Leo, and Larry is a Scorpio. They may each have *A Grand Madness* in May after all.

Thursday, April 22, 1999

U2 sent over a taped performance of Don't Take Your Guns to Town for the *Johnny Cash Tribute Concert* in New York City. A bit too prissy-sounding for my taste.

Tuesday, May 25, 1999

In the latest issue of *Rolling Stone*, Edge claims that the band is back in the studio working on a new album stripped down—in the manner of their 1980s style—to guitar, drums, and vocals. Quite hopeful.

Sunday, May 30, 1999

8:00 p.m. Dublin time. I've been up for twenty-nine hours now. My Heathrow-Dublin flight was an hour late due to an electrical shut-down of the entire airport. For Y2K (Year Two-Thousand) testing, I'm guessing.

On the drive out to Dun Laoghaire, we swung by the U2 studio on Hanover Quay. Directly across from the studio entrance, a concrete bench—put there, we presume, by the resident concrete company—has been cemented to the side-walk. How thoughtful.

Ice-cream at Tommy's and then down to Dalkey Harbour,

where we discovered that the Dalkey Island Hotel has been razed! Killiney Beach and then supper in the Library Grill at the Court Hotel.

Monday, May 31, 1999

We're sitting at Dalkey Harbour on a peaceful but chilly day. As we lunched in Dalkey's Laurel Tree earlier, a silver Mercedes slipped down the hill, Edge at the wheel. Round about four, George, Principle Management gateman, accepted a copy of *A Grand Madness*. Said he'd light a candle for its success. Bless him!

Thursday, June 3, 1999

Gerry at Principle Management took a copy of *A Grand Madness* to pass on to Paul McGuiness. Gerry had a late night with Bono on Tuesday, he said. They'd escorted eight or so children to an All Saints show. As a consequence, no one would be in today. Paul was off to London in the morning; Bono to France and on to New York City.

Saturday, June 5, 1999

Sitting in London, awaiting my 11:00 a.m. flight from Heathrow. Yesterday, I called U2's Principle Management offices. The receptionist, Alexis, told me to stop by after two and she would deliver four *A Grand Madness* copies to Larry's sister, Cecilia, who would pass them on to the band. The office was as cluttered as I remembered from a brief stop back in '93. Alexis, professional and distantly friendly, took the books as promised.

On a gloriously sunny day then, we set off for Powerscourt. As the great house had caught fire recently, entry was prohibited. But the gardens were dazzling, a vast expanse of velvety green lawn, rolling hillocks, bubbling fountains, and lofty canopied beech trees, their roots spread out like knotted feet. We drifted past bronze and marble statues a short while before heading out on the N11 for Avoca, the tiny County Wicklow village where the BBC's *Balleykissangel* is filmed.

Almost immediately, the day turned profoundly Irish, high-piled clouds sweeping in with a spray of rain and clearing to a ragged blue sky. At one point, a double rainbow curved up from out of the sea, one pale arc floating above a vivid lower one. Two full spectrums of glittering pastel light spanning the sky.

Here in Chicago now at nearly 7:00 pm. We've pulled away from the gate. While I have time, I'll get back to Avoca.

On the drive out, deep green forests alternated with emerald fields, roadways lined with butter-yellow broom hedges. Rain-dampened trees shone in the sunlight with ivy pouring off old stone walls, blazing pink/purple azaleas glowing from darkened forests. There were wide expanses of wild yellow irises, and farm carts selling strawberries.

For a brief half-hour outside Avoca's parish church—the very one from the series—blackbirds sang the sun down. In the dark wooded Vale of Avoca, we came across *The Meeting of the Waters*. Brown and brimming, the Avonmore (Abhainn Mhor "Big River") and the Avonbeg (Abhainn Bheag "Small River"), merge here. In a soft fleeting Irish rain, the air heavy with the scent of rich dark earth, wet stone, and peat fires, we read from a carved sign in the small public park there, a portion of the poem Irish poet and singer-songwriter, Thomas Moore, set to an old Irish air back in the early 19th century. I've put the whole of it here:

The Vale of Avoca

There is not in the wide world a valley so sweet
As that vale in whose bosom the bright waters meet
Oh the last rays of feeling and life must depart
Ere the bloom of that valley shall fade from my heart
Ere the bloom of that valley shall fade from my heart

Yet it was not that nature had shed o'er the scene
Her purest of crystal and brightest of green
'Twas not her soft magic of streamlet or hill
Oh no 'twas something more exquisite still

Oh no 'twas something more exquisite still

'Twas that friends, the belov'd of my bosom were near
Who made every scene of enchantment more dear
And who felt how the best charms of nature improve
When we see them reflected from looks that we love
When we see them reflected from looks that we love

Sweet vale of Avoca! How calm could I rest
In thy bosom of shade, with the friends I love best
Where the storms that we feel in this cold world should cease
And our hearts, like thy waters, be mingled in peace
And our hearts, like thy waters, be mingled in peace.

Coin offerings sprinkled the bottom of the inner shore where the two rivers met. Gifts of metal to a Celtic water spirit. Naturally, I added my own.

Speeding back into town, we once again, coincidently, caught Edge's silver Mercedes whipping by in the opposite direction, no doubt coming from Bono's in Killiney, where they'd been tirelessly comparing *A Grand Madness* notes!

After supper at nearly ten o'clock in The Court Hotel. We stopped once more on the beach in Killiney. The sea stood on the horizon sharp as a razor's edge. Houth, to the north, glittered with the amber of night lights. At quarter to eleven, the clouds broke over Dalkey Island and pale mauve-blue skies reflected on the luminous water with the radiant fluorescence of ultraviolet.

Our take-off from Dublin had the clearest views I've ever seen aloft. Green, green Irish fields above a bright turquoise sea, smooth as glass and shadowed with clouds. Boats carved long white arcs through the water, and widening river estuaries wore away the shoreline.

Friday, June 11, 1999

Just read in the Toronto *Globe and Mail* that Bono's *Jubilee*

2000 project is well underway. The Bible speaks of the fiftieth year of a reign as a Jubilee year, a time of "forgiveness and the freeing of slaves." The objective of *Jubilee 2000* is the cancellation of debt for the world's poorest nations. A worthy goal. But then what will keep the most corrupt of those countries from further exploiting their people once their debt has been lifted?

Sunday, July 11, 1999

Stuart Clark from *Hot Press* in Dublin rang up last Friday. He's prepping a radio show on music fans for *2 FM Radio* and wanted to talk with me as part of the show. He emailed later to congratulate me on the book. Called it "fresh and novel," and said "We thoroughly enjoyed it." The program airs live at ten o'clock tomorrow morning in Dublin. That's 2:00 a.m. here!

Tuesday, July 13, 1999

The *Hot Press* event went very well. I managed to remain calm, collected, and relatively articulate. It was actually rather fun.

Wednesday, September 9, 1999

A newsgroup post quotes Bono as saying the next album could be their last! I suppose that's true of any album, but it's never been voiced so pointedly before. He does seem to be more of a conforming "believer" these days. Yet no matter how rich and famous you are, you can only do so much—with or without any belief or faith. A vast chasm lies between the two, I think. "Belief is holding to a rock; faith is learning how to swim . . . . Faith is an openness and trusting attitude to truth and reality, whatever it may turn out to be. Belief is . . .a compulsive clinging to the idea that the universe is arranged and governed in such and such a way." [Alan Watts, *The Relevance of Oriental Philosophy, Philosophies of Asia Series* at *Alanwatts.com*]

As far as the Bible goes, I've found only the occasional fleeting glimmer of poetry, reason, and tolerance. Much of *Ecclesiastes*, for example, is quite poetic. Portions of the *Psalms* and the *Songs of Solomon*. Job, says, quite lyrically, "My root is spread out to the waters and the dew lieth all night upon my branch." A favorite passage from the King James Version, brought on by Moses' 'alchemy' on Mt. Sinai, reads, "And Mt. Sinai was altogether on a smoke."

Wednesday, September 16, 1999

With sighs of relief reverberating around the world, Bono has clarified his remarks about the new album. The band is working, he said, *as though* the new album could be their last.

Sue and Jane will fly to Dublin for the *MTV Europe Awards* on November 11.

Friday, October 15, 1999

We're on a flight to Chicago out of Glasgow after a second glorious stay at St. Clement's Croft in Rodel (Isle of Harris, Outer Hebrides, Scotland). In *Discovering Lewis and Harris* [James Shaw Grant, John Donald Publishers, Edinburgh, 1987], I came across this peerless description of a Hebridean beach: "One doesn't go . . . for a 'day at the beach.' One goes to see, to hear . . . and to feel the beauty and the power of the Western Ocean."

USA Today has U2's new album dropping the middle of next year. "Back to basics," songs on "the joy of being in a band." "Titanium soul," Bono says. Whatever that means.

Saturday, November 13, 1999

The band's next album will be out "late summer," a tour next fall.

Thursday, December 30, 1999

The *Freedom of the City Awards* will be given to U2 and company in Dublin on March 19. I've been toying with going over March 17 through the twenty-second, though I'd have only one day at home after flying in from San Francisco.

Friday, December 31, 1999

New Zealand and Australia passed through to the year 2000 without incident. No Y2K computer glitches at all. Experts have all been sent home. With building hopefulness, Dan and I watched the celebrations as they moved around the world. Maybe humankind can improve on the millennia we've left behind.

Monday, January 10, 2000

Library Journal reviewed *A Grand Madness* with a "recommended"! They receive over thirty-thousand books a year and only review about four-thousand.

Tuesday, February 8, 2000

Yesterday, Dave Fanning interviewed Bono on *2FM* Dublin. The new album is set to wrap up in May. Bono claims it's the one they've "always wanted to make," a "band's album." If you "like this band, you'll like the album." A lot of innovative groups around— Oasis, Radiohead—were "the boys," Bono said. U2 were "the men." Heartening, after the "artiste" feel of *The Million Dollar Hotel* (2000) and supermodel fashion-spreads.

Monday, February 14, 2000

Allied with *Jubilee 2000* efforts, Bono met with the Pope, who, eyeing his Fly shades with deep curiosity, tried them on. Cameras exploded. No photo will ever see the light of day, I'm sure. But what a great t-shirt that would make.

Tuesday, February 29, 2000

The "Freedom thing" opens 5:00 p.m. March 18.

Wednesday, March 1, 2000

Declan has snagged us each a *Freedom* ceremony ticket!

Monday, March 6, 2000

A wintry darkness with a hard and steady rain most of the day, a silvery light now over fresh snow on the front-range (Santa Catalina Mountains, Tucson, Arizona). The staccato of rain taps rhythmically on the sun-room roof.

I've finished an inspiring piece in the journal *Spirituality and Health* in which Maya Angelou talks about spiritual adventure. "Did it disturb your soul?" she asks.

Friday, March 10, 2000

One week and I'm off to Dublin again. We ate lunch today at Boudin's just up the road on Market Street in San Francisco. A yummy shrimp sandwich with hot chocolate for me, and Dan's beef stew in a bowl made of sourdough bread. Boudin's starter—the yeast and bacteria mix used to leaven the bread—dates to 1849. A smidgen is set aside before each baking to be used as the starter for the next batch.

I love this city, though at times it slips into artsy-fartsy, bucking the line between creativity and highfalutin' schmaltz. There's *Cosmic Cabaret*, for instance—an ex go-go girl sings physics lyrics in a nightclub; and *Music is the Game*—"an exploration of the rhythmic and sonic relationship between music and basketball."

Thursday, March 16, 2000

I'm outside on a mid-afternoon tea break. Firmly spring now. Limey green leaves budding everywhere, primrose and jasmine in bloom. The peach tree and the rock-garden aloe have infused the air with perfume.

I've unpacked from San Francisco, repacked for Dublin. I'll be collected for the airport at noon tomorrow. I also picked up the *Million Dollar Hotel* soundtrack. The film has not yet found a US distributor. The Ground Beneath Her Feet is exquisite, as is a gentle remake of For the First Time. And I do like Falling at Your Feet. But on balance, this compilation has a pinch too much Eno-esque avant-garde jazziness for my U2 taste.

Sunday, March 19, 2000

Just past noon. I'm "home alone" in Dublin, still a bit jet-lagged. Crashed last night about midnight, well after the *Freedom of the City* ceremony closed. I'd been up thirty-two hours by then. Landed at 11:30 yesterday morning, met Julie, and together we set off for the Ferryman on Sir John Rogerson's Quay, where we met up with others of our group. About three o'clock, Declan guided us over to the Smithfield area where we found parking beneath three glorious flowering fruit trees and walked over to the venue.

Smithfield Civic Plaza is on the site of the old Smithfield Market, which dates back to the 1600s, though the cobblestone pavement is only about a hundred years old. Each block had been removed, scoured, and reset with the restoration. A construction crane supported a video screen left of the stage. Whether this was intentional or more of an Irish thing, I can't say. Along one side of the open space ran a line of mast-like pillars, each spire topped with a gas flame. Two white metal 'sails' jutted out mid-way on each, so that, from a distance and bent as they were, they marched away like squared phases of the moon.

The *Freedom of the City* ceremony opened a venue surrounded by retail space, restaurants, and hotels. One of the latter, in the converted brewery of St. James, boasts an outdoor elevator in the old brewery's chimney, which leads up to an observation deck. Altogether, an impressive complex.

We stood in line at the proper entrance off King Street. When barriers came down, we managed standing positions second row from the front. Ahead of us, invited guests sat in chairs arranged between the front rail and the stage. I felt a tad bit of relief when spasms of entertainment would alternate with an assortment of on-screen videos. Standing had become a trifle prickly, and any movement dragged me back from the brink of collapse.

The first act, Juliet Turner, a young woman in her early twenties "from the North," sang some folksy bits accompanied by acoustic guitar. A fairly good group called Bill X1 followed, the singer's voice comparable to Radiohead's Thom Yorke. And then—with truncated flicks between—up came Dara, a male/female duet featuring top-notch violin and cello.

Last, Ronnie Drew, a lofty fellow in a pale suit and massive Colonel Sanders beard, played traditional Irish tunes. His next to last offering was Brendan Behan's The Auld Triangle, known to me primarily from the sixties Canadian duo, Ian and Sylvia (Tyson).

Shortly after Drew finished up, snippets of U2 videos began to scroll on-screen. Toward the end of these, a raucous cheer erupted from the crowd. The band had materialized on the upper balcony of the adjacent hotel. In good time after that, the Dublin City Council, along with the Lord Mayor, Mary Freehill, filed onstage in black and green robes and took their seats. U2 followed, behind a mace bearer and a sword bearer.

The Lord Mayor's speech was not particularly audible and some people laughed. Others shouted for her to get off the stage, which seemed anathema to the evening's purpose. Who would have thought, she asked at one point, that given their humble beginnings, U2 would have ended up where they were tonight. Onstage, Bono grinned and shrugged. Tonight, Ms. Freehill sportingly added, everyone was a Dubliner.

Each *Freedom* recipient stepped up in turn then to sign an "honor list." The first award went to Burmese dissident Aung San Suu Kyi, still imprisoned in Myanmar (formerly Burma). In her place, her son, Kim, on crutches, collected her prize—a dove made of Waterford crystal—and gave a short acceptance speech.

On receiving their own awards, each U2 band member, along with Paul McGuinness, was called on for some personal remarks. The trophy itself—a Joshua Tree in Waterford Crystal on Irish bog-oak—was quite striking.

Paul sat stiffly in his chair, arms folded across his suited chest. Serious stuff. "This is a great gift from a great city," he said at the podium, and thanked his wife, Kathy, and their children, Max and Alexandra. Dublin was exceptional, he said. Simultaneously a small town and the vibrant capital city at the heart of a great nation.

Ever the English gentleman, Adam's invocation, thanking family and friends, was next, brief and heart-felt. "To call Dublin home is a very special thing indeed," he said. And how grateful he was for the speed at which Dublin had dispelled the feeling he had of being a "blow-in."

Larry opened with a Gaelic shout-out he said his father yearned to hear from him on playing Croke Park. At one point, in a speech filled with spirit and good humor, he got himself completely turned around, alleging that U2 had given more to Dublin than vice-versa. But we all knew what he meant. He thanked his sister, Cecilia, for being "the believer," and honored his mother and a second sister, both of whom "couldn't be here." (Larry's mother died when he was about fifteen and he'd also lost a sister to leukemia, I think.) "This is even better than the real thing," he said, albeit dismayed that the *Freedom* award did not entitle him to drive in bus lanes or waive parking tickets. "I want to thank Adam, Edge, and Bono for being in my band."

Edge impressively included his ex-wife, Aisling, in his remarks, along with his children, his lover, Morleigh Steinberg, and his parents, Garvin and Gwenda. He "could have been living in Birmingham," Edge said. In 1962, Garvin, an airline captain, had been asked to relocate from Wales to either Dublin or Birmingham. "I thank them for what was ultimately a great call."

Bono's contribution was lengthier—surprise, surprise— delivered in a stream-of-consciousness style. He thanked a slew of people, including his brother Norman, Ali and the kids, and fellow Irish musicians Phil Lynott of Thin Lizzy, Bob Geldoff and the Boomtown Rats, and the Dubliners. He blew kisses to his family and proclaimed that the band did not really belong to any one community. Being a 'foreigner' in Dublin, this was singularly nice to hear. Among the freedoms they'd been granted, Bono said, was the right to graze sheep on St. Stephen's Green. He and Edge intended to exercise that privilege the very next day. How proud he was to have his father in the audience, he said, and how his mother would have loved to have been there.

Dublin was a city of "free thinkers, free drinkers . . . freedom to take off the blinkers." He liked that line so well that he repeated it, more slowly. "If there is one thing this city treasures above any other, it is freedom. Freedom to make noise, freedom to make a lot of noise, freedom to make your point, to say what you want to say, freedom to be a pain in the ass . . . freedom to criticize, the kind of freedom Aung San Suu Kyi has been denied. Freedom not to fit in, freedom to be uncool, freedom to be a one-off, freedom to believe in God when it's hard to imagine God believing in you, freedom not to believe, freedom spiritually, freedom sexually, freedom politically."

Even while Bono still spoke, Edge had left the stage. When

Bono added that they would "do a few tunes," Edge returned, guitar in hand, and they gave us a short acoustic set—With or Without You, Desire, and The Sweetest Thing, the last for Bono's mother, Iris—and One for John Hume, David Trimble, Gerry Adams, and Big Ian (Paisley) in hopes of getting the Irish peace accord on track again. "Our future as an island is in their hands."

In the end, everyone took a final bow and left to prolonged applause, appearing once again on the balcony of the adjacent hotel, Adam glad-handing the next-door neighbors.

Such a celebratory evening. I felt honored to be there, in a sprinkle of rain, under a misted and nearly full moon.

3:00 p.m. We're down at Dalkey Harbour. Sadly, they're raising condominiums where the old Dalkey Island Hotel once stood. Blackbirds are singing everywhere. We've just come from lunch at the poshly renovated Club Lounge, where, a few scant years ago, we plotted the cover of *A Grand Madness*.

6:30 p.m. Back at our B&B. We'll soon set off to meet the others for dinner at Dun Loaghaire's La Strada. After Dalkey, we strolled Killiney Beach. Barely a ripple stirred the silver surface of the bay. Butter-yellow gorse bloomed on Killiney Hill, with dripping red forsythia and wild daffodils everywhere.

11:00 p.m. We numbered ten at dinner. We ate at a long table by the front window. Lots of laughs and plenty of good food. In the course of conversation, someone mentioned Barry White. When I couldn't quite place the name, Barry was described to me as a "massive black man" with a thunderous voice. As if on cue, from the depths of the restaurant, a rumble of words rolled in from some fellow diner. We'd found our very own Barry, and from then on, each and every time this poor man's low, inarticulate growl emanated from the back room, we all fell to pieces. He may even have caught on, and, in the end we felt a sizzle of guilt, though not enough to stop.

Monday, March 20, 2000

1:00 p.m. We're outside the studio on Hanover Quay. Bono

has just gone in, having signed my copy of *A Grand Madness*!

We'd only just arrived when a sleek black Mercedes met us nose-to-nose. Jane was primed to toss the driver some unkind gesture when the fellow waved and we realized it was Bono. He drove past and stopped to chat with a couple of fans on the other side of the driveway. He waved then, still sitting in the car, so I sauntered over, leaned into the open passenger-side window, and said I would be honored if he would accept a copy of my book, which was a fan's-eye-view of the band.

"I'll just go in the garage," he said. "But I'll be right back out." True to his word, he reappeared a short time later. I repeated my "honor" speech and handed him a book, which he thumbed through. Really liked the pictures, he said. So often such photographs were "just crap." You could "join up all the dots."

I was just a "normal" fan, I chimed in. So the book embodied a "normal" fan's perspective. "As normal as a fan gets," Jane added and we all laughed.

Two foreign fans drifted over and after Bono had signed for them, he took up the book again and began a drawing on the title page, an up-dated self-portrait in a cowboy hat. His deep blue eyes were screened by thick black-armed eye-glasses that sported a dragon at each hinge, adorned with small red, green, and white stones, some of which were missing. Deep lines etched his pale, grizzled face and his shoe-black hair was spiked and punky. Over a dark t-shirt and pants, he wore a black leather coat spotted with animal poop. Sheep shit, we surmised, from that Sunday grazing on St. Stephen's Green.

Bono made special mention of the cheeky shot in the book that Sue had snapped at a meeting at the Marriott in Swansea, Wales back in 1995, when he had spoken at the Swansea Theatre. "You're allowed to grow a beard twice in a lifetime," he said with a smile. The pictures were "great," he added, and leaned toward me. "I'm sure the writing's no good at all." He laughed and said he'd leave the book inside for the others to see.

"Where are your sheep?" Jane asked then. "Is it roast lamb

tonight then?"

"Have you seen the headlines today?" Bono answered. "It's Ewe Two."

Someone brought up *The Million Dollar Hotel*. "The end is stunning," Bono said. "The beginning is good. But the middle's—a little long." He guessed that the film would probably see a US distributor by September.

Was a new tour likely? In the spring? It was. "Arenas," Bono said. "The last tour turned out to be a bit rusty at first," and they didn't want to rush things this time around.

As he continued to embellish each item put before him with relevant sketches, Jane suggested that he "must have missed his way," by which she meant his calling. When he left, I thanked him again for accepting a book—"even if you only look at the pictures."

On a recent TV broadcast, Bono and Edge had disclosed the specific quality each of them envied in the other. Bono spoke of Edge's patience. But he'd clearly shown us a great deal of his own.

Adam arrived about three-thirty and, with a short wave, went into the studio. Shortly after that, Edge drove up, stepped inside too, but came out again almost at once. Would he mind taking a copy of my book? I asked. After my "long-time-fan, fan's-point-of-view, taken-from-my-journals" intro, I told him that the book had been great fun to write. "Of course I had such a great subject to work with."

Wednesday, March 22, 2000

Finally, we're off on a twelve-hour flight—Dublin to LA—and on home to Tucson. Tomorrow, I'll be back in New York City! As we sail the Atlantic, I'll finish up yesterday's Hanover Quay events.

We'd only just arrived at the studio when Edge pulled into the garage. Shortly thereafter Bono drove up in his sharp, shiny black Mercedes. He sat there talking on his cell-phone for ages. Probably misplaced his garage door opener, Jane said, and was calling to be rescued. He wore the same outfit as Monday's, minus the sheep-shit jacket. As we'd had such a fine chat with him that day, we stood well out of the way as Declan leaned in and had his *Freedom* program signed. And then we all waved Bono off into the garage.

Next, in a small, chunky, green Mercedes, Adam pulled in from the opposite direction from which Bono had come. A bit grizzled, face lined, his chestnut hair clipped short, his eyes sparkling, he carried a Prada man-bag—as per Sue and Jane. Handsome and gentlemanly as ever, and clearly at ease, he wore a green-stone heart-shaped ring and a Claddagh on his fingers.

"How are you, Jane?" he asked, stepping out of the car.

"Fine," she answered. "You're looking well. You're not out grazing your sheep?"

Adam seemed puzzled by this reference. (He grazes a flock of sheep on his own estate.) No great advantage had come with "the *Freedom* thing," he confessed.

Smithfield had been a bit bizarre, Jane said. And Adam agreed.

In time, I pulled out The Book and asked Adam if he would kindly accept a copy. He was browsing through some of the photos when he suddenly asked, "Where are your children?" I was so taken aback by the question that I hardly knew what to say. (How did he know I had children? What was he implying? That I should be at home looking after them?)

"Oh, they're grown up," I answered. (Why do you ask? And what exactly do you mean by asking?)

"Yes, but where *are* your children?" Adam said again. On his third attempt, he explained that he'd read the foreword—by which he meant the dedication—and I was totally chuffed. (Bono had said he'd leave a copy in the green room for the others to see, and he apparently had.) My son, Dustin, was in Missouri working on his Master's degree in Materials Engineering, I said. And Danielle worked with disabled children in Tucson. We then talked a very short time about the difficulties of getting published, and Declan asked if a Slane Castle concert was in the works.

"You never know," Adam answered.

"Bono's been raving about the new album," Jane added. "Have

you been working hard?"

All the bass parts were finished, Adam said. He so wanted to get the whole thing wrapped up. But it was his favorite album so far.

What made it so, compared with the others? I asked.

Until the final mixing was done, it was hard to say, Adam explained. But it felt "very comfortable." Everyone was doing what they did best, rather than trying to do what others did best.

Close to 3:00 p.m. Larry drove up, waved once, went into the studio, and stayed there. Shortly afterwards, Sammy, [Larry's drum tech, Sam O'Sullivan, a skinny, red-headed fellow who almost always has a bemused half-smile on his face] came out and offered to take whatever we wanted signed inside. I gave him two books, a copy for Larry and my own for his autograph. Off Sammy went. In short order, he was back again. Larry, bless him, had signed everything.

Friday, March 24, 2000

1:20 p.m. We're sitting in Central Park [New York City] on a warm and sunny spring day. Trees stand bare but for one or two willows off across Heckscher Field. We've just come from lunch at the Carnegie Deli. Their famous pastrami on rye, with sauerkraut and dill pickles.

Gobs of people in the park today. Nearby, a group of elderly men are immersed in a game of bocce, tossing off small silver balls, rather like lawn bowling. A young fellow and his son are playing baseball behind us. The father bats, the boy catches. Their geriatric black-and-white cocker spaniel stands poised mid-field, stubby tail spinning like a propeller, tongue dripping. Completely ignored by his people, he's having the time of his life.

At Strawberry Fields now. Inside the John Lennon *Imagine* mosaic, edged in cut flowers for the Spring Equinox, snapshots and hand-written notes are scattered about, a Strawberry Fields Forever lyric sheet with a Lennon photo inscribed "Shine on 2000 Welcome Spring."

Let me finish up the Dublin trip while we laze about here in the sunshine.

Tuesday evening, we drove out of town for a meal at Declan and Mary's in County Kildare. Declan shared a *TFI Friday* [Channel 4, Dublin program hosted by Chris Evans] episode in which U2 perform an appealing acoustic rendition of The Ground Beneath Her Feet.

There followed one of the strangest and most fateful incidents I've ever experienced. We returned to Dun Laoghaire from Declan's, breezing past the studio on Hanover Quay just after midnight. Further on in town, as we idled at a stop light, a lustrous black Mercedes pulled up behind us. The light changed and as we set off again, this vehicle shot out to pass, tearing off into the distance. "There's a fellow in a big hurry," I said. Probably Bono trying to get away from us.

We braked for a second red light, and the black car, now directly ahead, crept forward, stopped, crept forward, stopped and—finally—we made out Bono's spiky-haired silhouette in the driver's seat. He reached up to adjust the rear-view mirror and waved. Of course, we all waved back. The light changed, and we set off again. At that point in town where two roads diverge—one to Dun Laoghaire, one to Killiney—Bono honked once, waved again, and sped off into the night toward Killiney. And we veered left to Dun Laoghaire and the sea.

An incredible coincidence! A minute here, a minute there—leaving Declan's, sailing past Hanover, flying down to Dun Laoghaire—and we'd have missed each other altogether. In the middle of Dublin City, after midnight, barely a soul in sight. A perfect ending to our Dublin stay. "Of all the gin joints, in all the towns, in all the world . . . ."

Saturday, April 29, 2000

U2 will support a protest over the creation of a landfill around *The Joshua Tree National Forest* in California. Eric Burden of the '60s band The Animals, who lives nearby in Palm Springs, is organizing a benefit concert.

Picked up some nice *Freedom* ceremony prints this morning.

Thursday, June 8, 2000

One of the U2 fan websites reports that the new album will be delayed a couple more months. Bono has extended his vacation in the south of France. He's no doubt stretched out on some glistening Mediterranean beach finishing up *A Grand Madness*!

Tuesday, June 20, 2000

Edge has told the Irish journalist Kevin Byrne that the album is about two months from completion. With production and marketing, this shifts the release date into October or November.

Wednesday, June 28, 2000

E-mail from Bono! At last!

Actually, a letter in his name went out to all the fanzines and on-line U2 sites suggesting that subscribers contact the members of the G7 [Finance Ministers from France, Germany, Italy, Japan, the United Kingdom, the United States, and Canada] ahead of their September 1 meeting in Prague on Third World debt. I did and received instant auto-responses from both Clinton and Blair. Hopefully someone is at least counting these emails.

Sunday, July 9, 2000

U2's new album will be released on October 31, Larry's birthday.

Monday, July 17, 2000

U2's new website is up and running.

Wednesday, August 9, 2000

Nearly 4:00 p.m. I have The Fables playing in my room as I unpack from Newfoundland. We had killer whales off Quirpon Island and humpbacks in Witless Bay, in addition to the L'Anse aux Meadows *Viking 2000* celebration.

Finally had a listen to about ten seconds of the new U2 single, Beautiful Day, on *U2.com*. Love it! Brings to mind the Berlin Bootlegs [stolen outtakes from *Achtung Baby*].

Wednesday, August 16, 2000

Just watched part of the *Democratic National Convention* at the

Staples Center in Los Angeles. Feeling energized by everything the Clinton administration has accomplished. A rousing Pride In the Name of Love was played at one point.

Saturday, August 19, 2000

Spirituality and Health ran a great piece by Rabbi Lawrence Kushner illustrating the spiritual malaise in the country these days. "There's a very compelling metaphor I heard first from Jacob Needleman. He says that there is a mountain and the mountain is very high, and the top of the mountain is being with God. But because the mountain is so high, its base is so big that it is in several different climate zones. And people have different traditions for how to climb the mountain. People in the tropical climate have a tradition that says wear short pants and a pith helmet and mosquito netting. And people in arctic climates have a tradition that says you wear a snow parka and goggles and boots. When the people in the tropical climates get about half-way up the mountain, it gets a little chilly and they have to go back for a sweater, and when the people from the arctic climates get about half-way up, it's getting a little bit warmer, and they shed their outer layer of clothing. When they get to the top, of course, everybody's dressed the same way. 'The problem,' says Needleman, 'is when people walk around the base of the mountain and argue about how to dress.'"

Friday, August 25, 2000

The new U2 album is called *All That You Can't Leave Behind.* Here's a track listing: Beautiful Day, Elevation, Walk On, Stuck in a Moment (That You Can't Get Out Of), Peace on Earth, Kite, New York, In a Little While, Wild Honey, When I Look at the World, Grace.

Dropped a note to *U2One.Com.* They're compiling suggestions for U2's new website, *U2.com.* How about posting tour schedules ASAP, so us working stiffs have time to make plans?

Wednesday, August 30, 2000

Downloaded an MP3 of the new U2 single, Beautiful Day. I *love* it! Eyes wide open to reality and yet still expressing a joyful spirit, the music as fine as the lyrics.

Friday, September 8, 2000

Watched a *VH1* live audience special with Larry and Bono, where Beautiful Day, the new single, was premiered. "Nice to meet the people we're going to be playing to" face-to-face, Bono said. "Real people, not computers all the time . . . ." Fans "there for the music."

Monday, September 11, 2000

Checking into Dublin flights. I may be off overseas later in the fall after all.

This snippet from Bono's *Jubilee*-days diary. He'd spent a day with President Clinton. Really liked him, though he usually "doesn't hang around people that tall."

Tuesday, September 12, 2000

Marsha found a cheap flight to Dublin in late October. I take that as a sign. She had a more expensive option on-screen and it disappeared even as we talked. Twenty-four hours to confirm. I'll have a long, deep think. Leaves Tucson at 7:45 a.m., arriving in Dublin at five-twenty the next morning. Still, cheap is good.

Wednesday, September 13, 2000

Sue and Jane arrive in Dublin on Saturday, October 28. We'll be up late on Sunday, so I'll crash that first day.

Sunday, September 17, 2000

It's a beautiful day! Bright blue skies and a balmy breeze rustling in the trees. Just came across this excellent Marcel Proust quote: "The real voyage of discovery consists not in seeking new landscapes, but in having new eyes." A great vibe for the new U2 album.

Tuesday, October 4, 2000

A roaring black thunderstorm plowed through town yesterday during the Presidential debate. I'm not sure people fully realize the dark days ahead if Bush defeats Gore.

Pre-sales have put *All That You Can't Leave Behind* at number seven on Amazon and it hasn't even been released yet. *NBC* has been given permission to use Beautiful Day for their Olympics coverage, provided they donate the fee to the *Special Olympics*. The band also lent the rights to I Still Haven't Found What I'm Looking For to a newspaper sold by the homeless in South Africa.

Lots of band activity in the UK and Ireland these days. Not much over here, though Bono was on *NBC Nightly News* yesterday talking briefly about *Jubilee 2000*.

Wednesday, October 11, 2000

A phone-in on-line event announced today. Fans could register for tickets to a U2 mini concert in Los Angeles limited to four-hundred people.

Wednesday, October 18, 2000

U2 performances in Belgium and Paris, tickets limited to four-hundred for each venue, drawn randomly from email submissions. Belgium is tomorrow night.

Thursday, October 19, 2000

We've entered an eleven-year high for sun storms, with massive amounts of negative ions hurled into space, disrupting communications. With the growing unrest in the Mid-east, my upcoming Irish junket comes at a rather inauspicious time.

The band played their promo concert in Paris today. Elevation, New York, Beautiful Day, Better Than the Real Thing, Stuck in a Moment, Mysterious Ways, All I Want is You, The Ground Beneath her Feet, and—BAD! Having heard about this for so long, I felt like I'd kept a lengthy and celebratory secret, and now everyone was partying without me!

Wednesday, October 25, 2000

The band will drop the new album in Ireland on October 27. They play *MTV*'s *Total Request Live* and then appear at Tower Records in New York City on October 30 and 31, with *CNN* and *USA Network* specials to follow Sunday and Monday. So while we'd hoped to catch the album release in Dublin, it'll be a done deal long before we get there.

Friday, October 27, 2000

Ready for Ireland but for sun-spots, terrorists, and fierce autumnal storms.

Yesterday morning, the lads gave a breakfast concert in LA for about fifty fans. They play *The Farm Club* tonight and then, after *MTV* and Tower Records, there's a London interview, which at least settles them on the continent next week.

Monday, October 30, 2000

We're off to Powerscourt Gardens [County Wicklow, Ireland] on a bright blue fall day, trees on the far side of change. Blue/grey clouds straggle by overhead at Sandymount, where the wind blows the crests off the waves. As we carry on, I'll get caught up.

The alarm failed Saturday morning and, at 7:00 a.m., Dan and I scrambled for the airport, hoping to make a 7:45 flight. He left me off at the curb, where I was further delayed by a baggage search. But with nothing to check, I careened into the appropriate gate with ten minutes to spare.

We flew Tucson to Dallas/Fort Worth and then on to JFK, where we idled an extra hour in order to account for the time change yesterday. Otherwise, we'd have arrived in Dublin at five-twenty the next morning, well before customs opened.

We'd coasted over Manhattan, the rectangle of Central Park below, the twin towers of the World Trade Center at a near distance. Out to sea for a U-turn before landing. The Atlantic flight to Dublin was a shaky one. The plane erupted in applause when we finally touched down.

3:30 p.m. On our return from Powerscourt. Massive gold-leafed beech trees—pale-gray trunks eight to ten feet in circumference—bordered the long drive to the great house and gardens. Views over the grounds swept deep into lush valleys and outward toward the Wicklow Mountains.

On my second listen to *All That You Can't Leave Behind*, I must say that I love it. Each band member does what they do best, just as Adam said, and, to me, the focus falls on living and searching for a life of "serenity without indifference." The Singer, having contracted with the best backing band imaginable, directs his attention to structure, lyrics, and delivery. Like *Pop*, *ATYCLB* draws from an array of styles—though in this case, they're all from U2's own past.

Tuesday, October 31, 2000

11:00 p.m. A blue-sky day filled with lumbering clouds and rainbow fragments, followed by cold and rain borne on a wintry wind. Touched base with Sharon in York this evening. She's decided to pop over for the tour opener in Miami.

Thursday, November 2, 2000

Bonfires on the beach for Halloween, and yesterday morning we saw a Dalkey van with a cardboard skeleton propped up in the passenger seat.

A bleary day with pearly-grey sky and lots of wind, the sea a marbled slate-grey. In Tucson, a rainy day is a great gift. Here, in seasonal darkness, it's just a dirty day.

Last night we ate supper at the Laurel Tree—a watery cream of broccoli soup with a salmon fillet in butter-cream sauce—and went down afterwards for a drink at the Queen's Hotel. Round about ten-thirty, beaten back by the noise level, we opted for another album run-through back at the flat.

As we made our way to the car, Jane spied a sleek black Rover flung haphazardly into the parking spot opposite ours. Beside this Dalkey car park, the Church of the Assumption looms, and, appropriately enough, we launched into some intense speculation as to who might be driving such a vehicle. Was Bono in the Queens pulling up his chair to a late dinner? Was the stocky bodyguard-type hovering in the doorway on the payroll of some A-list celebrity with whom he was dining? Wasn't Salman Rushdie in town?

We laugh now, but we sat there for some time, waiting patiently for whoever might own that black Rover to step up and claim it.

"Where the hell have you been?" we'd demand. "Do you have any idea how long we've been waiting here?"

We very shortly regained our senses and drove home.

Saturday, November 4, 2000

3:25 p.m. I'm in JFK, sitting at Gate 16 awaiting flight 105 to Dallas/Fort Worth.

U2 performed Elevation on *Top of the Pops* [*BBC* music TV program broadcasted from 1964 to 2006] last night, leagues ahead of any other performer, most of them Spice Girls clones all seemingly singing the same song.

My taxi ride to the Dublin airport featured an intriguing roadside sign that read: "Ears pierced while you wait."

Friday, November 10, 2000

I hope to have an *All That You Can't Leave Behind* review done by the end of the year. There's just so much to say about this album. Concert tickets go on sale either December 9 or December 16. Dan and I will be in Montreal then, but hopefully *Propaganda* [U2's official fanzine]will have member tickets available before that.

Tuesday's election is still on hold. Florida had a re-count, and Bush is only ahead by seventeen-hundred votes, an astonishingly low number. At least a hundred-million people voted. A law-suit involving illegal ballots in one Florida county has also cropped up.

Sunday, November 12, 2000

Bass Magazine printed an interview with Adam, now posted on Prarit's [Prarit Bhargava] U2 site [*Zoonation*]. One of the positive aspects of U2's success, he says, is their fan-base.

"We have great fans," Adam says. "They follow us through all sorts of changes, and in many ways encourage us to continue pursuing music that excites us."

Wednesday, November 15, 2000

The election is still unsettled. A re-count in West Palm Beach County, Florida, has the difference at three-hundred votes instead of seventeen-hundred. Understandably, Al Gore has asked for a manual re-count. He already won the popular vote by a quarter of a million people. The Bushies claim Gore only wants this re-count because he thinks he'll win. Well—duh! They're trying to stop the re-count. They'd have no objection if they weren't so afraid of losing.

The attorney general of Florida declined to grant a time extension for the re-count. But she was overridden today. She was a co-chair for the Bush campaign, so objectivity is not her strong suit. When a hundred-million votes are cast, with a difference of only three-hundred, ALL votes must be counted. They're waiting for absentee-ballots anyway.

Monday, November 20, 2000

U2 ticket sales have been moved into January. Sharon will be over for ten days, so we should manage at least three shows.

Tuesday, November 28, 2000

Someone asked Bono on a recent call-in radio interview if he considered himself a romantic. He likes romance, he said. But "it's important to flirt without going any further." Then someone else asked if he believed in love at first sight and he said yes. He'd fallen in love with Ali "at first sight . . . and last." How romantic!

Wednesday, November 29, 2000

Dan and I have finalized plans for a meeting in Washington in early March. We're home again by the seventh, the U2 tour to kick off on March 25. No definitive schedule as yet, but rumor has Charlotte and Atlanta after the Miami opening.

Thursday, November 30, 2000

I'm outside on a tea-break on a pleasant fall day. Leaves have dropped from the peach tree, and the pomegranate stands in brilliant yellow against a creamy-blue sky, high clouds inching in from the west.

I've been working up a review of the new U2 album *All That You Can't Leave Behind* (*ATYCLB*). There's "something magical about it," Bono has said of the album. "That's what we want from music. Magic."

Ditto for we fans.

Friday, December 1, 2000

U2 played a smashing version of Beautiful Day on the *My VH1 Awards* last night.

Meri, Lyn, Kim, and I have decided to try for a *Zoo Crew* reunion concert in Boston next year. [*The Zoo Crew* was the name of our *Zoo TV* road trip in 1992.] Wrapped up an *All That You Can't Leave Behind* review this morning, which will age while we're in Montreal.

Thursday, December 7, 2000

The presidential election is still being contested. The Florida Supreme Court will determine if the Miami/Dade/Brower County votes should be re-counted. In a previous Florida Court of Appeals trial, it was discovered that the Bush witness who invented the voting machine at issue had taken out a patent for a new machine. His was too unreliable, he said. Only a hand-count could be accurate. Yet the judge ruled against a re-count, hence Gore's appeal to the Florida Supreme Court.

Two Florida counties received applications for absentee ballots without proper ID numbers. Republican Party officials instructed the Republican supervisor to put ID numbers on Republican requests and send them back. Other applications were to be voided! If the Florida Supreme Court hasn't decided the case by December 11, the Florida Republican legislature said it would send up its own electors to the Electoral College. An "insurance policy," they said, so that even if Gore wins the election, Bush will still be president!

Friday, December 8, 2000

Today ballot-application judges ruled there were procedural problems, but the "sanctity of the ballots and the integrity of the election were not compromised." The woman who permitted ID numbers to be put only on Republican applications, voiding the rest, claims she thought she was just helping people to vote. No one can be that stupid.

The Florida Supreme Court has now called for a full re-count of under-votes in Florida.

Saturday, December 9, 2000

The full Florida re-count began today—in a state run by Bush's brother, Jeb. The U.S. Supreme Court granted Bush an injunction to stop the count until his appeal can be heard. This re-count "will cause irreparable damage" to his chances to be president, Bush argued. Well, no kidding!

U2 tickets on sale January 9.

Sunday, December 10, 2000

In the back yard, mid-afternoon, under a low blanket of clouds.

U2 played *Saturday Night Live* last night, Bono's voice a little raspy. He closed Beautiful Day with a snippet of All You Need is Love and made forays into the audience for an energetic Elevation, tacking on a snatch of We All Shine On for John Lennon. Instead of an ever-present cigarette dangling from his lips, Adam was chewing gum.

Tomorrow, the last election arguments will be heard at the Supreme Court. Sadly, I'm convinced that the fix is in, and they will decide against Gore. Republicans have been striving to rule America by stacking the courts and taking over legislatures for decades.

Monday, December 11, 2000

What credibility will the U.S. have to lecture the world about clean elections and the merits of democracy if we refuse to count the votes of all citizens, fearing "irreparable damage" to one's party's chances of holding the presidency? Such "irregularities"—bus loads of Republican voters allowed to vote after the polls closed; roadblocks in minority districts; students denied their franchise—these are the same things we expect international observers to monitor in other countries.

Tuesday, December 12, 2000

Sixteen inches of snow, and more expected in the Midwest. Highways shut down and airports closed.

The Supreme Court concluded their deliberations about 8:30 p.m. and gave the presidency to Bush! No surprise there. But to rub salt in the wound, they said the Florida Supreme Court erred in allowing a re-count without any specific criteria. The issue could go back to the Florida court, but it had to be fixed by today, leaving two whole hours for a re-count to be completed. Yes indeed, all votes *should* be counted. But . . . oops . . . we don't have time!

Thursday, December 14, 2000

A high of eighteen, low of seven [Fahrenheit] in Montreal!

U2 tickets on sale January 13; tour schedule out on the ninth.

Saturday, December 23, 2000

A calm day of blue skies and wispy clouds.

Rumblings about *Propaganda* releasing a "small number" of tickets to *U2.com* subscribers. Stuck in a Moment will be the second single in Europe, Walk On in the States. A new component has posted to *U2.com*. *The Oracle* answers queries about the band, one broaching Bono's driving. "Through the walls we hear the city groan," came *The Oracle's* response.

President Clinton visited Ireland recently to help jump-start Irish peace talks. "It's cold and dark," he said. "But I'm in Ireland again, and, as U2 say, 'It's a Beautiful Day.'"

Someone on Prarit's site described ending up in the U2 entourage room on *Saturday Night Live*. Irish accents swirled everywhere. All band members but one were there, and Val Kilmer drifted around completely ignored. Bono had stepped out for better cell-phone reception and hadn't yet returned. Someone—I think Steve Iredale—asked anyone and everyone if they'd seen him. He was "kind of short, wearing sunglasses," Steve said.

Tuesday, January 2, 2001

I've the *ATYCLB* [*All That You Can't Leave Behind*] album review done and sent off to Sue for *Eirinn*. It goes like this:

ALL THAT YOU CAN'T LEAVE BEHIND

*"The real voyage of discovery consists not in
seeking new landscapes, but in having new eyes."*
— Marcel Proust

OFTEN THE MOST profound experiences come from opening yourself to simply living life without looking anywhere but directly in front of you. In a sense, this is the essence of *All*

That You Can't Leave Behind. U2's official website has described the album as "four travelers caught with their baggage midway through their journey." *ATYCLB* is U2 midway through their creative lives, recorded in the present moment, with all that they can't leave behind. Where *Pop* pulled together current contemporary musical trends and gave them a layered and electronic, though thoroughly U2, rendering, *ATYCLB* recaptures the essential elements of U2's music, the very qualities and spirit that set them apart in the first place.

Bono's lyrics, multi-colored and yet full of shade and shadow, contain some of his best writing. Still passionate and powerful, his voice is deeper, richer, and more compelling than ever. Edge's lyrical guitar soars with minimal accents, and Larry and Adam lay down the perfect rock-solid foundation. A "comfortable" record in which nearly every tune builds to a soaring chorus, each band member doing what he does best, *ATYCLB* flows as naturally as sunlight, making it easy to slip inside each song. This is classic "big rock" U2 cut back to basics. They still haven't found what their looking for, but they're getting closer. "A song that I can sing in my own company;" a little peace of mind; some serenity without indifference.

"To be somebody you must last," the actress Ruth Gordon has said. And to last requires change—the freshness, courage, and inventive spirit so familiar in all of U2's work. This is the U2 album many of us have been waiting for.

BEAUTIFUL DAY's drum machine links it to U2's immediate past, while Edge's guitar brings back his trademark "watery bells" sound. Adam's bass supports this uplifting tune about noticing the rose in the vase as well as the dust on the table. Our pristine world in green and blue, as seen from space, is the same one teeming with strident and overabundant life. Rapacious oil fields are indistinguishable from sheltering Bedouin fires. Beautiful Day is classic U2—realism laced with hope and softened by grace. Without darkness there are no dreams.

STUCK IN A MOMENT – "A pop ditty about suicide" in

Bono's words, Stuck in a Moment—inspired by the death of INXS' Michael Hutchence—is my current favorite track. Quiet and soulful, with a splendid chorus and a simple but powerful keyboard foundation, Stuck in a Moment sounds like a hymn. Those who work among the downtrodden, the displaced, and the disillusioned—including lost souls like Michael Hutchence, who want what they haven't got even when they have everything—understand that "you don't want to kill yourself; you want to kill the moment." This is one of those moments. But "it's just a moment. This time will pass."

ELEVATION rises above all those Stuck in a Moment blues, Edge's fierce guitar leading the way. Brash and confident, Elevation struts in, pumps up the volume and the energy, and then, with a wild buzz and grind, struts out again. A clear concert opener, Elevation throws in a funky bit of rap, a sweet echo-y Mofo-styled suspended interim, and fabulous overlapping rhythms.

WALK ON, a profoundly hopeful and inspiring tune about personal courage and genuine heroism—specifically for Myanmar dissident Aung San Suu Kyi, but easily for anyone stuck in a moment—brings back more of Edge's minimally lyrical guitar. Opening with Bono's simple spoken words and followed by very early U2 sounds from Edge, Walk On has the quality of starting in the middle of something. And with its "stay safe tonight" and stirring chorus, Walk On would make a perfect concert or encore closing. There's also a hint of the afterlife. "Home, I can't say where it is, but I know I'm going home." Heaven is surely one of those places that have to be believed to be seen.

The end listing of all that you *can* leave behind—all that you fashion, make, build, break, measure, feel, reason, sense, speak, dress up, seek, create—reminds me of all that you can let go of in Bad—desperation, isolation, revelation, separation, condemnation, desolation. A definite favorite, Walk On says that falling down is not failure; not getting up is. "You don't drown from falling in water, you drown from staying there." Only when you give up and give in to defeat can you ever really be defeated.

KITE, another favorite, is summed up for me by something I once read on a tombstone in New England: "It is a fearful thing to love what death can touch." Though it begins like a carnival ride—which is sort of what life is like anyway—Kite, a sad song about chance and the vagaries of life, resonates with loss, uncertainty, and mortality. Edge's guitar shimmers, quietly saying only what needs to be said. Kite reminds me too of something I once heard from the comedian Jerry Seinfeld. "Life is truly a ride," he said. "We're all strapped in and no one can stop it. Sometimes you put your arms up and scream; sometimes you just hang on to the bar in front of you. I think the most you can hope for at the end of life is that your hair's messed, you're out of breath, and you didn't throw up."

IN A LITTLE WHILE must have been written with loads of love, gratitude, and hopeful promises, to Ali, Bono's long-time girl with Spanish eyes. When he's crawled in out of the heat or the cold, Ali has always been there. He fell in love with her the first time he saw her, "And the last," he's said—which says an awful lot about both of them. "In a little while, I won't be blown by every breeze," connects back nicely to Kite. I love the smooth guitar line, the easy drums, and the gritty rasp in Bono's voice, but in general, the style of In a Little While is not one I'm overly fond of.

WILD HONEY is another song I just love. Fun and folksy, simple and straightforward, with strumming Beatlesque guitars, Wild Honey is Ali's song too—one of Bono's hopeful promises. "My shelter and my shade," he sings. Ali is and always will be Bono's "harbor in the tempest." With an acoustic Staring at the Sun feel, Wild Honey just makes you want to get up and dance. Lyrically, it goes way back to freedom memories of a shared Irish childhood—innocent, buoyant days spent swinging through trees and "blowing in the breeze" like kites, full of promise and possibility. Light and lilting, Wild Honey is pure escapism—good times remembered; life when it was simpler and more natural.

PEACE ON EARTH – As beautiful and moving as it is—and Peace on Earth is one more album favorite—it just breaks my heart every time I hear it. The complexities of Irish history have been a part of an Irish childhood for centuries. This time it's Omagh. While most of *ATYCLB* builds to gorgeous choruses and pries a radiant hope out of the darkness, Peace on Earth moves with a mournful resignation, filled with desolation and grief, a weary surrender that's close to despair. Its hint-of-Christmas sleigh-bell sound opening feels a lot like Mothers of the Disappeared or Miss Sarajevo, two songs with similarly melancholy atmospheres. "Jesus can you take the time to throw a drowning man a line?" is another of those Wake Up Dead Man questions.

WHEN I LOOK AT THE WORLD – Because it asks the same question, When I Look at the World is the ideal tune to follow Peace on Earth. Out of sounds of "all kinds of chaos," heaven detaches and rises up with a sublime and steady rhythm-of-life beat, changeless and unruffled, Edge's guitar and the chorus both dissolving celestial sounds.

NEW YORK – I wasn't at all sure of this song on my first *ATYCLB* listen. But it's definitely grown on me. Exploding with energy, it's going to be absolutely stunning live. A fantastic accumulation of contrast, diversity, and possibility, New York is the perfect place for escape. The city is alive with temptation, opportunity, danger, excitement, virtue, vice, success; with sunken shadows, brilliant sunlight, and everything in between; the very best and the very worst of almost anything. Edge's wobbly guitar suggests a loss of balance, and Larry's driving tribal drums back Bono's concrete-jungle wolf-howls. Even if he's still working through his own wild and dark side—struggling to put the women and children first—the massive anonymity of New York must by now offer Bono some longed-for peace of mind.

"I heard your voice a-whispering, 'come away, now'," and the final distant "New York," seem like echoes of W. B. Yeats' *Stolen Child*. "Come away, O human child! To the waters and the wild with a faery, hand in hand, for the world's more full of weeping than you can understand."

GRACE is the antithesis of New York. Through all the noise, confusion, and frailty of the human condition, Grace rises up with a divine steadiness, seeing goodness, beauty, and simplicity in all things—an attitude we might all aspire to. Soft, restful, and ethereal, like Bass Trap or Three Sunrises, the serenity of Grace brings *ATYCLB* to a perfect close.

Edge has said that there is no single theme to *ATYCLB*, but if he had to pick one word, it would be "truth." Truth comes in many forms—"a child's smile, the feel of rain on your hand, the opening of a flower." Even the simple eloquence of folk music. More than once Bono has suggested that U2 may just be "a really loud folk band." Folk music captures the everyday—love, death, tragedy, relationships, joy, God—all that you can't leave behind. Often beautiful and moving—and always entertaining—folk music is the raw honesty, and "shared vision" of the moment. So it is with *All That You Can't Leave Behind.*

Wednesday, January 3, 2001

"The last time somebody listened to a Bush, folks wandered in the desert for forty years." Well put!

Bono has described his band members in an article in *Rolling Stone*. Adam, he says, is "a sage and the musical conscience of U2." Larry is "a man so handsome he will never be let sing in this group." Edge is "a Zen Presbyterian who finds Catholicism just too much glam-rock."

Asked how he would characterize himself, he said, "I don't know who I am. . . . That's the reason I signed on for this. . . .Isn't all art an attempt to identify yourself, really?" A familiar thought.

When his two girls were giving him long kisses on the lips, he was chuffed to think how much they loved him. And then he discovered that they were really just trying to find out if he'd been smoking!

My U2 tour is taking shape. March 22 through the thirty-first with Miami, Charlotte, and Atlanta. Boston with Meri. Phoenix in April.

Monday, January 8, 2001

"All Jewish feasts end in the same theme. We have been hated, scorned, insulted, condemned to ghettos and extermination camps—let's eat." (Jewish saying)

The U2 madness commences tomorrow with a formal announcement of the tour schedule, then pre-sale tickets for the first shows on Wednesday. I'll try for two first Miami. Next week it's two Phoenix and two Atlanta. Or two second Miami, which still leaves *Propaganda* orders open. Prop seats excelled for *The Joshua Tree* and *Zoo* shows, not so much for *Outside Broadcast* and *Popmart*.

Wednesday, January 10, 2001

It's *The Elevation Tour.* And so far we have *no* tickets! A hectic day of heightened desperation. Pre-sale time was advanced to 4:00 p.m. so *U2.com* members could get their passwords. Mine came fifteen minutes late. Dan's and Kim's not at all. I logged on to the Miami Ticketmaster site which overloaded. Forty minutes later, when I finally got through, everything had gone. Public sales start Saturday morning. If *Propaganda* puts theirs on-line too, we may have no shows at all. Disheartening, as I've wangled the opening show for the last three tours.

Friday, January 12, 2001

I'm before the fire on a bitterly cold day. Thirty-eight degrees with an icy rain.

Yesterday, I logged on for Boston's presale at exactly the time tickets went up—and they were all gone! My *Propaganda* order form arrived, and I fired off for two Miami and two Phoenix, Charlotte as an alternate. Danielle went for two Phoenix and two Boston; Atlanta as her alternate.

Saturday, January 13, 2001

Kim managed opening Miami tickets! Next week we have a repeat performance for Atlanta and Charlotte.

Sunday, January 14, 2001

Confirmation for the first Miami show. We're definitely in for the opener!

"We're really going to rock the house," Bono says in the latest issue of *Revolver*. "We're going for lift-off, and our band in full flight is something to see."

Monday, January 15, 2001

Meri has tickets for the first Boston show. Dan and I fly up Friday afternoon, back home Wednesday morning. A busy travel year ahead. U2 shows, a meeting in Washington, D.C., Canada mid-February, Vienna and Salzburg early fall, and then back to Mom and Dad's for Christmas.

Wednesday, January 17, 2001

On-line this morning, refreshing Ticketmaster for ten minutes up to sale time. Tickets "not yet available." And then abruptly, they were all gone! One Atlanta ticket on another site.

General Admission tickets aim to replicate the intimacy and excitement of many European shows. Larry says he's fed up with fans being so far away. Wants to "see the whites of their eyes."

Exactly what *Elevation* staging will look like is anybody's guess. But there's evidently a heart-shaped inner space with nooks and crannies.

Sunday, January 21, 2001

Two fairly good Charlotte tickets yesterday and another single for Atlanta. On-line ticket sales are like a silent riot. Tension and stress and wrangling with the competition. And not a sound.

Wednesday, January 24, 2001

Glanced at the newspaper [the *Arizona Daily Star*] this morning. A Jewish settler was sentenced to only *six months community service* and a $17,500 fine for beating and kicking to death an eleven-year-old Palestinian boy!

Thursday, January 25, 2001

All my U2 tickets are in. Atlanta and Charlotte hotels booked. Car rental tomorrow.

Saturday, February 10, 2001

Cecilia [Larry's sister, then working at Principle Management] sent Sue [editor of the U2 fanzine *Eirinn*] tickets for a two-thousand-person gig at the Astoria in London. Tickets distributed to all U2 fanzine editors. The band played seventeen songs, including Bad! Sue saw the lads afterwards. They were all "charming," she said. Bono glad-handed down the fan line, did a double-take when he passed Sue, and came back to give her a big kiss!

Monday, February 12, 2001

The European schedule out March 6; ticket sales on the ninth.

Thursday, February 22, 2001

A second Miami show March 26 failed to sell out, so I went on-line and snagged two tix behind the stage.

Wednesday, February 28, 2001

Packing for Washington; the cats suspicious. U2 in Florida fully sorted.

Friday, March, 2, 2001

Last night we ate at M & S [McCormick & Schmick's Seafood and Steaks, Washington, D.C.] Calamari and blasé fries, but a flavorful French dip. We ate in the bar, which is hung with apple-green stained-glass lamps, a central piece imprinted with "A Votre Santé" [To Your Health]. The redwood walls display an eclectic mix of sports and politics—portraits of old soldiers and framed documents beside faux presidential *Sports Illustrated* covers.

We drifted down Pennsylvania Avenue afterwards, to Lafayette Park, directly behind the White House. The Romans would have loved this solid, stalwart, monumental city, powerful and impressive by night or day.

Nothing official for U2 in Europe as yet, beyond a ten-hour festival at Slane Castle featuring the Red Hot Chili Peppers and Coldplay.

Friday, March 9, 2001

Confirmation of UK shows. I'll be gone two-and-a-half weeks mid-August.

Sunday, March 11, 2001

Flustered by the number of tickets given out to corporations, the band is looking for a second venue to Slane Castle.

Wednesday, March 14, 2001

Lime-green leaves on the pomegranate and a brown thrasher singing his heart out in the mesquite.

Ireland is pushing through legislation to allow a second U2 show at Slane. Lord Mountbatten, the castle's owner, is currently permitted only one concert a year.

Sunday, March 18, 2001

"God has some really weird kids," Bono says in an interview on *Beliefnet.com*. "I find it hard to be in their company most of the time."

Ditto!

"When those people get up at the Grammies and say, 'I thank God' I always imagine God going, 'Oh don't—please don't thank me for that one. Please, oh, that's an awful one. Don't thank me for that. That's a piece of shite.'"

We've booked the ferry to Dublin. A one-way flight goes for $130.

Thursday, March 22, 2001

"What is life? It is the flash of a firefly in the night.
It is the breath of a buffalo in the winter time.
It is the little shadow that runs across the grass
and loses itself in the sunset."

— Blackfoot Chief Isapwo Muksika Crowfoot

Backed away from my Tucson gate half an hour ago. A bouncy liftoff through rising heat. Two hours to Houston.

6:00 p.m. I'm at Gate C16 in Houston, awaiting Miami boarding. Gorgeous lime-green spring leaves glowed in sunlight among dusty pines as we cruised into Houston. Water, water, everywhere. Rivers and creeks and ponds, fields like worn, pale-green velvet, the city climbing out of a string of creepy, black cigar-shaped chimneys.

Friday, March 23, 2001

I'm settled in a suite at the Red Roof Inn by Miami International Airport, looking out on parking lots and a scattering of offices and industrial buildings. I arrived at eleven last night.

Decidedly *not* my kind of town, Miami does have some intriguing street names—Purple Parrot Place, White Seahorse Way, Yellow Toucan Road, and Panther Parkway.

Just after 3:00 p.m. and we're lazing by the pool at AmeriSuites in Plantation, Florida. The air smells of the sea, but the sun is red hot. I've no great impending U2 feeling as yet. There's a hockey game on at the venue at present, so the lads will rehearse tomorrow morning.

Sharon and I grabbed a shuttle here from the airport, an hour's drive for sixty dollars. I'm not much taken with the city, but our spacious suite has lots of room, and we had a tasty and inexpensive lunch at Einstein's—a garlic bagel with hummus, feta cheese, roasted red bell peppers, red onion, lettuce, and cucumber. Lyn and Kim joined us about an hour ago.

Saturday, March 24, 2001

10:00 a.m. We're outside the National Car Rental Center in Sunrise, on a gorgeous blue day of bright sunlight and high, puffy clouds. The silvery arena, surrounded by UFO-looking planters, has bright-green lighted windows. A modest group of fans has convened outside the main entrance, umbrellas raised against the heat. Broiling hot out here now, and the U2 tales are flying.

Sunday, March 25, 2001

We're in from TGI Friday's, where Sharon and I split a chicken fajita with house salad.

Yesterday, on a walk around the venue, we identified a more likely backstage entrance and slipped on over, entertained by a blue heron spear-fishing in a sea-grass pond. Car lots had closed after lunch at Applebee's, so we opted for the Sawgrass Mills shopping mall. By then, a crush of fans had amassed at the backstage entrance, among them "the lovely Barbara"—long blonde hair and an unrelenting mouth. Then came a Charles Manson look-alike with grey pony tail and beard, and a leathery-faced bleached blonde in white short-shorts. I passed the time in the grass, watching cormorants spiraling in the heated air.

When the doors opened, we found our seats in a sellout crowd of thirty-eight thousand, on the left side of the arena facing the stage—section twenty-six, row twenty-three, second tier. An inattentive corporate crowd packed the gap between us and the floor. The pointed end of a heart-shaped walkway, encompassing a small elevated stage, adjoined the larger one and faced the mixing desks. I'm guessing about three-hundred people could fit into the center space in front of the main stage. A dozen or so moveable screens at the back, along with several larger ones suspended overhead, comprised the staging arrangements.

The Corrs—three slim pretty Irish girls, their brother, and two guitarists—opened. After their first few numbers, one song seemed to blend into the next, their best, a rousing traditional piece on flute, fiddle, and drums. The lead singer, a slight bare-footed Irish waif named Andrea—no hips, no butt, no boobs—has been linked romantically, and I suspect falsely, with Bono. She does, however, have an uncanny resemblance to a younger Ali.

The Corrs wrapped up about seven-thirty, with U2 expected to start up in an hour. "Technical difficulties" pushed that arrival to after nine, and interim music included some Bob Marley and Radiohead's The Bends.

Here's U2's set-list: Elevation; Beautiful Day; End of the World; New Year's Day; Stuck in a Moment; Gone; Discothèque; Staring at the Sun; New York; I Will Follow; Sunday Bloody Sunday (with a bit of Bob Marley's Get Up Stand Up and Could You Be Loved); Sweetest Thing; In a Little While; Ground Beneath Her Feet; Bad (with a line or two of Walk on the Wild Side); Streets; Mysterious Ways; Fly// Bullet; With or Without You; One; and Walk On, with a small bit of 40's "how long to sing this song."

Yellow tape below us pointed to the stage. Sharon had just brought this to my attention when Adam started up the steps. Elevation, with the house-lights still on, established an immediate intimacy, and Beautiful Day followed, laser lights picking out Bono and Edge on the ramp. Bono's duel with Edge's guitar dominated End of the World, during which Bono backed up and fell off the stage!

The band played New Year's Day predominantly to fans behind the stage and Stuck in a Moment, dedicated to Michael Hutchence, had an especially expressive moment when Bono and Adam grazed foreheads, and again when Bono put his head on Edge's back. Black-and-white screen shots showed each band member in turn, Adam in dark camouflage. Gone followed, Edge in red light, Bono in yellow, Adam in green, and Larry in blue.

Pop had been recorded in Miami, Bono said. They'd have accomplished a lot more, he added, but for "having too much fun on the beach." Discothèque, "a riddle about love," followed, with a snatch of Staring at the Sun. And then, for New York, filmy draped screens unfurled from the ceiling, reflecting Bono's contorting silhouette in shadowy shapes, the Statue of Liberty among them. For an energetic I Will Follow, the audience went wild, and Sunday Bloody Sunday was a surprising high-point for me. Bono plucked an Irish flag from the audience, and there were lovely bits of Bob Marley's Stand Up and Could You Be Loved.

Four members comprised U2, Bono said on introducing the band. "You have some trouble counting here," he added, a poke at Florida's election snafu. Larry, in dark pants and t-shirt, was "the fellow who gave us our first and only job," Bono said. Moreover, he'd "had the same haircut for twenty years." Adam had "the biggest instrument in the band," a jab at the infamous European *Popmart* album cover which featured Adam full frontal nude. Edge, in a red/orange Miami Dolphins t-shirt, spangled trousers, and wool cap, was a scientist "with a brain so big he had to wear a hat; a man with more children than Abraham."

The Sweetest Thing and In a Little While for Ali came next, and then a fine acoustic Ground Beneath Her Feet. Bad—the prime offering of the evening in my view—followed, with four rotating lanterns and a flood of blue light. Bono wandered the stage, tacking on a snatch of Lou Reed's Walk on the Wild Side—"Holly came from Miami, FLA."

Streets was prefaced with a quote from Psalm 116. ["What can I give back to God for the blessings He's poured out on me. I'll lift high the cup of salvation. A toast to God. I'll pray. I'll complete what I promised God that I would. And I'll do it with you."] Streets made for a stunning performance, with the house lights up, wall to wall rejoicing, and a rising video wall of red light rolling with white at the rear of the stage. Twice Bono sprinted around the heart ramp, ending on the lowered video tier, which displayed the undulating silhouettes of Mysterious Ways' dancers, as it rose up under him. The Fly finished off the main set with "Love", "Me", "Believe" morphed into "Lie." Bono collapsed into the audience at the tip of the heart and was spirited away.

The encore opened with a raw and powerful Bullet the Blue Sky in red light. Someone passed Bono a sunflower here, which he handed off again. For Edge's spine-tingling guitar solo, Bono focused a hair-dryer-sized spotlight on Edge. Probably couldn't hoist that large stage lamp he'd used so many years ago for *Rattle and Hum*. For With Or Without You, the screens dropped again, covered in star charts. Afterwards, Bono thanked the audience "for following us all these years and for giving us a great life. Hope we didn't fuck it up. How was the first night for you?"

One next, and then the evening closed with Walk On. "Have we got the job?" Bono asked and received a resounding "YES!!"

I don't think anyone wanted to leave after that. After *Popmart*'s sketchy opener, this *Elevation* concert had achieved an exceptional high.

The after-show spectacle however, did not. One lone security

46   A GRAND MADNESS

guard faced down the crowd, one of which—a not-so-bright bulb in an ACDC t-shirt—screeched out "There's only one of him and how many of us?" And so a handful of one fan group's members rushed the entrance. The security guard called for help, and five flashing cop cars streamed into the parking lot, as another dim light started up a "fuck the cops" chant!

Monday, March 26, 2001

Sharon and I are off to the beach. A second Florida concert tonight and then up to Charlotte, North Carolina, tomorrow morning.

Early yesterday afternoon, we shuttled over to the airport for the rental car we will drop off in Atlanta. A Chevy Lumina, with "Clayton" on the license plate. [Clayton County, Florida]. We sped out on I-595 to the Everglades for an airboat tour of the swamp at Sawgrass, a "Recreation Park" somewhat on the ragged side. Animal occupants would "go home at night," a plethora of signs told us. Where exactly was "home?" we wondered.

11:30 a.m. On a blistering hot day, we're at Hugh Taylor Birch Recreation Park beach, A1A and Sunrise. A broad band of white sand stretches north and south, high-rise hotels to one side, the blue/green Atlantic to the other. A line of freighters stands off-shore with speed-boats churning the water in front. The crowds, the buildings, the traffic, the noise. And then up came Hugh Taylor, cool and green, with fig trees wrapped in sinewy tendrils, the sea glittering, warm and translucent. A spring day slipped from empty blue skies into towering black-bottomed clouds overflown by vultures and hawks.

While we soak up some rays, I'll finish yesterday's activities.

The Seminoles—predominantly Creek Indians—had a village at Sawgrass several centuries back. Seminole is a Muskegan word meaning "The Untamed People" or "The Runaways." The name describes various Native American tribes who were displaced by Anglo settlement, and thus retreated to the Everglades, adapting to a challenging new environment. They first referred to themselves as Seminole around 1775, and designated their area of swamp settlement the "River of Grass." To English settlers this same watery expanse of sawgrass islands—to which they gave the name "glades"—appeared to go on forever. Hence, the (For)Everglades. Much of Florida's drinking water comes from this region. "Gator Water," our guide told us.

Though the swampland is nearly devoid of trees, the Everglades still unfold with patchy island after patchy island of sharp sawgrass, barbed on one side. Water, water everywhere, but for a stand or two of dead eucalyptus-like trees planted by misguided environmentalists.

The high-point of our visit was three-year-old Scruffy, a female cougar with a noble face and doe-brown eyes. I made the most of an opportunity to scratch her about the ears, around her thick neck, and under her chin. When I rubbed her belly, she rolled on her side, put a paw on my arm, and began to purr, rich and low. Afterwards, the trainer put his forehead to hers, as Bono had to Adam's, and she rumbled some more.

There were reptiles and birds of prey with clipped wings. We even had a chance to stroke the soft, smooth, cool skin of a baby alligator. In the shop, a wide-eyed southerner raved about "all the signs" pointing to The End Times. Seven years left, he gushed with uncontrollable excitement. "If people only knew."

3:00 p.m. Here we sit in the venue parking lot opposite "the grassy knoll" where people milled yesterday. "The lovely Barbara" is in attendance once again.

3:45 p.m. Bono has just gone in to sound-check after signing autographs outside for about twenty minutes. Two o'clock Sunday morning, long after we'd left, people had been cautioned to keep calm and queue up along the curb, with the promise that *someone* would come out. Bono had. And so today, fans who'd presumably been there Sunday, scrambled into formation like a troop of obedient school-children.

"Irish people are Brazilians who can't dance," Bono wrote for one fan. And for the German fellow who'd given him a sunflower Saturday night, he squiggled "Sunflower" on the lad's t-shirt.

Someone asked him if he liked Chile. He'd been "poisoned there once," he said. Woke up alone in the middle of the night. No water. No lights. He thought he was going to die.

In open sandals and long pants, a checkered blue-and-white shirt, and a camouflage hat, Bono seemed comfortable, albeit a little weary. He'd just woken up, he said. Had he hurt himself when he'd fallen off the stage? "Only me pride," he answered. (His bodyguard had said earlier that he'd caught him, so Bono had never really hit the floor.)

Was anyone "at the show last night," he asked, by which he meant two days ago. Almost everyone said "yes." Patiently, he answered all of our questions, sketching pictures and self-portraits on canvas bags, on t-shirts and on tickets and photographs, before going back inside.

Tuesday, March 27, 2001

10:15 a.m. Sailing off on I-95 under a clouded sky.

10:15 p.m. We're in a Country Inn & Suites in Savannah, Georgia. We pushed through central Florida, reaching St. Augustine about three this afternoon. Much of Florida was lush and green. Other sections brown and brittle. Ponds of water lay scattered everywhere, rivers wide and brown and lined with high grass.

St. Augustine was quite pretty. The central area in Old Town, St. George Street, presented an accumulation of rather kitschy gift-shops housed in period buildings—wooden homes wrapped in long southern porches, and Spanish-styled ones dating to the late 18th century. The tide was out near a small fort being restored on the shoreline and the mud flats there were stalked by a handful of brilliantly white egrets, which would wiggle their long toes in the shallow sea-bottom before stabbing some crunchy morsel.

We ate at Angelo's Italian Restaurant in Jacksonville, the city off to the left in low late-afternoon sunlight, and then slipped into pulp-mill-and-swamp-gas country—Georgia. And so here we are in Savannah.

Wednesday, March 28, 2001

8:00 a.m. Still in the Country Inn & Suites, about five miles short of the South Carolina border, on a creamy-blue day, temperatures to drop to the low sixties later today.

10:00 a.m. While we're on the road to Charlotte, I'll wind up Monday night's Miami show, which both Sharon and I thought was better than Saturday's. Neither had much of the hype, turmoil, and blaring radio stations of *Popmart*'s opening in Las Vegas. Bottles had been disallowed Monday, possibly in response to a water-tossing incident Saturday night.

Seated behind the main stage, we nevertheless had an excellent view. A taped "X" below, indicated where Bono was to lie on the video wall for Mysterious Ways. Before U2 opened, Paul McGuinness escorted a shuffling old fellow and a young woman to the front of the stage, and snapped their photo against the crowd.

I found the Corrs quite talented this time around. If anyone told the singer they loved her, she said, she could say, and with all her heart, "I love U2." (Groan)

Here's the set-list: Elevation; Beautiful Day; End of the World; Discothèque/Staring at the Sun; Stuck in a Moment; New York; New Year's Day; Sunday Bloody Sunday; The Sweetest Thing; In a Little While; Angel of Harlem; Bad; Streets; Mysterious Ways; The Fly//Bullet; With or Without You; One/Unchained Melody; Walk On.

The Elevation opener ended with "I'm not your stepping stone," and for Beautiful Day, Bono drifted to the back of the stage and hovered there on the rim as though contemplating a jump. Adam played to Larry for the greater portion of the song. End of the World was accompanied by popping laser lights. Edge's guitar duel had Bono balancing himself in the crowd by the point of the heart where he afterwards performed an impromptu flamenco dance.

An outstanding Discothèque ended with a line or two of

Staring at the Sun. Multi-colored spotlights fired up the audience, our section in yellow. "It's hot here, if you're Irish," Bono noted. "In Miami there are 365 days of sunshine. We have thirty-six." All of that rain could sometimes spawn a sobering melancholy, he added. And "sometimes the blue turns to black," as it had for Michael Hutchence, to whom Stuck in a Moment was dedicated.

The New York staging and our unusual perspective reduced Adam and Edge to giant shadows one to either side of Bono, who, silhouetted on a separate screen, would bend and unbend like a troll.

With one single dash around the stage after Sunday Bloody Sunday, and a half-hearted ramble to the Mysterious Ways screens, Bono again dedicated The Sweetest Thing to Ali, who "had a baby in her belly."

Band intros followed. "Larry Mullen, not so junior, but he still looks like it . . . fan and father of Elvis." Adam, a "jazz man" dressed "like he just got back from Pakistan." Smoking hadn't hurt Adam, Bono mused. In fact no one had a problem with *Adam* smoking. It might be good for *Adam* "but not for anyone else." The bass player lit up a cigarette and sashayed down the ramp.

Edge, the scientist, was in constant contact with NASA. "Even his mother calls him The Edge. Good morning The Edge, how would you like your cornflakes this morning?" At the end of Angel of Harlem, Bono took a note from the crowd and feigned reading it. "Dear Bono, I love Larry."

Bad, with Ruby Tuesday, at the point of the heart, was outstanding, Streets another high-point. A young woman in low-slung stretch-pants hopped onstage for Mysterious Ways, repeatedly thumbs-upping her friends in the audience. She must have been a talker, as Bono kept "shushing" her. Their dance ended with Sexual Healing. Bono then ambled down the right side of the stage, quietly singing a line or two from The Fly, before that song kicked in. At the end, he leaped into the crowd and was whisked away.

A new video sequence marked the Bullet encore, though from our vantage point we couldn't see a thing. The song opened with gospel music, and then Charlton Heston [then president of the National Rifle Association] extolled the countless virtues of guns.

When Bono arrived in a blue suit, black appliquéd cat on the jacket shoulder, he delivered the whole of With or Without You to a young woman on the main floor balanced on her fellow's shoulders. They strained for each other and eventually the woman made her way to the stage for a dance with Bono, resting her head on his shoulder. Walk On, with a stunning "Hallelujah chorus," wrapped up the show.

2:35 p.m. We've just passed through Georgetown, South Carolina on #17, headed for Pawley Island and the seashore. Clusters of lavender wisteria droop everywhere like inverted lilacs, and lacy spring trees stand like pale reflections of their autumn glory.

Pawley, one of the East Coast's Barrier Islands, has an English vibe. Long, deserted, brown-sugar beaches and billowing waves. But with only a collection of high-end wood-frame homes—none of them of a B&B nature—we circled back to the mainland and carried on to Murrell's Inlet, where we ate at The Plantation Kitchen, a cozy clapboard eatery built in the nineteen-forties.

At the restaurant's entrance, a gorgeous live-oak draped in Spanish moss stood guard, and, from the front window, we gazed out to Garden Island, detached from the mainland by a reedy channel over-flown by soaring pelicans. Unlike most other area buildings, The Plantation Kitchen has no stilts for protection against storm surges. In 1989, Hurricane Hugo drowned the building in eighteen feet of sea-water.

As we ate—a basket of deep-fried clams and scallops with French fries and coleslaw—dark clouds amassed over the sea. Our brief seaside wander was cut short by wind and rain, and we headed north again.

9:00 p.m. We've settled in a so-so Howard Johnson's in Bishopville, North Carolina.

Thursday, March 29, 2001

1:50 p.m. We're in our room at the Clarion Hotel off #77 and the Billy Graham Freeway, in Charlotte, North Carolina. A cold rain has been dribbling all day, the high a measly forty-three degrees Fahrenheit. We left Bishopville this morning headed for Charlotte under grey skies. The road looped and undulated through early spring forests, cherry trees blossoming in pale pink and deep rose.

Our desert blooms predominantly in gold and yellow. Here the colors of spring are creams and ivories and pale cerise, roadsides splashed with rust-red grasses. Squared yellow "CHURCH" signs along the verges announced white-steepled Southern Baptist chapels or independents like "Testimonial Ministries."

Before we head out for supper, I'll jot down a word or two about Monday night's after-show events. Within half an hour of the concert's conclusion, three police cars convened at "the grassy knoll," one advancing to herd people off the hill. Security then announced that, if we were to "line up on the curb," the band would be out.

Adam arrived first, in khaki pants and a short-sleeved t-shirt. Bullet had been the best I'd ever heard, I told him when he reached me.

"Tonight or Saturday?" he asked.

"Tonight," I said.

"What did you think of the film?"

Well, of course, I hadn't seen a frame of it, but I answered— rather convincingly, I thought—that it had been "stunning," as I'm sure it had been.

For the most part, fans behaved well. One reedy Hispanic girl floated from one end of the line to the other and back again, stuttering and sobbing about having just touched Adam's hand.

A black limo inched along beside Adam as he walked and talked and signed, and in the end, he jumped in and was ferried away.

After a quick introduction of Larry, Bono claimed he couldn't stay long. "I'll show you why," he said and pulled Ali from a waiting limo, patting her very pregnant belly. She smiled radiantly at the applause she elicited.

They stood there, a sweet, smiling "proud parent" couple, and then Ali climbed back into the limo, and Bono commenced to shake a hand or two.

"It's nice to see you guys again," he told Kim and Lyn when he saw them. "How are you?" When he gave each of them a kiss, they were over the moon.

Larry started down the line from the opposite end. "It was a great show," I said to him as he signed my *ATYCLB* CD cover, and then struggled without success to extricate myself from the crowd. Before I knew it, Larry was signing my CD cover again. I stooped down to allow him to reach fans behind me and he rested his arm on the top of my head.

Edge, all in blue, appeared from the direction of Ali and Bono's limo, apologized for not being able to stay, and quickly left.

Saturday, March 31, 2001

11:00 a.m. I'm sitting in the Atlanta airport, awaiting a 1:00 p.m. flight to Houston. A twenty minute taxi drive to the airport on a dull grey day brought me here. An hour's ramble from check-in to Concourse D.

About midnight last night, we returned from our last *Elevation* gig to our digs at the massively opulent Hilton Atlanta Towers downtown. I'll write up that show now, before Charlotte's Thursday night, as it's sharpest in my mind.

Even warmer, more intimate and emotional than second Miami—which remains my favorite *Elevation* experience—the set-list was identical to the opening in Sunrise, but for 40 added to Bad. We reached the venue, Philips Arena, about four o'clock, having delivered our Avis rental to the airport and shuttling back to the hotel. One fellow on the Avis bus gabbed on his cell-phone the entire time. On, off, and in-between.

The Atlanta venue area has been renovated since 1992's *Zoo TV Tour*, with a spanking new parking garage and overhead walkways to both CNN and the Omni.

With one ticket to off-load, we found a young New Zealander who'd been scammed by scalpers. They'd shown him a U2 ticket for the going price—eighty-seven dollars. And he'd duly paid, only to be left holding a pass to some long-gone sporting event.

An hour before the gates opened, unsold corporate tickets were released. One man scored ten seats in the front row! Indefensible, given the experience of our Kiwi friend, and the too often dismal seats *Propaganda* had given long-time members.

In a silver-grey suit, Ali was still dancing in the celebrity section, chatting up Danny Lanois, when the band launched into *Elevation*, ending with the Monkees' I'm Not Your Stepping Stone. "Happy Birthday, Chantal," was worked into the lyrics of End of the World, with Bono's matador in devil's horns, and Edge in a #55 red t-shirt.

This evening was about a lot of things, Bono said before Stuck in a Moment. Jean Cocteau [French poet, novelist, dramatist, playwright, artist, and filmmaker, best known for his 1929 novel *Les Enfants Terribles*] had once asserted that "'friendship (was) higher than love.' I'd like to make this evening about friendship, 'cause we've got a lot of friends here in Atlanta and Georgia. This is for a friend of ours, a very, very close friend that's come over here for her birthday. For Chantal, for Steve Iredale, and for you, for hanging around. And for a friend we lost." [Michael Hutchence]

Gone was done up in colored lights again. Edge in red, Larry in blue, Bono in yellow, and Adam in green. New York was breathtaking, with larger-than-life graphics floating off into the audience. After Sunday Bloody Sunday—with Bob Marley's Could You Be Loved and Get Up Stand Up—Bono tripped over his Sweetest Thing piano part. "This is the fourth night," he said. "You'd think I'd know the piano part."

"Ali is in the building with a baby in her belly," Bono announced, and directed the first half of In A Little While to his wife, wandered off to collect a rose from the audience and handed it off to Adam. An exquisite Bad, with 40, followed The Ground Beneath Her Feet, and then up came Streets. This Bad/Streets pairing is a highlight of *Elevation* concerts for me.

The encore opened with Charleton Heston's gun rant—"a gun

in the hand of a good man is no threat to anyone . . . ." A devastating video sequence of destruction—war footage, leg traps, and bombs— kicked off Bullet, with Led Zeppelin's Whole Lotta Love. And star- charts glided over the audience for With or Without You.

One, dedicated to Coretta Scott King, included fragments of Losing My Religion and Everybody Hurts, for Georgia's REM, and before Walk On, Bono spoke about people he admired. "In my teens my hero was Martin Luther King," he said. "In my twenties it was Coretta Scott King." Walk On ended the show with spirit and celebration.

Pushing right along now with the Charlotte show [Charlotte Coliseum, North Carolina]. Sharon and I both felt a certain lack of enthusiasm here, beginning with all the lyrics Bono forgot. Too much post-show partying? Rain sluiced down both before and after, and it was very, very cold. Our seats, first section on Adam's side, by the heart, half-way to the stage, were top-notch in a sold-out crowd of nineteen-thousand. Still, this concert definitely resembled work.

Here's the set-list, with a few explanatory notes: Elevation; Beautiful Day; End of the World; New Year's Day ("Thanks for coming out in the rain."); a rather sad sounding Stuck in a Moment; Staring at the Sun; New York; Sunday Blood Sunday ("Blessed are the peacemakers."); The Sweetest Thing; band intros (Edge: "Crouching Tiger, Hidden Presbyterian"; "the very, very posh Adam Clayton, first manager of the band."); In a Little While (dedicated to Daniel Lanois); The Ground Beneath her Feet; Bad with Ruby Tuesday; Streets ("I want to take shelter from the dirty rain"); Mysterious Ways; The Fly; an outstanding Bullet; With or Without You; One; Walk On.

We wended our way back to the Clarion in the rain, and as Sharon fancied a drink, we dropped in to the hotel's Classic Sports Bar—scoreboards, section seats, and a bullpen—for red wine and a Samuel Adams. After a time, Sharon pegged the tall blond at the next door table as Mark Bryan [Hootie and the Blowfish guitarist].

A couple of young men at our end of the Bryan entourage,

who'd had more than enough to drink, drew us into conversation, and before we knew it, we were part of the clique. Sharon had once shared a pizza with Mark in London some years back, and Mark well remembered. Or at least he was kind enough to say so. They'd all attended the U2 show: Mark, his sister, with her husband, Mark's wife, and her brother, among others. Mark graciously shared snapshots of his children. We chatted briefly about the Hootie gig in Tucson. I'd read the notice in the paper just prior to leaving. "Of all the gin joints, in all the towns, in all the world . . . ."

2:30 pm. An hour and a half left of my Tucson flight. We arrived late into Houston, but the connecting flight had been held for me.

Friday, April 27, 2001

Nearly 6:00 p.m. I'm outside on a gorgeous spring day, black-bottomed clouds overhead, and a slight breeze. Oleanders, bottle-brush, and verbena perfume the air, and the prickly pear is on the cusp of blossoming, the pomegranate in small red trumpets.

Picked up July's airline tickets to Boston.

Sunday, April 29, 2001

U2 delivered a smashing show at America West Arena in Phoenix last night. About three-thirty, we picked up Danielle and a friend of hers who suffers from cerebral palsy. The Jefferson Street Grill had lapsed into a bar by the time we found a table. Guacamole and drinks arrived, but nothing in the way of a meal, so at quarter to eight we cancelled the order and left.

In a sell-out crowd of eighteen-thousand, our seats—left side, lower tier—were quite good. A warm celebratory inclusiveness defines *Elevation*, but this Phoenix show magnified the personal and intimate. The one-but-not-the-same, carry-each-other vibe commenced the instant the lads took the stage.

Here's the set-list: Elevation; Beautiful Day; End of the World; New Year's Day; Kite; New York; I Will Follow; Sunday Bloody Sunday; Stuck in a Moment; In a Little While; Stay; Bad/40;

Streets; Mysterious Ways; The Fly//Bullet; With or Without You; Pride; One/I Remember You; Walk On

Elevation worked in a welcome fragment of In God's Country. "Desert sky, dreamed beneath a desert sky, rivers run but soon run dry. We need new dreams tonight." Images of the band members flickered on-screen for Beautiful Day, and End of the World passed with strobe lights and the Bono/Edge bull/matador sequence. Edge's guitar knocked Bono to the floor and he swiped at it with flailing feet.

"Honey, we're home!" Bono said after New Year's Day. "You know a lot of folks think that we live in Arizona, you know what I mean. Island folk and desert folk, it's the same thing really. . . . But. . . . not. Anyway, we spent a lot of time here and just had an amazing time here, going right back to messing with your governor. What was his name again? Can we even remember it? Meechum or something. [Evan Mecham, Arizona's former "earth is flat" governor, was inaugurated in 1987, impeached in 1988]. But we remember Dr. King's name, and we remember Dr. King's day. This is a song about nearly losing everything. If you have somebody and you've seen them slip away or die on you, or if you've had a fright yourself . . . this is Kite."

Against the mesh curtains of New York, Bono, in a glittery black cowboy hat, mimed a gallop, slapping at his right hip. "For a long time, we used to tear this piece of material into shreds," he said of the Irish flag someone had given him around Sunday Bloody Sunday. "They're still kind of scary things, flags. But for the first time in a long time, it feels like, when you throw an Irish flag up to me, I can catch it and not feel ashamed."

After a moving Stuck in a Moment, Bono said he was going to introduce the band. "Something very difficult for a singer" to do, he added. This took nearly five minutes. Larry, the guy who started the band and never let them forget; Adam, the group's jazz man and musical conscience; Edge, with more children than Abraham, a man who could pilot the space shuttle, but preferred to "ride the number forty-two bus."

An acoustic In a Little While followed, and then Stay, a song they "hadn't played very much"—"Miami, New Orleans, London, Belfast, Arizona." Bad/40, in blue, slipped into Streets, with Psalm 116 and a wall of red light. The main set ended with The Fly.

An awesome Bullet flashed up words formerly spoken by the NRA's Heston. "A gun in the hand of a good man is no threat to anyone, except a bad man." With the last phrase, a little girl about two years old picked up a gun. Bono shielded his eyes and groped his way down the ramp.

One was dedicated "to Jerry Mele [former head of U2 security], a native of Phoenix, Arizona. He's been taking care of all you people. Jerry Mele had a bad accident in Mexico City. Some bad, bad, bad, bad things happened there." [In 1997, Mexico's security forces manhandled Jerry to such an extent that he'd had to retire.] "Two sisters, one brother," Bono sang at the end for his two little girls and big brother Norman. Walk on closed the show.

Saturday, May 5, 2001

The band pulled a runner to Las Vegas after the Phoenix show. Partied until dawn. Sheila [Roche, of U2's Principle Management] and Joe [O'Herlihy, U2 audio director] were both celebrating birthdays.

CNN will profile Bono tomorrow night on *People in the News.*

Thursday, May 24, 2001

In from a visit with Dustin in Missouri. The flight attendant out of St. Louis was Hispanic and warned repeatedly of items shifting in the "overhead beans."

U2 will have by now wrapped up Toronto's first *Elevation.* An especially good one, I imagine, as Bono and Ali welcomed their fourth child, a boy, on May 21. Meri emailed a photo of the three of them. Ali, forty-years-old and thirty-six hours from birthing the babe she's holding in her arms, looks phenomenal—sleek and trim.

I've finished a Phoenix review that will age while we're in Boston.

Tuesday, June 5, 2001

Blue and sunny with a cool breeze. This being Boston, the lads will likely step out to fans before sound check. But I just can't bring myself to go early.

We're in the garden of the Isabella Stuart Gardner Museum on Evans Way. Isabella was one of those wealthy women of America's past who roamed the world collecting things and then built a museum to house them. Mrs. G's wanderings were prompted by the loss of her only child, a son, who died at the age of two. I'm grateful that such people preserved so much over the years. But I'd really like to know who wove the tapestries, who painted the frescos, who sculpted the statues, rather than simply who had the wherewithal or chutzpa to acquire them.

The museum, a quiet enclave, designed on the model of a 15th century Venetian palace, has a tiled mosaic courtyard accented with filched Roman busts. The result duplicates the floor coverings we saw in Ostia Antiqua [the ancient seaport of Rome] and Pompeii. Rhododendrons and blue hydrangeas brighten various corners of the grounds. One sculpture of a young, stocky, and intimidating Roman soldier from the Imperial Period, around 150 A.D., might well have been inspired by the waiter in the Italian restaurant we ate at in the North End last night. The broad-face, the square jaw.

We reached the museum through Fenway Park, a slip of lush green just beyond the stadium, filled with geese and ducks and tall marsh grasses. Fenway is the wildest area in town, though like most cities of the Eastern Seaboard, "wild" is relative.

Wednesday, June 6, 2001

We're in the Boston airport for a noon flight back to Tucson.

The U2 concert review in the *Boston Globe* claimed Bono was "holding back" last night. None of us felt that at all.

We left for the North Station yesterday about four o'clock. Five minutes to Haines Convention Station, and then twenty minutes on the T [MBTA, the Massachusetts Bay Transportation Authority] to a corner of the Fleet Center venue. We've traveled to the North Station on the Green Line three times already, off-loading at a different spot each time due to construction. A ten minute ramble brought us to the North Church, where we met up with Meri and Rob. A Fleet Center vendor had pointed out the proper backstage entrance so they'd caught the band's arrival. Edge, Adam, Larry, and then Bono, who'd been held up in traffic.

After fish and chips in the super-crowded Harp pub near the venue, we went in. Dan and I waited in the outer corridor until P. J. Harvey closed and then found our seats in the second row opposite the stage, behind mixing desks and lighting equipment. Ned O'Hanlon and Maurice Linnane of Dreamchaser Productions were filming a U2 special, so that subtle lighting washed over the audience throughout the night.

Here's the set-list: Elevation; Beautiful Day; End of the World; Mysterious Ways/In My Life; Stuck in a Moment; Kite; Gone; New York; I Will Follow; Sunday Bloody Sunday; In a Little While; Desire/Gloria; Stay; Bad/40; Streets; Pride//Bullet; With or Without You; The Fly//One; Walk On

Edge's guitar swept Bono off his feet again in End of the World. He clawed at the strings, producing a wild dissonant screech. Mysterious Ways had a sweet snatch of the Beatles In My Life. They'd played "twenty-five years" in Boston, Bono said, and quickly corrected himself to twenty-five shows!

New York prompted a raucous chorus of "Yankees suck." Boston and New York City have been age-old rivals from colonial days. Bono stretched an Irish flag on the floor for Sunday Bloody Sunday, and standard band intros followed In a Little While, but for Edge, who, traveling by space-ship as a rule, had come with "only his yellow Les Paul." Some small talk touched on U2 being the best rock band in the world. "That comes from being Irish," Bono said.

An acoustic Desire ended with Van Morrison's Gloria and brought the band to the point of the heart. "Wild, wild horses can't drag me away," Bono tacked on to a sensational Bad/40/Streets sequence. He discharged his Psalm 116 recitation in complete darkness. At the end of Streets, he mimed flinging his heart out to each sector of the audience, and Pride finished the main set with three camera shots of the heart-shaped stage on the suspended screens.

Bono's statistic of 676,000 people killed by guns in the U.S. since John Lennon's assassination in 1980, kicked off the Bullet encore, and Heston's words popped up on-screen. With or Without You followed, and then the Fly saw Bono splayed on one of the lowered screens, like a bug squashed on a windshield.

A lot of talk about Africa introduced One, words about living free while "our African brothers" did not. A rousing Walk On brought the show to a close and the house lights came up with Grace.

12:30 p.m. We're off. The full green of western Massachusetts unfurls below. So pleasantly cool in Boston. Temps in the low sixties. A neat city, easy to navigate. Yet like many modern cities, few service people have the wherewithal to live there. A police officer near the Fleet Center hadn't a clue where the Old North Church was.

High-rise Boston flats go for several million dollars.

Saturday, June 9, 2001

Rollingstone.com reports that Wednesday night's Boston show featured a twenty-eight-year-old young man who'd been to several *Joshua Tree* shows as a child. He'd rehearsed Curtis Mayfield's People Get Ready, held up a sign to that effect, and shouted "People Get Ready" until—finally—Bono asked him what he was on about and the lad hopped onstage. Did he know the words? Bono asked him. "Sorry dude, that's your job!" he answered.

Thursday, June 14, 2001

The server for Edge's on-line June 10 live chat crashed from too much traffic.

Tuesday, June 19, 2001

The band plays New York City tonight, the second of two

shows there. Two more performances, in East Rutherford, New Jersey, follow at the end of the week.

Film-makers allegedly positioned only young lovelies up front in the GA section for one of the Boston shows. Hand-picked by U2 security, we hear. How much fairer to reward whoever has the staying power to manage the front of the line, no matter their photogenic attributes. That the band might want to see new faces is immaterial.

Wednesday, June 20, 2001

Nearly 5:00 p.m. Our summer heat is on, with vague and distant rumblings of thunder. Yesterday, a light evening rain put the monsoons on schedule for St. John's Day [June 24].

Monday, June 25, 2001

Sue has a floor ticket for London's *Elevation* show. I'll be on my own in the stands.

Monday, July 9, 2001

The European *Elevation* tour opened in Copenhagen on Friday. Same set as the U.S.

Monday, July 23, 2001

After years of ill health, Bono's dad, Bob, has "taken a turn for the worse."

Wednesday, July 25, 2001

U2 will return to the States in October or November. No mention of Australia, New Zealand, or Japan. A running boycott of Mexico after the Jerry Mele incident.

Thursday, August 9, 2001

12:05 p.m. I'm in the Tucson airport, on the first leg of a trip that lands me in Manchester [England] tomorrow afternoon.

3:25 p.m. In LAX, Tom Bradley International Terminal [Los Angeles]. Dispiriting and oppressive, the city rises at a distance from a blanket of yellow smog. A long hike here from my arrival gate, with only vague responses to directional questions.

"Just off to the left," someone said.

"Down a floor to the blue corridor."

A balloon vendor finally pointed out the requisite shuttle and now the klatch of bubbly high-school girls beside me is discussing down time in Dublin.

Friday, August 10, 2001

11:45 a.m. At Gate A15 in the Dublin airport, on a bright blue day. "We'll forgive you," Irish Customs said when I told them I was just passing through. We flew in across the island, and then out over the Irish Sea for a U-turn before landing, brilliant green fields on the horizon as we banked. Nine boring hours from LA and I'll leave for Manchester in another two and a half. Aer Lingus Customer Service sorted my Luxemburg Airlines flight. Twenty-four hours plus on the road now.

5:30 p.m. In room #305 in Manchester Central Travelodge. The flight to the UK was short and pretty, on a smallish jet with plush grey-leather seats. I'll hold on until Sue comes in from Carlisle.

Our spacious room has no air-conditioning, and, with windows flung open, it's quite noisy. The city bristles with red brick and chimney pots, Boddington's Crown Tavern lies just across the street, a broad brown river in back.

Saturday, August 11, 2001

Nearly 1:00 p.m. Just back from lunch at the nearby Café Rouge. I rallied until seven last night when Sue left to meet a couple of German friends.

The day's a tad doleful, with sprinkles of rain from a dull grey sky. I do like Manchester, polished modernity adjacent to picturesque Victorian stonework. Out the window, the languid River Irwell flows between darkly time-worn walls.

5:00 p.m. In from a meal at Bar Med, a nearby tapas restaurant, after a jaunt to the Lowry Hotel. Rumor had the band staying there. A short while ago, the limo idling outside hauled away a Gallagher brother [from the Irish band Oasis].

Julie pulled in from Southampton an hour ago. With her train delayed, she'd missed her connection and ended up in an unmanned

station surrounded by empty farm fields. A taxi brought her to
Bristol, where she managed a second train for Manchester. Seven-
hours she'd been traveling, longer by several hours than a flight from
Toronto to London!

Sunday, August 12, 2001

It's just after 11:00 a.m. We're due to check out in an hour.

Here's the set-list from last night's outstanding Manchester
show: Elevation; Beautiful Day; End of the World; Discothèque/
Staring at the Sun; Kite; New York; I Will Follow ("for Bob Hewson,
tough old . . .fucker")/Sunday Bloody Sunday; In My Life/Stuck in
a Moment; In a Little While; Desire; Stay; Bad/40 (with a line or
two of Oasis' Champagne Supernova); Streets; Mysterious Ways;
The Fly//Bullet; With or Without You (a snatch of Love Will Keep
Us Apart, from the Manchester band Joy Division)//One (dedicated
to Noel Gallager); Wake Up Dead Man; Walk On.

Kelis, the opener, was intensely forgettable, all ear-splitting
"augghhh"s. Our seats, at the top of the section next the stage, Edge's
side, were exceptional. Moreover, the Manchester Evening News
Arena has a steepness that allows for an unmatched perspective.
Though wistful with warmth and intimacy, as a tribute to Bono's
dad this concert exuded a profound melancholy. Coming to term
with an imminent death. Elevation opened with the house lights
still on, as usual, and Beautiful Day and End of the World were both
energetic, Bono challenging and then in awe of Edge's guitar chops.

After thanking fans for their patience, a hush fell over the crowd
when Bono broached the subject of his dying father. He'd composed
Kite, he said, only to discover that it had likely been given to him by
his father, who now, at seventy-five, had only "a few days left in this
world." With "I'm not afraid to die; I'm not afraid to live," Kite took
on all the reflective sadness, inevitability, and reluctant acceptance
of "you just never know."

They were having a fine time in Manchester, Bono said after
Staring at the Sun. And nice to know they were having a great time

while they were still having it. Not finding out about it later. The band had played for eleven people in the Beach Club, years ago. And now here they were again, Larry's little Elvis savoring his first ever U2 show.

England and Ireland were two lands separated by a slim slip of water, Bono said after I Will Follow. "Great men" were doing "great things" and should not stop. [Jerry Adams' Provisional IRA had dropped out of the Good Friday Peace Accords because of the arrest of some of their terrorist cohorts. I myself have never considered Adams 'a great man'.] For Sunday Bloody Sunday, Bono positioned an Irish flag on the heart stage, and ended with Get Up Stand Up. In all the many, many years Sunday Bloody Sunday has been performed, few glimmers of optimism and hope have blossomed in our world. How long *must* we sing this song?

A tidbit of In My Life was followed by In a Little While, which improves by leaps and bounds when performed live. Edge took up the last lines. An exuberant Happy Birthday to Edge followed, the birthday boy glad-handing the front ranks. All I remember of intros was Adam being once again declared "the poshest member of U2."

I do relish the quieter rendition of Desire on this tour. Afterwards, the great Manchester group Joy Division was extolled. They were the "best band on the planet," Bono said. "Second to U2." There followed "in tribute to Frank Sinatra", a lovely Stay, which segued into Bad, blue lamps revolving on the upper periphery of the heart. Bono's Psalm recitation introduced a no-holds-barred Streets.

Mysterious Ways and a fitting Fly ended the main set, Bono flattened on the lowered screen, calling to mind both Dire Straits' The Bug and Stevie Nicks' Sometimes It's a Bitch.

The first encore began with a tribal wailing of sorts, and a list of members of the UN Security Council [the United States, Great Britain, Germany, China, and Russia], scrolled on-screen, lapsing into the world's five biggest arms dealers—the very same bunch. Thundering tanks, little boys with sub-machine guns, drilling military units, and detonated bombs introduced Bullet, and Bono strode past the screens, shielding his eyes.

A great many "thank you"s followed With or Without You before the second encore got underway with One. "Thanks for coming from far and wide to see us," Bono said, which I really took to heart. More work remained to be done for the *Jubilee*, he added. "You have a right to take to the streets." Civil disobedience had a noble history. But not "the stupid shit happening now. You know what I'm talking about." [A reference to the rioting then taking place at the G8 Summit in Genoa, Switzerland.]

One, dedicated to Noel Gallagher, also went out to "an old country"—Africa, with mention of the African HIV-AIDS epidemic. We should all be involved, Bono said. "Even a rich fat bastard like me." A touching Wake up Dead Man and then Walk On brought the show to a close with a string of gloriously ecstatic "hallelujahs."

Monday, August 13, 2001

3:30 a.m. I'm at Sue's in Carlisle, just in from U2's second Manchester show. Arrived about an hour ago. We've been chatting over tea.

11:00 p.m. A grand day altogether. Sue had a fanzine photo pass last night, so Julie and I rode the #62 city bus into Carlisle to hand off her photo chip. Had cheese and ham toasties for lunch at Scotchgate while awaiting photo development, and then took in a Pre-Raphaelite exhibition at Tullie House.

The Pre-Raphaelite Brotherhood, a group of seven mid-19th century English artists, challenged the then-current depiction of country folk. Artistically, they reverted to the age "before Raphael," and took their inspiration primarily from the Middle Ages. Some themes and styles proved too classical or Biblical for my taste, but for the most part, I loved the collection.

Those artists influenced by or associated with the Brotherhood especially impressed me. The dark, moody etchings of Samuel Palmer, for example. Moon-rises and shadowy country lanes. Ford Madox Brown, Fred Griggs, and Charles Ricketts. I was dazzled by nearly every canvas, studying lines and light in charcoal, chalk, watercolor, oil, gauche, pastel, ink, and pencil.

Tuesday, August 14, 2001

10:00 a.m. Leaving Penrith on the 9:47 Bournemouth to Birmingham, under a lowering but still textured sky. Verdant green fields and late-summer trees.

And now chugging through the Lake District. Clouds have draped themselves on balding hilltops and fireweed blazes along the tracks.

3:00 p.m. In our room—#221—in the Holiday Inn Express, a half mile from the NEC [National Exhibition Center] in Birmingham, a venue connected to both the Birmingham train station and the airport.

Wednesday, August 15, 2001

10:35 a.m. On the 10:31 Birmingham to Edinburgh, headed back to Carlisle. The railroad banks all along our route are heavy with late summer grasses and feathery fireweed.

Of my three UK *Elevation* shows thus far, first Manchester remains my favorite. One of the most emotional U2 shows I've ever seen. They must serve as something of a catharsis for Bono at this difficult time. Not many people would or could share such pain and loss so openly.

Second Manchester was quite the opposite. Explosive, angry, and aggressive. Fans in the heart spoke of technical problems. But it seemed to me it was more a case of the straw that broke the camel's back.

Last night's Birmingham show differed again—the sound much improved over the first two shows, Bono and company in top form, laughing and acknowledging specific audience members.

12:20 p.m. Coming into Warington Bank Quay. Clouding up, with a high creamy overcast as we travel north. Barges, long and narrow and brightly-colored, plied the canals in the south.

Leaving Wigan Station, past rows of stalwart, cozy, red-brick row-houses, thick with chimney pots. The sky's gone white, a haze of fog in the middle distance among the trees.

6:00 p.m. Back at Sue's. I came by taxi from the train station about three o'clock. On her way to work, Sue left me off at the Market Place, where I dropped off yet more film, passing the time in The Bookstop, an old used-book store. Left with a lovely tome called *The Crying of the Wind*, by author/artist Ithell Colquhoun [Peter Owen Limited, London; 1955]. A travel book really, centered on the mystic side of Ireland—a "darkling landscape" with heaps of "time-honored" paganism.

Leaving Lancaster, our Birmingham train sped across the wide, brown, tidal River Lune as it flowed out to the Irish Sea. Shortly afterwards, we crossed a broad stretch of coastal flats across from which we could just make out the gentle roll of the Cumbrian Hills. From a small village there, Sue's sweet little dachshund, Toffie, hails, raised by a woman who'd sold her, only to discover her new owner was abusive. By threatening exposure to the RSPCA [The Royal Society for the Prevention of Cruelty to Animals], the woman rescued Toffie, returned her to good health, and passed her on to Sue.

A stop at Oxenholme. Grey-slate roofs and lowering skies. Banks of bracken follow the tracks, and on the hillsides, snaky stone walls enclose flocks of sheep. Directly or by preventive measures, a great many of them were lost to the recent hoof-and-mouth epidemic. The smell and the pall of smoke from burning bodies spread everywhere. In desperation, many farmers took their own lives. For centuries ewes have taught their babes territorial lessons, so that, instinctively, no one strays beyond their appointed grounds. Sadly, much of that knowledge has been lost.

We're back into the Lake District—cerise fireweed exploding over railway banks, balding hills behind, lush fields in vales edged with late summer's yellow-brown grasses. Penrith by 2:00 p.m., and shreds of blue sky just as we pulled into Carlisle.

We've had a gentle rain now since six o'clock. If the weather holds, I'll stroll along the Eden tomorrow and update the journal.

Thursday, August 16, 2001

A dull grey day. With all of my UK *Elevation* shows behind me, I have to say that first Manchester remains my favorite. Perhaps of all time. Though I've said that before. *Elevation* stands as a natural progression to *Popmart*. Friendship, without the distraction of gigantic arches and mirror-ball lemons.

2:00 p.m. Sitting on the bank of the River Eden. In a flood of sunlight, I drifted through the King Moor Nature Preserve behind Sue's flat. The sky has clouded over now, and the riverside has thickened with a splendid, bushy orchid. The whole area seems busier than I remembered, all hammered thuds and racing motors, the river with a rolling rush to it, as it spills over a small weir.

While I have the time, I'll dive into second Manchester. We left the Travelodge noonish, had a late breakfast at the RSVP restaurant, where we camped out until about four o'clock. Always up for a magnified coincidence while "on tour," we were chuffed to be seated at table 40.

Outside the Manchester Evening News Arena, we huddled under brollies on a dismal, dreary, bleary day, staying just long enough to see the lads arrive for sound check in four identical silver Mercedes. Paul McGuinness trailed after in a police car. A mediocre pizza and then in for the show.

Here's the set-list: Elevation; Beautiful Day; End of the World; New Year's Day; Kite; Gone; New York; Out of Control; Sunday Bloody Sunday; Wake up Dead Man/Stuck in a Moment; Sweetest Thing; Rain; Staring at the Sun; All I Want is You; Streets; Mysterious Ways; Pride//Bullet; With or Without You; One

Before the show even began, Bono knelt and crossed himself, which he's done before on occasion. I suppose he needed that, as his performance—explosive and aggressive—felt like the antithesis of Saturday night's concert. Yet all that anger gave this performance an energy and power that left us feeling guilty for having ridden the crest of his grief.

We could see Sue in the pit, very near the point of the heart.

She had a fanzine pass for the first three numbers. Norman was there too, his wife in tears. We thought then that perhaps Bob had died. But there's been no official notice as yet. Bono looked old and grey and strained, Sue said. And "his trousers were very, very tight."

2:20 p.m. I've been driven inside by a manic motorcyclist. I'd been serenely seated by the blackish river on a moldering log capped with bright green mosses. A fly-fisherman stood hip-deep in the rapids mid-river, near a small marshy island. Several gigantic maples swayed overhead and impenetrable ivy darkened the ground, while sunlight glittered on the surface of the water. Blackbirds soared above, with a pair of eider ducks cruising below the weir.

But back to Manchester. Some intense dueling came with End of the World, and a tremendous cheer rose up for New Year's Day. Gone next, and then Bono spiraled out of control for Out of Control. A ticking time bomb, he flung himself about the stage in hopes of dissipating some of the anger and negative energy he must have accumulated. He kicked over his microphone stand and spear-headed it toward the crowd. The Statue of Liberty he devised against the screens for New York, fingers splayed for a crown, created something troll-like and shadowy. Most of Wake Up Dead Man he sang motionless, on his back. And for The Sweetest Thing, he strained to focus on his piano part.

All I Want is You in place of Bad displayed great anguish, though Streets remained extraordinarily celebratory. And then, with Mysterious Ways, the poor lad raged again, shouting and pacing and flailing his arms.

Bullet opened the first encore with the familiar NRA quote— still so fitting in light of the Provos' refusal to disarm. A dark-haired woman onstage for With or Without You laid her head on Bono's shoulder and he kissed her hand before sending her off. Confused words marked the start of One and Bono spent ages just staring at the floor. At the concert's close, Adam and Edge glad-handed the front rows. And with a terse "Goodnight, God bless," Bono stormed off the stage. Everyone rallied for a Walk On that never came.

In a sense, Bono collapsed right along with the show. Yet his passion and anger fashioned an incredibly potent performance, a mammoth fire-works display that fizzled out in the end.

Out of the darkness, as technicians swarmed the stage with flashlights, a disembodied voice sang a lengthy I Did it My Way. I thought at first it was a croaky Bono after a Louis Armstrong vibe. The actual singer, Dutch artist Hermann Brood, had thrown himself off the Hilton Hotel in Amsterdam a few weeks ago. He'd confided in Bono that he meant to kill himself. But he was prone to such outbursts, and Bono hadn't taken him seriously.

I Did it My Way came across as Bono's way of acknowledging the mixed emotions brought on by a dying father. Bob Hewson had clearly done it *his* way. A hell of a way to end a show though. Like driving off a cliff. Like jumping out a window.

Friday, August 17, 2001

9:00 a.m. I'd penciled in a walk to the nature preserve this morning, but I'm feeling a bit chilled. As we're off to London tomorrow, I'll make a stab at Tuesday's NEC Birmingham show.

We left the Holiday Inn about half three and found the backstage with ease, a spacious area cordoned off with a permanent metal barrier backed by a sidewalk and a line of summer trees swarming with flying ants. Sound-check included an instrumental Bad.

Round about four o'clock, Larry—Sullen Mullen, Sue says—arrived in a silver Mercedes, and came out to fans. Rarely did he glance up or even crack a smile, his thin face deeply furrowed, his lean body rattling about in a pair of baggy, nylon, parachute-like trousers.

Beside me, one fan asked Larry's bald and booted body-guard if he—the body-guard—would take a photo of him—the fan—with Larry. Stiff and unsmiling, and seemingly none too pleased, Larry acquiesced. When he turned to me, and I told him that the album and the concerts were wonderful, he paid not the slightest attention. Yadda, yadda, yadda. Heard it all before.

Looking fit and well, Adam and Edge then worked opposite ends of the line. I reiterated my lengthy conversation with Larry, and Adam, bless his heart, smiled with a gentle "thank you." Congenial and relaxed, they spent a good deal of time out with fans, Adam in sweater, slacks, and shoes in what Sue refers to as a "shitty brown," Edge in black cap, bluish t-shirt, long aubergine vest, and ratty blue jeans.

Sound check progressed after they'd gone in, Edge on vocals. His gentle voice doesn't really lend itself to a passionate delivery. He's much more at ease with his low-key Stuck in a Moment contribution, and the confidence in his voice was palpable when he reached that point. In time, he teased out some awesome guitar overlays against Stuck, as if demonstrating that this was his real forte.

About six o'clock, the silver Merc outside the backstage door was dispatched with Dennis Sheehan [U2's lighting director] riding shot-gun. In short order, the car returned. Bono, leaning out the left rear window, raised a bottle of Vittel. That would be that, we thought, given the late hour. And then Julie whispered, "he's coming over." And indeed he was.

In dark trousers—the bottom legs of which were gathered around his ankles—a lightly-striped blue shirt, black silk-textured jacket, and a camouflage cap worn backwards, he began to sign autographs five or six fans to our left. His hair, thick and longish in back, had a ginger hue much closer to his natural color, and he wore tinted metal-rimmed glasses.

"And how are *you* today?" he asked me, his gaze worn, his features lined and grizzled.

"Just fine, thank you very much," I answered, appending a new-album's-great-concerts-wonderful-thank-you-for-everything spiel.

"Our last album didn't have many white spaces," he remarked as he inscribed my CD cover, and I agreed.

"He's nicked me pen," Sue murmured then, as Bono moved on, taking her gold felt-marker with him, and he passed the pen back to Julie.

The Sweetest Thing video shoot, Fitzwilliam Square, Dublin –
September 20, 1998

Dreamchaser's
notice board for
The Sweetest
Thing video
shoot, Dublin –
September 20,
1998

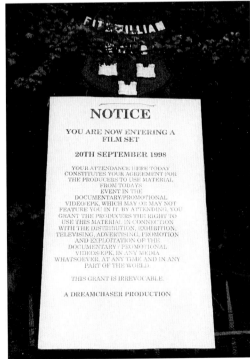

NOTICE

YOU ARE NOW ENTERING A
FILM SET

20TH SEPTEMBER 1998

YOUR ATTENDANCE HERE TODAY
CONSTITUTES YOUR AGREEMENT FOR
THE PRODUCERS TO USE MATERIAL
FROM TODAYS
EVENT IN THE
DOCUMENTARY/PROMOTIONAL
VIDEO/EPK, WHICH MAY OR MAY NOT
FEATURE YOU IN IT. BY ATTENDING, YOU
GRANT THE PRODUCERS THE RIGHT TO
USE THIS MATERIAL IN CONNECTION
WITH THE DISTRIBUTION, EXHIBITION,
TELEVISING, ADVERTISING, PROMOTION
AND EXPLOITATION OF THE
DOCUMENTARY / PROMOTIONAL
VIDEOS/EPK, IN ANY MEDIA
WHATSOEVER, AT ANY TIME AND IN ANY
PART OF THE WORLD.

THIS GRANT IS IRREVOCABLE.

A DREAMCHASER PRODUCTION

Ebb Tide at Colliemore Harbour, Dalkey, Ireland – September 22, 1998

Surf Fishermen on Killiney Beach – September 26, 1998

The Wicklow Mountains from Powerscourt Gardens, Ireland – June 4, 1999

Powerscourt Gardens – June 4, 1999

The Meeting of the Waters, Vale of Avoca, Ireland – June 4, 1999

The *Freedom of the City Awards*, Dublin – March 18, 2000

Adam at Hanover Quary – March 20, 2000

Edge at Hanover Quay – March 20, 2000

Bono signs *A Grand Madness* at Hanover Quay, Dublin –
March 20, 2000

The *Imagine* mosaic at Strawberry Fields, Central Park, New York City – March 25, 2000

National Car Rental Center, Sunrise, Florida, opening of the *Elevation Tour* – March 24, 2001

Birch Recreational Park, Fort Lauderdale, Florida – March 26, 2001

Bono signs autographs at sound check, National Car Rental Center – March 24, 2001

Larry, after-show, Miami – March 26, 2001

Adam, after-show, Miami – March 26, 2001

Edge, after-show, Miami – March 26, 2001

Bono, after-show,
Miami – March
26, 2001

St. George Street, St. Augustine, Florida – March 27, 2001

The Fleet Center, Boston, Massachusetts – June 4, 2001

Manchester Evening News Arena, Manchester, UK – August 11, 2001

U2 *All You Can't Leave Behind* billboard, Manchester, UK – August 11, 2001

Band on-stage , Manchester, UK – August 12, 2001 (Sue Fell)

Bono on-stage , Manchester, UK – August 12, 2001 (Sue Fell)

Larry meets and greets, Birmingham, UK –
August 14, 2001

Bono signs autographs, Birmingham, UK – August
14, 2001

Bono pre-show London – August 19, 2001

The London Eye – August 20, 2001

Slane Castle, Ireland – August 25, 2001

U2 Karlsplatz UBahn metro station, Vienna, Austria – September 23, 2001

Thomas and Mack Arena, Las Vegas, Nevada – November
18, 2001

Décor in Harrah's Casino, Las Vegas, Nevada – November 18, 2001

As he inched his way down the line, some of the fatigue dropped away by degrees, and he began to laugh, stopping to chat on someone's cell-phone. And then, headed for the backstage door, he hesitated at a clique of fans near the car-park kiosk, clearly charming the socks off a grey-haired woman there. He suddenly darted forward, kissed her on the cheek, and she beamed.

The bald and booted body-guard put a protective arm across Bono's shoulders when he set off again. With his head bowed like a little boy who'd been hurt on the playground, everybody loved him. The night's concert had much of this same warmth, vulnerability, and good-humor.

12:20 p.m. Lunch break in a narrow clearing on the King Moor Sidings Nature Preserve Trail. I'm seated on a throne-chair I've discovered carved into a sawed-off tree trunk. Though quite young, the woods here—once a siding for the railroad—call up dark knights on heavy horses, velveteen mantles flashing in a woodsy copse. Late summer hangs in the air, with crows cawing from tired-looking yellowing ash and silver birch. Leaves rustle with the sound of crumpled paper, and the feathered seed parachutes of the fireweed towering around me, drift everywhere.

Here then is the set-list from Birmingham's high-spirited and celebratory show: Elevation; Beautiful Day; End of the World; New Year's Day; Kite; Gone; Desire; Stay; Bad-40; Streets; Mysterious Ways; The Fly//Bullet; With or Without You//One; Walk On.

Edge was especially on fire for this performance, Stay and Sunday Bloody Sunday the best I've heard in some time. Using binoculars, Sue informed us that when Bono stepped out into the audience for Elevation, some woman groped him. The duel in End of the World came to a sudden stop when Bono dangled an arm around Edge's neck and then reached down to still his guitar strings.

At one point, Bono danced briefly with a young man who'd scrambled onstage. The lad kissed Bono's hand before leaving. Round about I Will Follow, Bono confessed to having "slept on the floor last night," as he had in the band's early days, when they'd regularly crashed in gardens, and on lawns and couches.

Forced to sleep in their van one exceptionally cold night, Alsatians had been brought in to sniff out drugs, they assumed. Adam had terrible gas in those days, so that all the poor pooches came up with was what had "come from Adam's arse." Why had he been telling this story? Bono asked himself. He couldn't remember. Maybe it just arose from being in Birmingham twenty years later, he surmised.

The Bad/Streets combo remains the high-point of *Elevation* shows for me. With "I want to feel sunlight on my face," the stage fires up in yellow light, giving Streets even more of a lift.

A dark-haired girl came to the stage for The Fly. Bono cradled her head as they danced, and then collapsed at her feet. The second encore opened with One for Africa's twenty-five-million HIV-positive inhabitants. And then, with Walk On's "hallelujah"s it was all over again.

9:00 p.m. Ready for an early night. We had an exceptional meal at the Golden Pheasant Chinese Restaurant earlier, a pubby place in faded peach. It's clouded over now, with a light rain.

With the entire Dublin docklands slated for development, Hanover [U2's Dublin studio on Hanover Quay] has been put up for sale, we hear. News too of a Catholic priest tagging along with Bono on tour. Issues of a dying Catholic father, I imagine.

"So I was just on the phone with my old man," Bono said at the second Birmingham show. "And sort of said how useless I felt not being there for him, and he replied, 'Sure, if you'd be at home you'd be useless anyway.' He's a tough fucker."

Monday, August 20, 2001

12:35 p.m. On the London to York train out of King's Cross Station, Coach R. My reservation says D, but I flew in here by the skin of my teeth and jumped in the first open door. This is the last major haul of my luggage until Sunday, when I fly back home. I've a smoked salmon and lettuce sandwich and a cup of tea from the trolley. Unfortunately, behind me, the female half of an elderly couple is reading the newspaper to her hard-of-hearing spouse.

Sue set off for Carlisle about nine-thirty this morning. With no choice in trains, she missed our London Eye experience. Jane and I took the Wandsworth line to Waterloo Station, where I checked my luggage, and then we reached the Eye in a rather round-about fashion.

The huge glass pods of the slow-moving, over-sized Ferris-wheel-like construction called the London Eye, each accommodate fifteen to twenty people. They rise from the bank of the Thames, opposite the parliament buildings, affording outstanding panoramic views up and down the river, north and south. We were eight, including Mark and Alan, members of NU2, a talented English U2 tribute band. Back at Waterloo Station, an enormous queue had formed for checked luggage, and with massive confusion over which tube to take, we opted for a taxi to King's Cross.

1:15 p.m. Coming into Peterborough now, with apologies for a delay due to an unforeseen stop at Stevenage and the breakdown of another train. King's Cross Station has closed behind me due to a gas leak.

I've settled in more fully now. Time to jot down a word or two about last night's U2 show, the second of two at Earl's Court, and my only GA [General Admission] experience this tour. Both London shows started and ended early, likely due to the residential nature of the surroundings. "Please Work Quietly" signs were posted everywhere in a rather dingy area of yellow-brick flats, "Chris and Paul was here," scrawled on one low wall.

We arrived at the venue about nine in the morning, in slashing-down rain. We flashed our tickets at a small window, were given red ECO (Earl's Court) wristbands, and instructed to wait under a side canopy. When the rain let up, we would be herded into prepared enclosures at the back of the building.

The queue situation remained haphazard until a Cockney bloke from venue security took charge. In a maroon Showsec UK jacket, the lean East-ender, thin and wiry, with short sandy hair and a knotted face, spit out pithy explanations as to what would happen and when. When he'd repeated himself to one group, he turned to the rest of us with "Where do they get their fucking fans from?" An American woman, vastly disturbed to find herself with a GA number in the low one-hundreds, moaned and wailed to excess.

About one-fifteen, having been shuffled into pens, we commenced a lengthy wait for U2 wristbands. Rain came and rain went, and around three o'clock, said bands appeared, and we were set free. Around the corner, at the Tournament Pub, our drinks arrived, but our lunches never did, and we cancelled and grabbed a chicken sandwich next door.

When Bono cruised in to the backstage entrance in his silver Mercedes, accompanied by "Baldy" [the "bald and booted" bodyguard], the crowd surged. In a bluish-green un-pressed shirt, light brown trousers and cap, he climbed out of the rear seat to back himself up against the car door.

I stood well out of the way and learned later that he'd called both Debbi and Jackie "sweetheart." Had a flicker of recognition for Sue, too. She emerged walking on air.

Afterwards, when GA ticket-holders were conducted to the floor in groups of twenty or thirty, we managed to attain the heart enclosure, which holds about three-hundred fans. We gathered in front of Bono's main mike, near the left side of the heart, where the End of the World duel takes place, sidling ever closer as the night progressed. Edge, Adam, and Larry remained in full view, Bono reduced, on occasion, to the knees up.

Here we go again, but this was just the best U2 show ever! Time in the heart was like being in some small intimate club. Heart to heart. Eye to eye. Bono was buoyant and energetic, though at one point he clutched his lower abdomen. Sue learned later that he'd injured his ribs in Paris and had been advised not to tour for two weeks. An incredibly high aftermath left us all exhilarated and "euphorically content."

2:20 p.m. Shouting moppets and a barking dog out of Doncaster, the cathedral high on a hill, nuclear power plants, creepy and futuristic, puffing steam right and left.

Tuesday, August 21, 2001

10:30 a.m. In Sharon's back garden in York. Pulled into town on a bright-blue sunny day, high spotty clouds, and a stiff breeze. Several urchins on the train made the going rough. One little boy's mother pronounced him "a right little bugger," and I had to agree. My eyelids finally stopped twitching, when they'd shifted several seats forward.

News on the telly at breakfast yesterday of an intricate crop-circle, discovered in an English wheat-field, composed of lines and arcs and multiple discs. The construction of such an involved arrangement could hardly have gone unnoticed, I said. What could any alien message possibly have been?

"U2 were fantastic last night," Jane answered. "Send more men."

More on second London before lunch. Here's the set-list: Elevation; Beautiful Day; End of the World; Discothèque/Staring at the Sun; Kite; New York; Sunday Bloody Sunday; Wake Up Dead Man; Stuck; Ground Beneath her Feet; All I Want is You; Streets; Mysterious Ways; Pride//Bullet; With or Without You; Angel of Harlem; One; Walk On

Experiencing the best band in the world in a "club setting," lent an air of intimate familiarity to this show. But the performance was electric in and of itself.

P. J. Harvey opened, a deathly pale waif with long choppy hair. She and the members of her band joined us later in the heart. For U2's opening, we held positions some thirty feet from the main stage. Elevation ended with a tribute to The Clash—"London Calling from the outskirts in."

Jane and I were beside the heart ramp for End of the World's superb dueling. "We're having an amazing time here in this city," Bono said before Kite. "People have been really generous to us. So thank you very much. This song I want to sing for my father, who is very sick at the moment. It's interesting . . . I didn't get on with my father for most of my life really . . . But I've made some kind of peace with him, and I'm really glad for that. So he was an opera singer. He had a pretty good tenor voice. In fact he has told me that if only I had his voice, I could have really done something with my life. This is Kite. This is for Bob."

Discothèque included INXS' Devil Inside, and a long chat introduced Sunday Bloody Sunday, touching on the troubled relations between Ireland and England. "What we want from you is repentance," Bono said. "And we'll give you forgiveness. But we won't go back." Long moments passed then as he tried to coax fans on the second tier into sharing their Irish flag. The heart crowd roared its encouragement, and Bono himself mimed tossing the flag down. But the owner just never got a clue.

"The Irish are really thick," Bono said, shaking his head and walking off. Another flag reached him from the point of the heart. "Twenty-nine people out shopping in a place called Omagh," he finished, hinting at Peace on Earth's IRA murders in Omagh in August of 1998.

Introducing a spirited and energetic Out of Control, the band's first single, Bono reverted to his long-gone teen-age self and referenced Stories for Boys and its B-side, Boy/Girl. The skit referenced the media, those talent scouts who make or break a career with such ease. As a band, the lads had shopped around, hoping someone—anyone—would listen to their song. "It's important to us," Bono said. "One day my head's going to be so big it's going to take Earl's Court to fill it."

For Mysterious Ways, Bono swiveled his hips with such finesse that someone handed him a fiver [a five pound note], which he tucked into his waistband. Someone else offered him a twenty-pound note which he looked over with a smile and handed back. "Right down and dirty he was," Sue said.

The Ground Beneath Her Feet, "stolen" from "The Salman

Rushdies," was also played at the point of the heart. A rich and sweet Wake Up Dead Man followed, and then Stuck in a Moment, "a song about something I would have liked to have been able to say to someone while he was still here." [Michael Hutchence]

In place of Bad, we had a splendid All I Want is You on the heart ramp, accompanied by Bad's rotating blue lanterns, and the arena convulsed for a fist-pumping Streets. Pride ended the main set with Bono flinging his heart out to the crowd.

A water bottle Bono dropped into the front row somehow worked its way back to Sue, who said she suddenly felt "a wet slithery thing" in her hand. The Italian man beside her, slapped his wrist, shouting "I give you my watch! I give you my watch!" A cup of water Bono drop-kicked into the crowd came back to hit him on the head.

As usual, the first encore opened with Charlton Heston and Bullet. For such a fan-centered performance, the emphasis on guns and celebrities seemed eerily appropriate. "I can make wounds that won't heal," Bono sang, focusing his spotlight first on the band, then pivoting to the audience, ranting Mark Chapman's "John, John, I just want an autograph!"

Entertainers of all stripes must wrestle with a craving for adulation from fans. If Bono had been scarred at a young age by his father's indifference, he might yet feel the sting, struggling to please a man of such opposite temperament.

Star charts and constellations floated above us like a planetarium show for With or Without You. The encore finished with *The Joshua Tree*'s "We'll shine like stars in the summer night; we'll shine like stars in the winter night. One heart, one hope, one love."

A rousing sing-along of Angel of Harlem came with the second encore. A lot of people have been "on the road with us over the last months," Bono said. "I look out here and see all these faces I've seen before. People I've seen in Miami. People I've seen in Paris. People I've seen in Germany. You've been on tour too . . . And they haven't been sleeping in fancy hotels either. But they're paying for our hotel rooms, and I'd like to thank you for that."

An outstanding Walk On closed the show. "This was an amazing, amazing, amazing night," Bono added, as the lads glad-handed the front row.

3:00 p.m. I'm on a lunch break in Sharon's back garden again. High feathery clouds streak a blue sky.

Sue's taxi from London dropped her at the wrong station and she missed her train altogether. As King's Cross Station closed just after I left, Jane missed her train as well. Thousands of people poured into the streets, as a result of a gas leak that affected the underground, Victoria Station to Chelsea.

3:30 p.m. Blazing hot now, a cool breeze and a bank of dark clouds crawling in from the west. Trains speed by beyond the moor. A race-track nearby as well. From a steady stream of announcements—none of which I can decipher—a muffled voice builds and builds in tone and speed and pitch, and then there's a massive appreciative roar.

Sweet little Sammy, Sharon's elderly cocker spaniel, has kept me company all day. Blind and deaf, he stumbles down the pathway to the back deck, snuffles up the stairs with stress and strain, and snuffles down again.

6:00 p.m. Sharon just in with news from Declan that Bob Hewson passed away four o'clock Monday morning. And Bono set for another London show tonight. Performing as his father lingered may have been therapeutic for him, a way for him to mourn. How hard it will be for anyone to cheer tonight.

U2 management convened to discuss going forward with the tour. Would Bono be persuaded that it would "look bad" to continue? Most people have to work through such loss quite literally, and I'm certain he'll soldier on. But how broken he must be. Though we may prepare for the inevitable, the actuality always comes as a shock. We're a bit like voyeurs, I suppose. And yet there's a privilege in sharing someone's grief, especially when they themselves have chosen to share it.

10:00 p.m. Looks like we'll drive to Liverpool Thursday night. If not, in order to catch the 8:00 a.m. ferry to Ireland, we'd have to leave York at five in the morning.

Wednesday, August 22, 2001

10:00 a.m. I'm outside with a cup of elderflower tea on another bright blue day, a jacket and raincoat this time yesterday. I savor these recuperative days with wanders on the moors and walks along the river or through the woods.

Before heading out to Hob Moor, I'll jump right into the first London show last Saturday. We came to Euston by train, hopped the tube to Victoria Station, took a cab to the Holiday Inn Express, London/Wandsworth, and a second taxi to Earl's Court. Julie, Jane, and I rode together in a cab driven by an unkempt fellow smelling of alcohol. Careening through the backstreets of London, zigging and zagging, he pulled into a cross street without looking.

Rooting around in my bag, I felt a thud and heard a crack as our left front headlight popped and a car struck the front passenger door. Two further jolts followed. The dinky red car that hit us had bounced off a van, hitting a silver Mercedes parked on the corner.

People poured out of flats, jotting down plate numbers, makes, and models. Involved drivers, together with the Merc's owner, exchanged insurance information. Our driver, totally unruffled, tossed off an occasional "it'll only be a minute." Never once did he ask how we were, except for Julie, who was in the front seat. He simply motored on to Earl's Court, where we pried open the front door to set Julie free.

Larry arrived at the rainy backstage entrance, and Sue listened in as Baldy advised him to "watch out for the blonde with the ponytail." Larry grunted, took a brief run at signing autographs, and went inside.

When Adam stepped over to fans, I waited out of the rain, under a tree, while Sharon gallantly put up her umbrella to protect him. "Hello, Jane. How are you?" he said to Jane when he reached her. "You're looking well. Nice to see you again." In the end, Baldy pulled up a brollie of his own and walked Adam back to his idling car.

Here's the first London set-list: Elevation; Beautiful Day; End of the World; New Year's Day; Kite; Gone; New York; I Will Follow; Sunday Bloody Sunday; Wake Up Dead Man; Stuck in a Moment; In a Little While; Desire; Stay; Bad; Streets; Mysterious Ways; The Fly//Bullet; With or Without You//One; Walk On

The strongest, most exceptional portion of this show was the I Will Follow/New Year's Day/Sunday Bloody Sunday sequence. Streets made room for a Get Up Stand Up ending, and there was further talk about the band's early days. How Larry always traveled with his own sleeping bag in order to avoid hotel sheets. How Bono developed a "bad knee" so he could ride shotgun. How Adam's mum hauled them around in a van.

Bullet was blistering, and One came with thanks to both "the Almighty" and "the spirit of music." After Walk On, the lads made a circuit of the heart with waves and smiles. And then once again, it was done.

We walked over to MacDonald's for a late night snack afterwards, catching a scrawny red fox jogging fearlessly about the city streets.

Sharon, Julie, and Marian left the next morning. (Marian is completing her Ph.D. in sociology, her thesis being *The Social Implications and History of Acne*. "Thoughts on Spots," you might say.)

Just after noon on a hot blue day, and I've finished lunch here on Hob Moor. Wide and flat, brownish grasses amid the green, Hob Moor is actually a common, crisscrossed by ancient track-ways. But for the hoof and mouth plague, cattle would be grazing here.

Off the edge of the moor, I crossed under the railroad tracks through a black tunnel lined with graffiti of the "Danny wuz ere" sort. On the other side, a vast swathe of green called Knave's Bank unfolded. Wild flowers and blackberry bushes abutted the asphalt path, and at the far end, by the main road, stood a gnarly boulder, another, hollow-topped, at its base. During the plague, camps on the moor took in the sick, and traders used this basin to "disinfect," with "holy" water and herbs, any goods they'd brought for the afflicted.

As I returned to the moor, a lanky fellow came striding in from the far side, a massive log balanced on his right shoulder. In a long grey hooded tunic he might have belonged to any one of countless centuries on the moor. But as he came closer, I could see that he was wearing flaming-red high-topped sneakers.

Boundless and empty but for the odd walker, worker, or dog runner, the moor is a wonder. Trees fringe its borders, with the Minster and village houses at a distance. Gangs of blustering magpies sail below a blanket of black-bottomed clouds.

9:00 p.m. In from supper with Jane at Gringo's Salsa Mexicana in Leeds. A tasty but irregular chimichanga fashioned with an odd assortment of veggies. Another long and busy day tomorrow.

Looking forward, I've reached my limit with hanging out before and after shows. What more could we possibly want beyond a genial chat with Bono in some Irish pub? I'd natter on about life and living, poetry, and the writing life. Jane says she'd like to show the lads some of their old videos. "The one where Bono takes a flagpole and jumps off the stage bonking Adam on the back of the head. And remember that video where it looked like your head was on fire?"

Thursday, August 23, 2001

I've repacked for the Dublin ferry.

Sammy is dead-knackered from tracking me all day yesterday. He'd sniff me out to be sure I was who he thought I was, then drift toward the door and back again, angling for ham snacks. When I finally got up, he would squint back again and again, just to reassure himself that I was indeed following him inside.

I've just read an excellent *NME* [*New Music Express*] article from last October, by a Sylvia Patterson. She describes Bono as a "strange, funny, serious, bright, melancholy, and nonetheless formidably optimistic man." Well said!

Bono describes *himself* in the piece as a "champagne socialist . . . . I've certainly found a place where I can face myself . . . I've had some mad times alright. And there's mad times to come." The album is about "the fire you pass through (in life)." All the straw and wood is burned away and "you're left with eternal things like friendship and laughter." All that you can't leave behind.

9:30 p.m. On the drive to Liverpool, yellow-gold lights left and right spread out over the hills. Up ahead, the reddish haze of a crescent moon.

Friday, August 24, 2001

Quarter to eight in the morning. We're in a queue for a Liverpool-Dublin ferry. Our company is the Seacat, at the Sea Packet Terminal.

Shopping our way into York yesterday, we nipped into the Minster, where the choir was practicing. Sumptuous artistry all around—the intricate choir screen, the tapestries, sculptures, and embroidered kneelers. Of the latter, the three coiled snakes of St. Hilda was my favorite. Barred protection for the stained-glass windows has left them quite congested looking. Strolling the wall then, I picked up a fridge magnet in a little shop in a dark and windowless corner of Monk's Gate.

8:30 a.m. Filing aboard.

Nine now, and we're churning past Liverpool. Not much of a skyline. In the past, I've always had to brace for the banks of wind and biting cold of a Scottish ferry. But it's a mild day in Liverpool, grey and overcast.

We left York at eight o'clock last night and reached our hotel in Netherton just after eleven. Nearing Liverpool, the sky lightened to a pale watery orange, and we motored down the ring road to the dockland ferry terminals. The area suggested a larger, battered and beaten, Dublin. Loading equipment and stacked containers crowded the sprawling lots, and dingy yellow lights glossed blackened windows and squalid brick walls. Shades of Whitechurch and Jack the Ripper.

At the ferry's car park this morning, we were directed to a disinfectant wash aimed at preventing hoof and mouth disease from invading Irish soil. A company man on the ramp then advised us to flip on our hazard lights as we drove into the ferry's bowels. A heads-up to the loaders below that a woman driver was on the way, he laughed. A moment or two we idled on the ramp while the muddy Mersey bubbled below. On shore, the Liver Building rose up grandly, with "Penny Lane" splashed on a passing bus.

Our ferry, the *Rapide Luxembourg* does clip along. Anything swept overboard disappears in the blink of an eye. The great white swath of foam in our wake has sea-birds hovering and bobbing left and right. The grey Irish Sea lies calm and flat, oil platforms poking up here and there, the vague hills of Wales to the south. When I flew into Manchester two weeks ago, ships anchored at varied distances sat like toothpicks on a blue plate. The sea has thickened somewhat off the ship's sides.

10:30 a.m. The captain has advised that we're now running on three engines! The main one conked out. No one knows why. Already delayed by an electrical communications problem between the bridge and the engines, we may have to call at Holyhead for another ferry.

Noon. On-shore management has indeed re-routed us to Holyhead. No berth availability there until after three o'clock, so we'll have to bob off-shore a spell. They've hatched a plan to tinker with the failed engine in a way that has never been tried before. Something to do with a starter engine.

3:00 p.m. Back in our car, but still on the *Rapide Luxembourg*. That one-off starter engine approach apparently worked. Now, however, some turbines are on the fritz.

Two hours later. Choppy and windy with a spit of rain. Turbines functioning, we have Dalkey Island and Bray Head behind us now. The spike of Killiney Hill's monument pierces a grey haze to one side. Howth floats off the other. We've proceeded up the Liffey to the docklands, colossal blue cranes everywhere.

Berthed beside the signature twin towers of the Liffey power station. Off-loaded and disinfected.

We're headed for Declan's in the rain, around The Point and down the quays. Cranes, cranes, and more cranes. Principal Management across the river, where the *Seaborne Pride* lies at anchor.

Sunday, August 26, 2001

In Los Angeles International, awaiting my Tucson flight. Five hours before my ten and a half-hour Dublin to LA departure, Sharon and Jane dropped me at the Dublin airport, where I had a light breakfast.

The flight went smoothly, each seat with its own entertainment center. I weathered several movies and played trivia games.

On a bright sunny day, in contrast to the smogginess here in LA, we banked westward leaving Dublin, and crossed the island. Ireland expanded below in haphazard fashion, green fields shaped by stone walls and hedgerows. Iceland came up next, black and barren, with a sweeping interior plain of glaciers. And in time, we overflew the Canadian Prairie Provinces, Montana, the Great Salt Lake, and the rugged Sierra Nevada.

4:30 p.m. We depart for Tucson in forty-five minutes. Just long enough for Dublin pre-show notes.

From the Dublin ferry, we hurried out to Declan's and passed a few pleasant hours there with him, his wife, Mary, and their angelic seven-week-old son, Owen. Mary prepped an unbeatable chili/pasta dinner.

At Amberly then—our Blackrock B&B—we off-loaded our luggage and rendezvoused for drinks with Sue and Julie at the Court Hotel in Killiney. Back to Blackrock by eleven.

Seven-thirty Saturday morning, we breezed out to Declan's again. An enormous travelers' enclave of heaped garbage and shabby campers augmented an already bleary day. Declan stood on the roadside with his young cousin, David. Mary, bless her, had packed sandwiches in two large cookie tins. David works for a crisps [potato chips] factory—a "potato factory," Mary said—and so we left with a fine supply of nibbles.

Setting off for Slane just after eight o'clock, Declan hurled down roads thick and thin, in road-rally fashion, Sharon struggling to keep pace. By Dun Boyne Village, we knew Slane Castle—in a lush valley above the River Boyne, thirty miles north of the city—was within spitting distance.

Close to nine, we parked in a cow-plotched field opposite a VIP lot and hiked the half mile of intermittent tote-bag searches to the heart queue. There, we grew several thousand strong before being sectioned off, a second group taking form behind us.

We stood and we stood and we stood, in an on-again/off-again rain, the ground too littered and dirty for sitting. At eleven o'clock, we were shifted onto an expansive grassy slope ringed with barrier fences and vendor stalls. From here, we made our way to the bottom of the hill, where we found excellent positioning adjacent a wooden wall on the right side, fifty feet or so from the stage. We'd missed out on the heart and learned later that the group behind us had been led to a second entrance which brought them to the near left side, so that some of them made the heart. Still, we had a clean and unobstructed view of the main stage and ramps, and after settling in, I trekked to the loo, a dismal, never-to-be-repeated experience.

The all-ages crowd formed a figure eight, wide and deep before and beside the stage, bottle-necked above, and then spilling into a second vastness of green lawn. Fans wearing leprechaun hats, bell-tipped fool's caps, Irish flag cloaks, priestly frocks, and Cardinal robes peppered the throng. Inflatable fingers, willies, and even chairs, floated everywhere, helicopters and hot air balloons hovering above.

When Relish, the first act, opened under a scorching sun, I'd already stretched out in the grass. JJ72 followed, fronted by a helium-voiced young man. And then Kelis, a large woman with a colored sponge for hair, offered up a semi-decent Sweet Dreams [Eurythmics]. "This next song is also from my new album," she then explained. I'm a Junky for Your Love was the title, as I recall. "I hate you so much right now" figured in there somewhere too.

Coldplay took the stage about four-thirty. "There's been a lot of talk about this next song. Maybe too much talk. This song is Yellow," the singer, Chris Martin, said, echoing Bono's former intro of Sunday Bloody Sunday. Larry, Ali, and Jordan formed a small clique on the left side of the stage during Coldplay's excellent set, and further left still, Bono danced with his second son, little Eli, in his arms.

The Red Hot Chili Peppers launched about six o'clock and played a lively fifty-minute set, Anthony Kedis tearing around the stage, tumbling and jumping. At one point, he asked members of the audience to take off their shirts, and I'm sure that somewhere a woman or two complied. For the most part though, fans had newly purchased t-shirts, or clothing they'd already removed for the heat, and we whirled these overhead "like helicopters."

As the set progressed, Kedis announced that it was "that time in the show" when a dedication should be made. He indicated a lone woman in a lime-green security vest high in the emptiness of the hill between fenced off audience sectors. "That security person," Kedis said. The woman responded with a vigorous wave, and the crowd thundered its approval.

Friday, August 31, 2001

10:00 a.m. Back in my office again, things very nearly in order.

I arrived home about six-thirty Sunday evening. Slane was a dazzling and magical experience. The best U2 show I've ever seen! [Not again!] A mixture of positive celebration and heart-rending poignancy.

Here's the set-list: Elevation; Beautiful Day; End of the World; New Year's Day; Kite; A Sort of Homecoming; I Will Follow; Sunday Bloody Sunday; Wake Up Dead Man; Stuck in a Moment; In a Little While; Desire; Staring at the Sun; Bad; Streets; Mysterious Ways; Pride//Bullet; With or Without You//One; Walk On

The stage's simplicity recalled *The Joshua Tree* tour—four overhanging screens with static, black *All That You Can't Leave*

Behind song symbols. Pouring over the hollows and rises of the castle grounds, the capacity crowd of eighty to a hundred-thousand—depending on the newspaper consulted—roared with ecstatic abandon. The castle rose in grey turrets to the right, one single light blinking in a high-placed window.

Under a half moon in a darkening sky, the band arrived for Elevation about eight-thirty. Bono genuflected and crossed himself. His father's funeral had taken place only the day before, the coffin shrouded in irises in honor of his wife.

"Jesus, this is beautiful." Bono gazed out over the tumultuous crowd, a boundless sea of color fading off to our left. "Thanks for coming out. I want to thank the sun for shining," he said. "I want to thank God for taking my old man away from his sick and tired old body and giving him a new one. And I want to thank you for your patience. It's taken us twenty years to get to this moment." [U2 had supported Thin Lizzy twenty years before, at Slane Castle's first concert, in August of 1981.]

Kite—a song "I thought I wrote for my kids, but now it feels like my old man wrote it for me and my brother"—was dedicated to Bob Hewson.

Not having gotten on with his Dad, Bono's sense of the importance of communication in relationships must be paramount. People knew Bob's heart through his words, I've read, though they must have been frequently unemotional and head-centered. After Bono had fallen off the stage in Miami, for example, Bob had rung him up. "Have you fallen off any more stages?" he'd asked, with a father's need to know. Very much a man of his generation. Like my own father. Not one to be overly emotional or demonstrative.

"The last of the opera stars, when be-bop drove the big cars," Bono finished, highlighting the era of his father's life.

The audience raised cigarette lighters for Kite, some fans brandishing lit scraps of paper, drinking cups, or rolled pieces of cardboard, so that a sizeable number of ground fires had to be snuffed out afterwards.

Recorded at Slane in 1984, A Sort of Homecoming excelled. Bono could have brushed up on the lyrics, I suppose, but the atmosphere and emotion were over-the-top. I Will Follow included "amazing grace; I was lost, now I'm found."

Some stirring remarks about Ireland's relationship to her recent immigrants popped up at one point. "We won't go back," Bono said. "We're bigger than this small island. We're bigger than our past. We're bigger than racism." And then he segued into Omagh and Ireland's historical penchant for internecine violence.

After In a Little While, he presented the band. "Wearing his number seven shirt is the Edge." Larry, "the man who started the band and the man who on a daily basis may finish it." Adam "the poshest member of the band, a man fit for a castle." Mention of Thin Lizzy came here as well. "When we started off, it was unimaginable that we'd be headlining Slane." When they'd supported Thin Lizzy, "we were crap." (Dublin is mulling over a Phil Lynott statue. Lynott's mother was in the VIP section.)

Another emotional Bad included a fragment of Coldplay's Yellow, and a wash of red light announced Streets, white spotlights bouncing off the hillside audience. "I want to dance, dance, dance to the end of the race."

For Mysterious ways, Bono pulled a young woman up from inside the heart enclosure. They strolled together to the tip of the heart and then Bono danced with her a long moment before sending her back into the crowd. Utterly star-struck, she still managed a belly-dance before she left.

Pride ended the main set, Bono, "in the name of love," throwing his heart out to the masses. "Thank you for coming all the way out here. Thank you for giving us your love . . . we're not going away."

The first encore opened with Bullet. Here, Bono took a pacifist stance against guns and lambasted Irish terrorist organizations, the UDA [Ulster Defence Association], the IRA [Irish Republican Army], and the UVF [Ulster Volunteer Force].

A great deal of talk about Bob Hewson launched the second

encore. On a bedside vigil at the hospital, Bono had fallen asleep, roused by the sound of his father's voice. Bob beckoned him over. "This is a prison," he whispered. "I want to go home." Was he expressing a literal desire to be taken home, to quit the forced confinement the hospital had become? Had life itself become such an enforced torment that he was beyond ready for an "eternal home"? It hardly matters which.

Before One, Bono thanked his father for "giving me the voice I'm speaking to you with today." A voice that would go down to his children and his children's children. Overhead screens blinked with those One video elements that featured Bob—the teeter-totter, the flapping overcoat, the stepping off-camera. These resolved to Bob's portrait. "Bob Hewson 1925-2001."

Bob had understood the relationship between the First World and the Third, Bono said. In reference to the validity of the *Drop the Debt Campaign*, the Irish should never forget they'd been refugees themselves once. All people deserved to live in dignity. "If I learned anything from my father, it's that." One then wrapped up with the Supremes When Will I See You Again.

A celebratory Walk On closed the show with hopeful joy and then, accompanied by a fifteen-minute fireworks display over the moonlit banks of the River Boyne, The Unforgettable Fire welled up. Showers of light and color blossomed across the sky, explosive underfoot. The perfect ending to a perfect show.

The Unforgettable Fire had been recorded at Slane Castle back in 1984. This new one, with burgeoning lights in the skies overhead, heralded the end of the European *Elevation Tour*. A grand Dublin homecoming. The final celebration of Bob Hewson's life. The last incomparable night of an Irish wake.

We slogged our way up the great hill, through a farm-yard, to the cow-plotched field where we'd abandoned the car. Hour after long hour we waited then for the VIP section and others to empty. With the Navan road blocked, Declan deftly guided us back to Blackrock by an alternate route and we arrived home just short of three a.m. Sunday morning.

What a night! What a show!

Saturday, September 1, 2001

4:30 p.m. Overcast. Low grey clouds and a light breeze in the palm trees, with rain to the south. A fallish feel in the air. Trees changing color. Dan watching football.

My overseas *Elevation Tour* remains so fresh and distinctive, culminating in the exhilaration of Slane Castle. An ethereal experience, replete with hope and joy, despite the pain. Bono embodies his life in his art, so that his grief and his art can never really be separated. Such a privilege to have shared both.

Friday, September 7, 2001

Last night, U2 accepted the *Video Vanguard Award* at *MTV*'s *VMAs* [*Video Music Awards*]. They're far ahead of the game in my book, with rap, hip-hop, and rap/metal so prevalent these days. Oodles of long, thin men in over-sized shirts and trousers, clutched at their crotches, and leggy, skimpily-clad young women gyrated in endless dance blocks. Britney Spears pranced about in vague lace, a thick pale-gold boa constrictor draped over her shoulders. I couldn't make out a word of her breathy delivery.

On an elevated blue stage that lowered to floor level by degrees, U2 performed a medley of Elevation, Kite, and Stuck in a Moment, with one false start when juice failed to reach Adam's amp.

Tuesday, September 11, 2001

Oh my God!!

Early this morning, terrorists flew two domestic planes into the twin towers of the World Trade Center in New York City!! Those buildings hold fifty-thousand people, and they're guesstimating a low murder count of ten-thousand! A dark, dark day!

Danielle called this morning with news of the first attack and we switched on the TV just as the second plane hit, in real time.

"I can't believe the news today. I can't close my eyes and make it go away."

Thursday, September 20, 2001

7:20 a.m. At Gate 17 in Sky Harbor International Airport [Phoenix], on our way to Vienna, Austria. Our Atlanta flight leaves in an hour. "You don't have to be a victim," the *CNN* announcer declared as I came back from the loo. Ah, the World Trade Center, I thought. Incomprehensively, she went on to extol the many merits of Rogaine.

8:50 a.m. On our flight to Atlanta, heading into another of the U.S. cities terrorists had targeted. In Phoenix, our pilot had stepped out from the cockpit well before departure time to say that we, a mere handful, were all accounted for. If everyone was in agreement then, "we might as well be off."

Yesterday, I called Marsha, our travel agent. "God willing, I'll talk to you when we get back from Vienna," I said. "God willing, I'll be here to talk to," she answered.

I'm into a book called *Sacred Spaces* by Margaret Silf. The first section addresses the Celtic Knot as a symbol of infinity, weaving all aspects of our lives into a whole. "We all know how we feel when circumstances shake our certainties and we feel like curling up again in the fetal position to get ourselves put back together . . . . Simply become aware of the weaving process that never ceases in you. The weaving has been going on day by day, hour by hour, silently and surely. And it still continues. Every day we live is a further weaving of God's Dream in our own lives."

5:45 p.m. A huge American flag unfurled from a window of the Atlanta control tower as we landed.

Saturday, September 22, 2001

So much more to say about the Hofburg [the former Imperial Residence, Vienna, Austria], an astonishing collection of elegance and pomp that expresses the power of the Hapsburgs over their six-hundred-year reign. The Austrian president lives here now. We entered the precinct through the St. Michael Portal, a classical façade with a pale blue-green dome. Back to our hotel then on the underground, our line to the Rathaus [the City Hall] is U2!

9:00 p.m. In from the American Embassy. Huge cement pylons on the periphery protect the building, and armed guards are everywhere. We placed a bouquet of roses on the makeshift shrine, to honor Trade Tower victims. Four or five-thousand, it's presumed now, from over ninety countries.

Wednesday, October 10, 2001

Home again. I missed the internet broadcast of U2's concert at Notre Dame [Indiana] last night. They opened with Beautiful Day, performed What's Going On—a new single for AIDS in Africa—and Peace on Earth. In the course of an especially poignant show, New York City firemen, policemen, and other first-responders were brought to the stage.

Sunday, October 21, 2001

Breakfast on the east patio, on a warm and sunny day. Last night, we watched the *Concert for New York City*, The Who's We Won't Get Fooled Again, the highlight. WTC victims' families, rescue and cleanup crews, could all breathe again to some small degree.

Bono and Edge, slated to appear, never arrived. When everyone gathered for an encore/finale featuring Paul McCartney, he made firm mention that this was indeed the end of the evening.

Thursday, October 25, 2001

Sunlight glistening on the cereus has left them a mass of luminous, feathered fringes. I've hardly gotten much work out. Editors, reeling from the recent anthrax scare, are dumping everything, something they've no doubt dreamed of for decades.

I'm bidding on an eBay ticket for U2 in Las Vegas. Dustin is there November 15 thru November 18. I'm there the seventeenth to the twenty-first, though I doubt that our paths will cross.

Bono and Edge were "unavoidably delayed" for the *Concert for New York City*, when an anthrax scare erupted at a daughter's school.

Monday, November 5, 2001

A band of blackness just rolled in from the west, with bomb-blasts of thunder. Last night, the Arizona Diamondbacks won the

World Series. A relief to have those games on. Even *I* watched. More and more we're getting back to normal. A couple of days ago, a woman on *Larry King Live* said that New York is really "a small community. There's just a lot of people there." That attitude will see us all through this calamitous time.

U2 play Phoenix November 23, Thanksgiving weekend. I considered driving up Friday, then back out to Cave Creek [Chiricahua Mountains, southeastern Arizona] on Saturday. But it's one hell of a drive.

Saturday, November 17, 2001

8:00 a.m. On my flight to Las Vegas. Ate supper at a nearly empty Mexican restaurant at the airport, National Guard troops everywhere.

9:00 p.m. In our room, M657, in the Mardi Gras Tower of Harrah's Casino. Sharon and Jane just in from the UK.

Sunday, November 18, 2001

Lazing by the pool at the Flamingo Hotel. Too cold for swimming. Angela, a tiny Greek waitress, served us breakfast this morning at Harrah's buffet. A strange town, Las Vegas, she said. Women so phony if you shook them, their boobs could fall off. And sometimes they were men.

Monday, November 19, 2001

1:30 a.m. Yet another incredible U2 show!

1:30 p.m. I'm perched on the steps of Caesar's Palace, Sharon and Jane off to the Wal-Mart Superstore on the bus. Finding a spot to rest your dogs in this town—without gambling—is a challenge. After another hefty breakfast at Harrah's, during which 11 O'clock Tick Tock was played, we passed another hour or two at the Flamingo pool.

After the gig last night, we hiked the three miles back from the venue [Thomas and Mack Center] in just over an hour. As we approached the hotel, U2's Joe O'Herlihy and Dennis Sheehan passed by, out to take in the action.

Idling now in an alcove of the outdoor adjunct to the Bellagio

Hotel and Casino. A fountain-filled lake stretches before me, with a line of white-balustraded Parisian-style villas in Pompeii gold on the far side—Hermes, Giorgio Armani, Olives. The lamp-post beside me is playing Italian music.

I've shifted over to the Desert Passage Shops at the Aladdin Hotel, where I'm *seated*, with a coffee, at a garden table outside Teuscher's. The Java Jacket on my decaf warns that this is a "hot beverage." Duh! I'm in a pink-pillared central court with bleeps and chimes, chinks, and electronic whiz-bangs echoing from the casino opposite. Shops are selling enormous quantities of upscale "stuff," much of it jewelry. The constant racket keeps your mind bouncing off the walls, the whole town top-heavy with gargantuan larger-than-life thematic casino/hotels that leave the impression of having been built by gigantic extra-terrestrials.

Hallelujah! I've found a bench. Outside the Paris Las Vegas. The French do like to sit. The Arc de Triomphe squats to my left, with a short Champs Elysees, and the Eiffel Tower climbs up behind me.

In a lounge chair of the Parisian's lobby now. Mosaic tiled floors. Enormous cut-glass chandeliers. Floral carpets. Candled wall-sconces and an assortment of gilded this and that. The floors are tiled in ice-blue, with dark-edged creamy carpets in pink and blue curlicues. Everything, everywhere, accented with giant vases of ruby-red roses.

The constant casino *boings* would drive me up the wall. Clinking, bleeping, eating, drinking, shopping, gambling. It never stops. One specific background hum keeps you constantly on your toes. A note that says, "Any minute now something exciting is going to happen. You wouldn't want to miss it now, would you?" You're on the edge of your seat. Literally. In any other context, this would be anxiety.

Inside the Parisian proper, the ceiling is painted 'summer sky at twilight.' Lamp-posts on cobble-stoned streets front cafés and shop facades, each replete with gambling paraphernalia.

But on with the show, now that I'm back at Harrah's.

On our trek to the backstage entrance for sound-check, we passed the Heart fans—some of them still asleep. Many had been there since Thursday night, stretched out with air mattresses, sleeping bags, camp stools, and awnings.

University of Las Vegas security officers just moved us to the far end of the road, threatening with arrest those fans who'd hidden out in an adjacent parking lot. A Bono clone, balding and overly thin, materialized, along with a bespeckled female McPhisto, both of whom we noticed later on inside. Asked again to shift position, we discovered a cement bench secured to a wall. When yet another officer ordered further retreat, we hesitated, and in short order a string of black limos and vans came around the corner, Edge smiling out one open window.

Back at the main gate, local band Mercy Lady Day implored support for an upcoming CD release party. After the frenzied *Popmart* Las Vegas opener, the sparse crowd belied a U2 concert.

Round about six, inside the venue, we ordered pizza and a chicken fillet, and retreated to a spot near a service elevator and a first-aid station. When Sharon grabbed a few winks on the floor, several UNLV policemen stopped by to make sure she was alright.

When No Doubt wrapped up, I took my seat. With an unobstructed view on Edge's side, mid-way down the heart ramp, I had only three rows in front of me, a narrow gap, and then the ramp itself, which extended three-quarters the length of the floor. I was one seat from the side rail, beyond which, ten to fifteen feet away, rose the staircase by which the lads would reach the stage.

Tuesday, November 20, 2001

Windy this morning. Out by the Flamingo pool once again.

Here's the Las Vegas set-list: Elevation; Beautiful Day; End of the World; New Year's Day; I Will Follow; Sunday, Bloody Sunday; Stuck in a Moment; Kite; Wild Honey; People Get Ready; Please; Bad/40; Streets; Still Haven't Found; Pride//Bullet; What's Goin' On; New York//One; Wild Horses; Walk On/Can't Help Falling in Love

Elvis impersonators were sprinkled through the crowd, a number of them in the Heart enclosure. One of these, with a Priscilla Presley clone, sat just right of the stage in the first row. Beautiful Day had a lengthy "heart" and "soul" improvisation, together with the lines "to California, out to Nevada, into the desert" and "see Adam Clayton right in front of you." Sunday Bloody Sunday hit home with "bodies strewn across a dead-end street." Bono clasped an American flag to his chest.

Kite—for "anyone who's lost someone"—had a slew of Las Vegas memories beforehand. Frank Sinatra, who'd "slagged off" U2's duds, boxing-match tickets Bono had given to REM's Peter Buck, who ended up sitting beside Sugar Ray Leonard, "a perfectly normal spaceship, a mirror-ball lemon."

The young woman in shades invited to play guitar for People Get Ready, performed with great poise and confidence. When Edge, her favorite, backed down the ramp, she followed, and both he and Bono gave her a kiss before she went back out into the crowd.

Please, with its "September, streets capsizing, spilling over down the drain. Shards of glass, splinters like rain," had, of course, been written for the Irish Troubles. How fitting for 911. Some remarks about fundamentalists creating god in their own image—"small, tiny people"—followed. How "proud and humble" the band felt to be touring America "at this time . . . . We wouldn't want to be anywhere else."

Bad came as a welcome surprise. A celebratory Streets next, and MLK's "I have a dream" speech, with love lobbed out to all sides of the venue.

Bullet opened the first encore with a tuneless wail and an odd chaotic mix of lines, chunks of lines, and crisscrossed lines on-screen. Gwen Stephani of No Doubt accompanied Bono for What's Goin' On. "In New York I had some trouble with too many choices," Bono ad-libbed in New York. "I lost my luggage. You lost your wife . . . . Even Las Vegas loves New York."

Passengers and crews of the doomed 911 airliners scrolled on-screen for the second encore, One, dedicated to Elvis Presley. "You know, in a city that's so full of fantasy and wild imaginings," Bono said. "I would like for a second to think that the same imagination that brought you this city could imagine a world that would be a fairer place for more people living in it. And I think that that might be the only fitting memorial for the lives that were lost on September 11."

One closed the show with Can't Help Falling in Love.

The healing energy of this very American performance eased our national heartache, if only for a moment.

Wednesday, November 21, 2001

Awaiting a 10:00 a.m. flight home to Tucson here on Concourse C. Jane and Sharon are over at international departures, Concourse D.

Tuesday night, Jane and I scoped out the nine-fifteen "eruption" of The Mirage's volcano. Against a build-up of jungle drums, bubbling-water "lava" flared up in orange light. Arcs of fire sprouted from gas valves and flash pots exploded.

Afterwards, we took the tram over to Treasure Island, where a crowd had gathered for the 10:00 p.m. sinking of a pirate ship. To the Venetian next, passing a billboard ad for hypnotist/magician Justin Trance. I realized then—quite suddenly—that I was all Vegas-ed out!

We did however prowl the Venetian again last night, riding the inside escalator up to the Canal Shoppes, where a fake blue sky upheld slow-moving summer clouds drifting over a piazza of outdoor cafés and gondola-laden canals. One of several stone bridges displayed a decorated Christmas tree around which Renaissance-costumed members of an Italian light opera company performed. Boatmen serenaded in the striped shirts and caps of real Venetian gondoliers, and women with whitened faces, hands, and feet froze on cobblestones like statues. Palaces, one with identical oriels to the Ca' d'Oro in Venice, lined the canal and the lion of St. Mark was everywhere.

From The Venetian we sauntered over to the Paris Casino's Saint Alexandre Bridge and rode the glass-walled elevator to the top of the Eiffel Tower, half the size of the Paris original. From here, we had a grand view of the lights and the color up and down The Strip. Also enjoyed the dancing-waters on The Bellagio's lake. I'm not fond of operatic voices, but the mellow tenor to which the waters swayed and swirled, white chutes and fine sprays lit with varied hues, was quite magical.

Untold miles we hiked in Caesar's Palace, in search of some escape. We finally stumbled on a bold Exit sign, marked For Emergencies Only. But just to the right, a small unmarked *Alice in Wonderland* door allowed us a rush to freedom.

Thursday, November 22, 2001

10:00 p.m. Settled in Stone Cottage at Cave Creek Ranch [Chiricahua Mountains, Southern Arizona]. After a top-notch thanksgiving dinner at the house, we arrived at the end of a glowing orange sunset. About an hour ago, we drove up to Vista Point by Cathedral Rock. A half-moon with an icy halo hung above the pink rhyolite cliffs. In a wild rush of wind, the faces of the mountains morphed into black silhouettes. Dark craters like the iris of an eye transformed the moon into something sentient, a safe and warm Spirit of the Universe.

There's a U2 show tomorrow night in Phoenix . . . and I won't be there.

Friday, November 23, 2001

There's a U2 show in Phoenix tonight and I won't be there!

Stretched out on the granite outcrop across the creek, on a slope of the mountains, we have a vast view up and down the canyon, east and west. We ate a picnic lunch beside the creek outside of Paradise and are settled now in our L.L. Bean chairs, feet propped on a log. The creek, strewn with rusted sycamore leaves and studded with pinyon pine, juniper, and manzanita, burbles by.

With a good twelve hour drive there and back, I know I was

right to forego U2 in Phoenix tonight. But it's not been easy.

10:30 p.m. After supper, we drove up to Vista Point. All the things that happen in the world and all the things that *have* happened and *will* happen, and the canyon and the mountains remain. Day and night, year after year, always changing, always the same. What a pleasure and a privilege to have such peace, such wildness, to be able to refresh the spirit and renew the soul.

A shooting star flashed across the sky just at the time the lads must have taken the stage.

Sunday, November 25, 2001

Stopped for gas in San Simon on our way home. A fellow in a U2 t-shirt there reminded me that, once again, there was a U2 concert in Phoenix last night. And I wasn't there!

Wednesday, November 28, 2001

The Las Vegas Elvis impersonator Bono dedicated One to— as "promised" (along with Quincy Jones)—was Mark Hussman, whom Bono had met at a party just a few weeks ago.

Friday, November 30, 2001

George Harrison died in Los Angeles yesterday. He'd traveled to New York on a "last ditch effort" to ward off brain cancer. He passed away at the home of a friend "conscious of God and fearless of death." George believed that one of the most important things in life was the search for God. I hope he's found what he was looking for.

Saturday, December 1, 2001

I've finally wrapped up a review of the Phoenix Elevation show way back in the spring. [Specific numbers, covered earlier, have been omitted.] I call it, appropriately,

WHEN LOVE CAME TO TOWN

Way back in the 1980s when U2 played their first arena shows, Adam described the band as "stripped down . . . straightforward and honest." Stripped down only applies to the current tour when compared to the technological extravaganzas of the *Popmart* and

Zoo tours. Flamboyant and full of light—as it should be—*Elevation* shows come complete with lasers, spotlights, and strobes; with filmy curtains and drifting projected images. Six suspended screens show off the band in black-and-white. But "straightforward and honest" doesn't get any better.

When the *Elevation Tour* rolled into Phoenix on April 28, I'd already had the privilege of experiencing the two opening shows in Sunrise, Florida—followed by concerts in Charlotte, North Carolina, and Atlanta, Georgia. Though nothing short of stunning, the Florida shows, by a perceived necessity, pressed to make a point, to prove something, to blow away the competition and the critics with unparalleled and ready showmanship and talent. On a scale far more massive than the mini-tour of their relatively recent promo-gig past, the band felt compelled to "reapply for the job," having gotten "lost along the way," as Bono confessed in Charlotte. By Atlanta, the fully evolved passionate spirit of *Elevation* had kicked in and it would only get better and better. This is not to say that Florida was lacking in any way, only that the band was now done with the hoopla and media expectation of an opening night, and so free to relax and focus on what they wanted from their own performance—"an evening about friendship."

By now, thanks to the internet, *Elevation* shows are the stuff of legend—warm, inclusive affairs, intimate and communal, and yet—typical of U2—still incomparably passionate, powerful, and uplifting. U2 is the consummate live band. When they play live the goal has *always* been elevation. But the spirit of love and friendship permeates and further energizes the atmosphere of *Elevation* concerts, while pre-eminent musicianship just blows the roof off. These shows are about being together—audience and performer—one but not the same. The artificial separation built into both the *Popmart* and *Zoo* tours has vanished. No matter where you find yourself in any venue, the celebration will surround you—an extraordinarily engaging, expansive, and personal experience.

Elie Wiesel has said that life is not made of years, it's made of moments. What an extraordinary moment *Elevation* is! A moment to elevate the soul and forget the mire of the world. U2 have made a career out of making themselves comfortable wherever they happen to be, and they've proven time and again that they can go anywhere. "You have to jump off cliffs all the time and build your wings on the way down," Ray Bradbury has said. He was speaking about the writing process, of course, but from U2's past, they're obviously equally at home with that challenge. And as *Elevation* proves, as they continue to grow, they're only going to get better and better. (The older the fiddle, the sweeter the tune, an old Irish proverb says.) In long ago but not forgotten *Joshua Tree/Rattle and Hum* days, B.B. King used to ask U2's audience, "Is there love in the house?" Well yes . . . there is. Mutual love. And lots of it.

Monday, December 3, 2001

I've just learned that U2 will play the half-time show at the Super Bowl in New Orleans on February 12.

Friday, December 21, 2001

A couple of quotes while I wait for Dan to call, the first from Stephen King, who writes, "You can't deny laughter. When it comes, it plops down in your favorite chair and stays as long as it wants."

The second, from Bono, comes from a *Gentleman's Quarterly* article: "Sunrises are God's hit singles. Do the big number first and then just get on with the rest of the show." Except for an off-putting remark about the Dalai Lama, I quite enjoyed the piece. His Holiness had asked Bono to participate in a festival celebrating "Oneness." Bono "sniffed . . . the unsavory whiff of 'hippiedom,'" and declined. "One, but not the same," his response read.

For someone who's cozied up to the Pope, who, as head of the Roman Catholic Church has dealt the world a rather large dose of pain and suffering, that's a rather unfair attitude. The Dalai Lama and the Pope are cut from the same cloth, both the eventual fallout of competing political parties. The Roman Church, then the Roman and Celtic Catholic Churches, and finally the Roman Catholic and

Eastern Orthodox Churches on the one hand; rival Tibetan tribal Lamas on the other.

Saturday, December 29, 2001

Making my way through Chet Raymo's *An Intimate Look at the Night Sky* [Walker Books, London; 2001] Light travels at 186,000 miles a second, and yet our nearest galaxies lie millions of light years away. One Deep Space photograph from the Hubble Telescope includes at least a million galaxies. Eighteen-hundred such photos would be required to encompass the entire sky. Hundreds of billions of galaxies, each with hundreds of billions of stars. Meteor storms with 150,000 shooting stars per hour. Our last known super nova arrived in 1987—my first year of U2.

Wednesday, January 2, 2002

A quiet New Year's Eve, just the way we like it. The full moon topped the Rincons, in line with Jupiter and Saturn. Peter Jennings' special included a pre-recorded New Year message from Bono. "See you next year," he said.

I'm holding him to that.

Monday, January 14, 2002

NSYNC garnered Best Group at the *American Music Awards* and they were booed! U2 should have taken that category.

Monday, February 4, 2002

"As the rain dropping from the sky wends its way toward the ocean, so the prostrations offered in all faiths reach the one God who is supreme."—*The Bridge of Stars* [Marcus Braybrooke, Ed.; Duncan Baird Publishers, London, 2001]

U2 played the Super Bowl half-time show in New Orleans yesterday, on a heart-shaped stage erected in less than six minutes by five-hundred high-school students. They performed Beautiful Day, MLK, and Streets. In tribute, the names of all 911 flight victims and lost first responders scrolled above the stage for MLK.

At a press conference Wednesday, Bono spoke of the position

he played in Irish football. He was a "hooker," he said. Adam claimed his favorite sport was flower arranging.

Thursday, February 28, 2002

Just in from a meeting in New Orleans. Between bouts of catch-up, I watched U2 at the Grammys. Nominated for eight awards in seven categories, they took four—Best Pop Performance Duo or Group, Best Rock Performance Duo or Group, Record of the Year, and Best Rock Album. Decent competition this year too. Bob Dylan up for Best Album. The soundtrack from the Cohen brothers' *Oh Brother, Where Art Thou* won.

Sunday, May 19, 2002

Here's Bono's intro to Adam Harbinson's *Wit and Wisdom* [Adam Harbinson; 2001]: "I'm still amazed at how big, how enormous a love and mystery God is, and how small are the minds that attempt to corral this life-force into rules and taboos, cults and sects . . . . Mercifully, God transcends the church."

Monday, May 20, 2002

Details from Sue's latest Dublin stay. A handful of fans were waiting outside Hanover Quay when Bono leaned out the front door. "Are you going to come in?" he asked. And they did! "Hello darling," he said to Sue and she was over the moon, once again.

Sunday, May 26, 2002

Bono visited four African countries with U.S. Treasury Secretary Paul O'Neill. In Ghana they sat on "gold-plated thrones" in a "marble-floored palace." How about food, medicine, and education for Ghana's citizenry instead?

Monday, June 24, 2002

Last weekend, Edge married dancer Morleigh Steinburg in a castle ruin in the south of France.

Monday, September 9, 2002

U2's new single, Electrical Storm, a gorgeous tune, had been given by Bono as a wedding present to some radio personality who promptly aired it on-line.

Thursday, October 10, 2002

MTV's *Bono and Chris Tucker: Aiding Africa* aired last night. A pander to organized religion, but then that's likely who's footing the bill. How many of Africa's issues might be alleviated with the promotion of birth control? And yet "Just say no!" ruled the day.

Walking into an open elevator, Bono addressed the viewer as the door closed on his shoulder. He gave a quick laugh and a sharp *ow*, but never broke his stride.

Tuesday, November 5, 2002

Watched the video for Electrical Storm this morning—a literal interpretation that conveys the struggle to sustain the "love and only love" of a once fairy-tale relationship. Here's my review for Sue.

ELECTRICAL STORM – A Review

I'm always relieved when new U2 music agrees with me. Electrical Storm is no exception. Though Bono's lyrics are thinner than usual, the sound and the sentiment, the quiet introduction, the gorgeous swirling center, the ring of Edge's guitar, and the passion in Bono's voice, are all exceptionally focused and sublime. The gentle minor strum of Edge's opening guitar duplicates, though with a different rhythm, Bob Dylan's Man in the Long Black Coat, a song that clearly describes the possible consequences of a relationship that's failed to recover the "love and only love" of its early days. Like rising summer heat, stress and strain—family and professional needs, demands, and obligations; children; severed interests, causes, involvement, and philosophies—can all surround, obscure, and sometimes crush the soul of any relationship, leaving couples standing back to back instead of side by side.

If such circumstances can overwhelm ordinary lives, how much more so those of the limelight rich and famous? Metaphorically or otherwise, going to places no one else has been and seeing colors

THE ELEVATION TOUR   125

that have never been seen must be a special challenge under constant paparazzi scrutiny.

But just as an electrical storm can shatter a broiling heat-wave, returning the atmosphere to its vibrant and lucid core, so too, if they're lucky—in or out of fame—lovers can recover the single-issue magic, the "love and only love," of their beginning. "If the sky can crack, there must be some way back."

The final thunderclap of Larry's drums says that the hope and the possibility are very real. May there be more like this one on the way.

Saturday, November 1, 2002

Just picked up an on-line interview with U2 in real time. Larry groused about fans at the studio keeping Bono from his work. Bono, bless him, said he didn't mind at all, seeing it as a way for fans to show their respect for the music. He knows how fans feel. As an admirer of the Beach Boys, he'd gone to Brian Wilson's boyhood home in California, just to see where he'd lived.

Listened to U2's second *Best of U2* album. Excluding My Blue Room and Summer Rain, the boring B-side dance remixes could meet with a steam roller and I'd hardly miss them.

Friday, November 21, 2002

The Hands That Built America, U2's contribution to Martin Scorsese's *Gangs of New York*, is stunning.

Sunday, December 1, 2002

On behalf of his organization, *DATA* [*Debt Aids Trade Africa*], Bono's "on tour" in the Midwest—Nebraska, Ohio, Indiana, Illinois, Tennessee, and Kentucky. He preached a sermon at St. Paul's in Lincoln, Nebraska, and offered these wise words: "Religion reduces God . . . . It's what's left when God leaves the room."

How will that sentiment play out in U2's next incarnation?

2.
The Vertigo Tour

*"Until you make the unconscious conscious
it will direct your life and you will call it fate."*
— Carl Jung

Saturday, February 15, 2003

U2's new album will be released at the end of the year, as per Edge at Hanover. A tour next year.

Wednesday, February 26, 2003

An El Nino event brought an ice storm to the lower Midwest, dumping snow in New England. Here, after a light rain, we have blue skies and sunshine.

Bono and Edge performed The Hands That Built America on *The Today Show*. People need to appreciate that many Irish immigrants to America were as much the thugs of their day as are those of today's Third World, Bono said. *The Gangs of New York*, which Dan and I took in over the weekend, confirmed that. The film excelled in sets, costuming, and execution. But I didn't give a rat's ass about any of the characters. Such vicious tribalism explains a lot of the violence endemic to contemporary American society.

Thursday, March 20, 2003

Bush's Iraq war—based on lies and deception—has begun. What a sad day for the country, the world, and humanity.

Sunday March 23, 2003

U2 delivered their Best Song nomination, The Hands That Built America, at the *Academy Awards* in Los Angeles. Bono, appropriately, changed the lyrics to "late in the spring, yellow cloud on a desert skyline, some father's son, is it his or is it mine?"

Thursday, May 22, 2003

Sue has frequented Killiney's Court Hotel for a good many years, and here, on the cusp of its November closing, both she and Bono were there at the same time.

Sunday, May 25, 2003

Jane and Sharon stayed at the Ferryman in Dublin over the weekend. At Hanover with Declan, they met Edge, who was wild about Declan's baby.

Friday, August 15, 2003

"Don't worry about roses having thorns.
Rejoice that thorns have roses." — Ziggy

Via Denver and Chicago, Dan and I have arrived in Cleveland, Ohio, for the Rock and Roll Hall of Fame's U2 exhibit. The Cleveland terminal was dark but for subdued green flares glowing here and there. We idled on the runway while EMTs, entering from the rear of the plane, removed an ailing passenger. Dan suggested that a handful of psychologists should probably have accompanied them, at the ready to treat passengers who were thus prevented from elbowing their way into the aisle. Several agents with flashlights and glow-sticks directed us out the back door.

A massive blackout had darkened the entire Northeast corridor, New York City to Cleveland. First rumors fingered a lightning strike on an electrical plant in Niagara Falls, Ontario, but final blame fell on an explosion at a power plant in upstate New York.

Through unlit streets, our taxi crept to the Wyndham Cleveland Playhouse Hotel, where we registered by lamplight, and then, armed with light-sticks, we hiked up to our tenth floor room. Early this morning I sensed a flash of light, and rolled over to find the room's digital clock flashing. The power failure had begun almost as we reached the Tucson airport yesterday, and yet we'd traveled over seven hours without hearing a word about it.

Cleveland is a steel town fallen on hard times, and our hotel, encircled by empty store fronts in metal and concrete sky-scrapers, stands at the edge of the theatre district, on Euclid.

8:45 p.m. We drifted down Euclid to 9th, and then walked north to Lake Erie, which smelled like fresh uncooked corn. The Rock and Roll Hall of Fame, a geometric glass building designed by I. M. Pei—of Louvre glass-pyramid fame—rises by the Port of Cleveland beside the Cleveland Browns Stadium. We idled in the meager shade of the Science Center, until the museum opened at noon, and then, while everyone else milled about on the lower level, we headed upstairs.

In a thick heat-haze screaming with seagulls, we ate on a balcony on the third floor where we'd stopped for hot dogs and bottled water. (The city's water supply has been shut down.) A large movie screen flashed U2 videos in the Second Decade exhibit on the empty sixth floor, and Dan and I had a private dance to Desire!

Four enormous album covers graced the sixth floor's upper walls—*All That You Can't Leave Behind*, *Pop*, *Achtung Baby*, and *Zooropa*. Glass enclosures displayed collected material, much of it from Paul McGuinness—sketches of stage concepts, promo posters, lyrics, periodical covers, and itinerary books. Brian Eno's production notes brimmed with mathematical formulas, lyric comments, and doodles, and in the four corners of the room hung an assortment of concert costumes. In the margins of Bad's lyrics, Bono had jotted down thesaurus "t-i-o-n" words—justification, vindication, generalization, formulation.

On the First Decade fifth floor, fanzines—three of them Sue's *Eirinn*—layered the wall above a guest comment book and a *DATA* sign-up sheet. I very much admired Larry's impressive pack-rattedness. One of many items he'd squirrelled away was a press release written by Adam for *The Hype* and signed "Charles Clayton, Manager." Adam identified Bono as Paul Heuston and described himself as "a precision bass player (who) thrives on disorganization and mistakes and has been deteriorating ever since." Larry had also retained a no-doubt much regretted rejection letter from Arista Records.

The fourth floor show-cased work from Steve Averill, along with collections for Bob Dylan, the Pretenders, and Bruce Springsteen. One telling note here read, "Ok guys. Hands off all food except cereal and drinks. The Boss".

Saturday, August 16, 2003

This morning, on a bleary, dreary day, we prowled the permanent downstairs exhibit at the R'n'R museum. The Jimi Hendrix selection included a smattering of his drawings. (He was wise to stick to music.) Born in Seattle, Jimi moved to the Mayfair District of London, staying in a house once lived in by the composer Handel. "I didn't know this was Handel's pad," Jimi wrote. A short Hendrix film, on a loop, featured his Johnny B. Good and Voodoo Childe.

Jim Morrison's relatives had donated baby foot-prints, a birth certificate, and report cards, one of which had an S for satisfactory in everything but self-control, for which Jim had garnered an N. Beside a note concerned with Morrison's indecent exposure charges, was a letter in which his father claimed he hadn't seen Jim for at least five years after Jim finished college. Mr. Morrison emphasized how hard he'd struggled to dissuade his son from a performance career. He had "no talent." Perhaps Jim's considerable problems stemmed from his relationship with a military dad so averse to his poetic soul. The museum overflowed with costumes, itinerary books, album covers, lyric sheets, posters, letters, and much more.

As we made to leave, a young boy passed by with his parents. "What's so great about U2?" he asked them.

Where do I start? I thought.

Debra Winger—an actress who abandoned her career for its high-stress, youth-oriented attitude—once said "I guess I've turned the word 'passion' into whatever it is that melts your heart." That's as good a place as any to start.

Thursday, October 30, 2003

I was honored to be asked by the on-line U2 fan group *Interference* to contribute to their upcoming fifteenth anniversary celebration of the release of *Rattle and Hum*. I sent off a review of the closing Tempe shows just this morning. It's already been posted.

STARS IN THE WINTER NIGHT

"We'll shine like stars in the summer night;
We'll shine like stars in the winter night;
One heart, one hope, one love."

There's a great glowing wide-eyed expectancy whenever I think about Sun Devil Stadium in December of 1987. Another time. Another place. Can it be nearly two decades since U2 came back to Arizona to close out *The Joshua Tree*, a tour that had opened there nearly a year earlier? Concert footage from Sun Devil was to be the centerpiece of the transitional film that would become *Rattle and Hum* a year later—a record of U2's bid to illuminate the myth of America, to celebrate the country's musical heritage, and update the essence of U2 on celluloid. "A kind of photograph," Edge said.

A lot has happened in the world since those all-too-brief winter nights in Tempe. Gone is the World Trade Center in New York City. And though Palestinians and Israelis have continued to kill each other with persistent and vigorous regularity, in 1987 we looked out, metaphorically, on the hills of El Salvador, where now we have the minefields of Afghanistan and Iraq. Iran-Contra and government subterfuge under Reagan/Bush filled the newspapers in '87. Today, it's WMDs and government subterfuge under Bush/Cheney. In 1987, AIDS had just come to Africa and the world's glance suggested it just might tackle the threat. Today, Africa's AIDS crisis has reached plague proportions and the world is still dithering. "It's not what you're dreaming, but what you're gonna do."

On the plus side, South Africa has slipped the bonds of institutionalized segregation and repression, and genocide has been capped in Bosnia.

Meanwhile, U2 went from being the biggest rock band in the world to being . . . well . . . the biggest rock band in the world. In the early '90s, following those now-legendary Sun Devil shows, they dreamt it all up again, waking up to the multi-media extravaganzas of the *Zoo TV*, *Outside Broadcast*, and *Zooropa* tours, and the gimmickry and color of *Popmart*. All of these were incredible experiences and accomplishments, but the new millennium brought us *All That You Can't Leave Behind* and a band that's come full circle from the passionate soulfulness epitomized in Tempe. "Life presents us with all the possibilities of finding our way back home."

Rattle and Hum director Phil Joanou successfully shot Tempe for "intense and epic." Yet those lustrous December nights had a seeming simplicity that turned a vast stadium space into something intimate and communal, like the *JT* tour itself. "It was like—throw out technology," Adam said.

And for the most part, they did. The staging was simple, a wide white wing to either side that spelled out U2, and straight-ahead twin performances that were exceptional—sublime and uplifting.

The first night, December 19, was cool and cloudy, with a fine hazy rain. Joanou would later call it a "fucking disaster." But that's director-speak from a film-maker's point-of-view. Few fans who were there would agree. That mystical rain created powerful atmospherics that wrapped the night in inspiration and hopefulness. Under a half-light red-orange sky shredded with cloud, the gigantic blue/black-bowl venue filled often with flickering golden light, and the stage swirled under a tea-rose pink mist. The view from a dozen or so rows back from center-stage was extraordinary. As always for me, Bad was a highlight, along with Edge's blistering Bullet solo, and the red screen and strobe lights of Streets.

Producer Michael Hamlyn would declare the next night, December 20, "the best show of the tour." And they got it all on film. There was an epic Bad, nine moving minutes of El Pueblo Vencera tacked on to Mothers of the Disappeared, a stirring One Tree Hill, In God's Country for our lush Sonoran desert, a gigantic party-time It's Christmas, Baby Please Come Home, and a rousing Jingle Bells serenade-of-a-closing.

The energy and excitement made the night incomparable

and exhilarating. One enormous Christmas party with fifty-five-thousand of your closest friends. In the end, when It's Christmas in Killarney came up over the sound system, snapping electrical surges still swept through the crowd and no one wanted to go home. It was "a great show," Joanou would say. An understatement of gigantic proportions. "We nailed it visually and they nailed it musically and the crowd was great."

"Life can only be understood backward, but it must be lived forward," Danish physicist Nels Bohr has written. In retrospect, I understand—as much as it's possible for a fan to understand—the permutations and continued blossoming of a vibrant and living band like U2, as it moved from the innocence of *Boy* through the heart of *The Joshua Tree*, to the soulful maturity of *ATYCLB*. And looking back on those two brilliant winter nights in Tempe, I'm hungrier than ever for whatever's next.

Wednesday, November 26, 2003

Bono spoke recently at the Canadian Liberal Leadership Conference. "The Canadian voice is hard-wired in my heart," he said. "I'm a fan."

Wednesday, November 31, 2003

Monday night, I watched the recent AIDS Concert from Cape Town, South Africa. Nelson Mandela and Oprah Winfrey sat onstage in high-backed thrones, like a king and queen before their subjects. AIDS is killing far more black South Africans than white, and yet, for this free concert, barely a black face could be seen in the crowd of thirty-thousand. Bono and Edge performed a rather tired One and I found Bono's other numbers strikingly forgettable.

Friday, September 17, 2004

*"There is only one great thing . . . to live to see in huts
and journeys the great day that dawns and the light
that fills the world."*— Inuit Song

Far removed from the gentle rains of Mo'orea and Huahini [French Polynesia] last month, a powerful thunderstorm idled over

Tucson in the middle of the night. Gobs of water eroded segments of the front yard.

In a recent interview, Bono held his own against Bill O'Reilly of *The O'Reilly Factor* [former *Fox TV* talk-show]. Geared for more of an argument, O'Reilly succumbed to a Bono charm offensive and potential jabs were deflected into questions of compassion, ideals, and possibility.

Notice of U2's new album in *USA Today*, the first single to come out at the end of September.

Thursday, October 21, 2004

Danish money in hand for Christmas with Dustin in Copenhagen.

Picked up a copy of *Blenders*, with a U2 cover story. The tour will open in Miami on the first of March.

Monday, November 22, 2004

The U2 single, Vertigo, arrived in the post today. The "B Side", Neon Lights, captures the glitter of a big city by night, but there's not much to it.

Thursday, November 25, 2004

Snagged a Limited Edition of the new U2 album, *How to Dismantle an Atomic Bomb*. I was blown away to find *A Grand Madness, Ten Years on the Road with U2* nestled on Hanover Quay's bookshelves, right beside *Propaganda*, as part of a photo collage by Adam in a booklet show-casing Bono's creativity.

Monday, November 29, 2004

I've finally finished a review of *How to Dismantle an Atomic Bomb*. There are some extraordinary songs here, focused on God, love, faith, life, death, peace, and truth. The album strikes me as an extension of *All That You Can't Leave Behind*. Songs echo each other as commentary or counterpoint. *ATYCLB* sought to separate out those significant aspects of life that can't be jettisoned. *HTDAAB* [*How to Dismantle an Atomic Bomb*] testifies to how difficult that process can be. Explosive in the aftermath of his father's death, Bono is deconstructing himself, struggling to achieve some semblance of former completeness, which in spiritual circles, might be called his "authentic self."

HOW TO DISMANTLE AN ATOMIC BOMB

As with most of U2's best work, *HTDAAB* is an existential album filled with the contradictions and complexities of life.

VERTIGO – This song seems the antithesis of Elevation, which lifted us high enough to fly. With all the temptations that come from getting everything you want, you run the risk of losing your balance. Though it's not a favorite, Vertigo is growing on me and it's the clear choice to open the show.

MIRACLE DRUG – I can envision Miracle Drug, a hopeful tune that's the flip side of When I Look at the World with its unanswered questions, as ending the main set. More classic minimalist Edge guitar here. Thoughts too about how the Divine operates in Bono's writing. The songs are "in your eyes. I see them when you smile." Many artists, in every medium, feel they've been given a gift, that something Divine works through them.

I love the emotion and the uplifting hopefulness of this tune. The old saying that you only fail when you give up is restated here with "the only failure is when you quit." Bono himself has said that this song is about Irish writer and cerebral palsy victim, Christy Brown, who was deprived of oxygen at birth and ended up completely paralyzed. A miracle drug allowed him to move his neck enough to type with a special device attached to his head, and great poetry spilled out of him.

SOMETIMES YOU CAN'T MAKE IT ON YOUR OWN – This is classic U2 with Edge's watery-bells guitar and some of Bono's most passionate lyrics. Father and son—Bono and Bob—were at odds much of the time, and yet they were "the same soul." The *ATYCLB* counterpart is Stuck in a Moment, with its "I'm not afraid of anything in this world" and "You gotta stand up straight, carry your own weight." Sometimes that's just too hard. Sometimes you can't make it on your own.

LOVE AND PEACE OR ELSE – With a great bluesy guitar from Edge and some Exit-like whispers, this song is going to be extraordinary live and it should open an encore. *ATYCLB*'s Peace on Earth, so deeply Irish and so full of resignation and despair, is contrasted and expanded on in this updated view of world violence. Filled with anger, determination, and demand, Love and Peace or Else focuses on the Mid-east in particular. A strutting tear-down-the-house number, anchored in exploding rhythms from Adam and Larry, the song's only weakness, to me, is a contrived bridge. But menace and danger are all over this one, including the distinctive, threatening whirr of a rattlesnake, along with the deep rumbling explosions of war. In Peace on Earth "they say what you mock will surely overtake you and you become a monster so the monster will not break you." In Love and Peace or Else "we're gonna break the monster's back."

CITY OF BLINDING LIGHTS – Chiming away with the same twinkling key-board/guitar as the musical poem Neon Lights, this is a much fuller anecdote of New York City before it became all that it became on *ATYCLB*. When the lads first arrived in the city, they came with an open innocence, a newness, an excitement, the enthusiasm of possibility. They were shielded, to some degree, from the city's reality. When you fly over or into any large city, you're wide-eyed and overwhelmed by the glitter, the beauty, the vastness of city lights. You're separated from all the murder and mayhem going on down below. Musically, this song has the same excitement, the same night-time twinkle of a city that can be deeply missed.

The simplicity and blissful ignorance of the band when they first arrived, their innocence and openness, the positivism, the possibility and belief, they're all here. What happened to that "authentic self," to that early inner beauty? "Time won't take the boy out of the man," Bono sings, determined to recover the enthusiasm, energy, and curiosity of those earlier days.

This song's *ATYCLB* twin is New York with its "too many choices," its heat, vices, and temptation. City of Blinding Lights is the newness of pure possibility, a striving for the energy of original innocence. "Oh, you look so beautiful tonight" is a phrase Bono used on his NYC audience all those years ago.

ALL BECAUSE OF YOU – An uplifting rocker, whether it's meant for God, Ali, Bono's parents, or anyone or anything else. Fans are going to love the "all because of you" chorus. After Bono's primal scream, Edge's solo and Larry's drums are especially wild.

"The end of all things is to get back to the place you started from and discover the place for the first time," to see old things with new eyes. Like many of us, Bono is constantly struggling to uncover and understand the Divine through new eyes, and in the process, to rescue his "authentic self." If it's all because of God—a "by the grace of God" sort of thing—this song's twin might be *Elevation*'s Grace, but in an active sense rather that the gentle passivity of Grace.

A MAN AND A WOMAN – My least favorite, this number sounds generic and clichéd. ("How can I hurt when I'm holding you." Groan!) Adam's bass lines hum, and I love the acoustic nature of the song, but I can also too easily hear some cringe-inducing duet. Like In a Little While, A Man and a Woman seems to comment on Bono and Ali's relationship, the "theme" of trying to get back to the authentic self—"I've been trying to feel complete again" versus "blown by every breeze." "That little girl with Spanish eyes" versus "brown-eyed girl across the street."

A Man and A Woman and In a Little While are my two least favorite songs on *HTDAAB* and *ATYCLB* respectively, though I do like the line about not taking a chance at "losing love to find romance." I think that says a lot about this particular relationship, about Bono and Ali's mutual faithfulness, and the depth and power of their love.

CRUMBS FROM YOUR TABLE – This song about old doubts didn't grab me right off and still doesn't. Its twin might be *ATYCLB*'s Beautiful Day, an optimistic song that finds joy and beauty in all things, though Beautiful Day is much better. I'm not sure what to make of the lyrics, beyond the doubt and the contribution of others, not feeling worthy, and so forth. I especially like "with a mouthful of teeth, you ate all your friends and you broke every heart thinking every heart mends."

ONE STEP CLOSER – This one has an ethereal otherworldly Grace-ness quality to it, though lyrically it's closer to the philosophical introspection and atmospheric sadness and inevitability of Kite. Edge's guitar is so serene and gentle. The story goes that at Bono's dad's funeral, Bono mentioned to Noel Gallagher that in the end his dad hadn't known if he believed in an afterlife or not, and Gallagher said, "Well, he's one step closer to knowing." This song comes across as a direct reference to the spiritual path this whole album seems to be a part of. Something's at least in sight now. It's just across the road, it's just around the corner, it's just up ahead.

I like the use of Larry's drums at the end, after the "can you hear the drummer slowing?" Life moves on, just as in Kite there's the inevitability of a passing life and the approach of death. "Who's to know where the wind will take you? Who's to know when the time has come around?" It's just around the corner, it's just across the road, it's just up ahead.

ORIGINAL OF THE SPECIES – This cautionary tale for our children builds beautifully from Edge's ringing keyboard through to a slow-building anthemic ending, with a calming mid-section. Because it has the same sense of early authentic days, of what used to be and what still is in the heart, it has some of the same "night lights" quality of Neon Lights and City of Blinding Lights. Like Wild Honey, Original of the Species sounds like the reality of who Bono and Ali are together, though I've heard it was actually written for Edge's eldest daughter, or for young people in general.

"Please stay a child somewhere in your heart" and "slow down, the end is not as fun as the start," goes right back to One Step Closer. The lyrics "I'll give you everything you want except the one thing that you want," is much like So Cruel's "I gave you everything you ever wanted. It wasn't what you wanted," which touched on Edge's relationship situation.

YAHWEH – This one is fabulous! Yahweh should end an encore and wrap up the entire show. It's the passive side of Walk On which demanded you "be strong." Here you turn it all over to some Higher Consciousness. A bit too "Christian-rock" for me at first, it did what the best of U2 always does, it asked a question—"Why the dark before the dawn?" Why not have beauty from the beginning?

"Still I'm waiting for the dawn," Bono says. He still hasn't found what he's looking for, but he's getting closer. And as long as he's still looking, I know we'll be getting more incredible music from this band.

FAST CARS – Fast Cars is unlike anything else that's on *HTDAAB* in the same way that Ground Beneath Her Feet was separate from the rest of *ATYCLB*. Both come after the story has been told. "There in the desert to dismantle an atomic bomb," Fast Cars says. This flamenco/castanet Hispanic sound also closes the album in terms of the "uno, dos, tres, catorce" of Vertigo. After all the heavy complexity-of-life stuff, Fast Cars comes as something of a relief. Forget all that heavy stuff, let's party!

I do love this album. Songs on all of U2's albums could be mixed and matched, as Bono so often writes about the same or similar themes. *HTDAAB* seems more obviously connected to *ATYCLB*, as though it's a commentary of sorts, like *Zooropa* was to *Achtung Baby*, or *Rattle and Hum* was to *The Joshua Tree*. The rhythm and the flow—even the syllables of the titles—thoroughly mesh.

HTDAAB is Edge's album too, in terms of the emphasis on his pure sound. In fact, all the instruments work so well as part of whatever specific story is being told. A lot of anthemic writing here too, with words at the forefront. The bridges remain the weakest part of many songs to me. When they're not there, as in Original of the Species, it's something of a treat. Otherwise, there's occasionally the feeling of work. "We need a bridge here. Let's build one."

How to Dismantle an Atomic Bomb is in many ways a "born-again continuance," spiritual transformation being a lengthy process that often takes a life-time, even when you have the advantage of knowing you're on one. It's a middle-age album too—presenting a changing world in which our parents die, our children grow up, and we become more aware of our own mortality.

But, as always, the best U2 has a dark side, and so, just as they do and should, introspection and doubt lie alongside the love and the hope and the strength of the human spirit.

Monday, December 6, 2004

Propaganda membership at *U2.com* guarantees two concert tickets, so at least I'll get to a couple of shows.

Wednesday, December 15, 2004

The *Vertigo Tour* schedule comes out in January, so I at least won't have to think about it while we're in Denmark.

Sunday, December 26, 2004

A dreadful series of tsunamis hit Asia today, the death toll already at 150,000!

Wednesday, December 29, 2004

9:50 p.m. Up early this morning for the pickled-herring-laced breakfast buffet at our hotel [The Admiral Hotel, Copenhagen, Denmark]. Afterwards, we set out for the House of Amber in Kongens Nytorv, the square at the top of the Nyhavn canal. A stunning assortment of amber there, from all around the world— insects sealed in raw nuggets, sculpted animals, sailing ships, and polished trinket boxes. A million years for resin to become amber.

Just as we entered the shop, U2's Everlasting Love came up on their speakers.

Sunday, January 23, 2005

9:00 a.m. Fifty-nine degrees [Fahrenheit] out there today. A winter picnic on tap for Molina Basin [Santa Catalina Mountains, Tucson] this afternoon.

The U2 tour schedule comes out tomorrow morning, pre-sale tickets on Tuesday.

Tuesday, January 25, 2005

What a dismal experience ticket sales have been. The band hustled to outsmart brokers and scalpers who, in turn, doubled-down, using computer software to block legitimate customers. Thousands of tickets have already been posted for resale on eBay.

I have no ticket for either Manchester or Glasgow, snagged one for London, and two for the opening show in San Diego, March 28.

Wednesday, January 26, 2005

A brief appreciation of the Full Wolf Moon last night, one bright light in the scramble for U2 tickets.

Saturday, January 29, 2005

Grateful for any show at all at this point. I have two tickets each for San Diego and Anaheim, though we need three. San Diego completely sold out this morning. Tomorrow, I'll look into Staples [Anaheim, California]. Jane managed Manchester and London, and will attempt Dublin tomorrow, while Sue tracks down a Glasgow for me.

Mid-June, a few days ahead of the Irish gigs, I'll fly from Glasgow to Dublin.

Monday, January 31, 2005

The quest for tickets continues. New *U2.com* memberships include access to tickets. They moved the deadline to Monday night and one scalper successfully signed up for a hundred memberships!

Friday, February 4, 2005

San Diego, Anaheim, and LA all sorted. Larry apologized for the ticket snafu, finishing with a "fuck off" to fans who'd begun to question the band's integrity.

Sunday, February 13, 2005

Great to be home in Tucson again, after a short sojourn in Kitchener [Ontario, Canada]. Cool and cloudy here, but no deep snow drifts or icy winds.

I watched some of the Grammies earlier today. U2 nominated in two categories, both of which they won.

Wednesday, March 9, 2005

Larry, bless him, has taken control of ticketing for the fall leg of the *Vertigo Tour*. *Propaganda* members were to have ticket codes reinstated. Mine never did show up.

Thursday, March 10, 2005

Outside on a gorgeous spring day, light breeze and a blue sky.

With her *U2.com* code, Sharon will try for Miami tickets on Tuesday. On Saturday, Sue will look into Boston.

Friday, March 11, 2005

Finally heard back from *U2.com*. They researched my *Propaganda* enrollment—I've been a member since 1986—and sent me a new pre-sale code.

Friday, March 18, 2005

Ali's new clothing line, Edun, will be specific to Saks 5th Avenue. That excludes me and everyone else I know.

Sue came up with U2 Boston tickets for October 3, and Sharon snagged excellent seats for Miami in November.

Took in part of the Rock and Roll Hall of Fame ceremonies last night, the Pretenders and Buddy Guy both with first-rate performances. U2's induction went on for well over an hour. Bruce Springsteen delivered a twenty minute intro, the lads played a few tunes, and then each gave an acceptance speech, wives and significant others all in evidence.

Bono addressed the Martin Luther King/Governor Mecham fiasco in Arizona during *The Joshua Tree Tour*. He'd received death threats, he said, and recalled looking up onstage to find Adam "ready to take a bullet" for him.

Sunday, March 27, 2005

10:45 p.m. In our room, #229, at the Holiday Inn San Diego/ Mission Bay, just across the road from the fifteen-thousand seat San Diego Sports Arena.

Monday, March 28, 2005

11:00 a.m. Lazing by the pool while Sharon and Jane—in seventh heaven—shop Target, Mervyn's, and Ross Dress for Less.

2:00 p.m. On our return to the hotel from a tempura lunch at Yakitori's Japanese Restaurant, we found fans already queued up on the pavement, spread out with a colorful collection of folding chairs.

Tuesday, March 29, 2005

11:00 p.m. We set off for the opening *Vertigo* show last night about seven-thirty. The staging was straightforward—four overhead screens and a ramp, identical to the *Elevation Tour*'s, with the addition of red lights. *Popmart*'s light-bulb screen had been dismantled, reconstructed, and dropped down like an electronic curtain.

Here's the set-list: City of Blinding Lights; Vertigo/Stories for Boys; The Cry/Electric Co.; An Cat Dubh/Into the Heart; Beautiful Day; New Year's Day; Miracle Drug; Sometimes You Can't Make It On Your Own/No Regrets; Love and Peace or Else; Sunday Bloody Sunday; Bullet/The Hands that Built America/When Johnny Comes Marching Home; Running to Stand Still; Zoo Station; The Fly; Elevation//Pride; Streets; All Because of You; One// Yahweh; 40

A shower of glitter rained down with the opener, City of Blinding Lights, to which Arcade Fire's "now that I'm older, my heart is colder," had been appended. The bead curtains sparkled with red light. Vertigo followed. "I'm at a place called San Diego," Bono sang, adding a line or two from Stories for Boys.

A snatch of The Cry followed, and when mention was made of a return to where the band had started, the album cover for *Boy* floated on-screen. An awesome Electric Co. took the concert into U2's customary high-energy range. In blue and purple light, Bono prowled the walkway for An Cat Dubh, stroking an imaginary cat, setting an imaginary bird free.

Beautiful Day, in the four colored squares of the *Elevation Tour*, included a line from Blackbird—"You have only waited for this moment to arrive." For a rather tiresome New Year's Day, Bono strained to reach a young woman in the back tier who very nearly toppled over the railing.

"Here we are—a great, great, great, great night for us," Bono said before an emotional Miracle Drug. "It's a miracle. Thanks for waiting in line, for putting up with the difficulty of getting tickets." A man of lights strode digitally on-screen for Sometimes You Can't Make It On Your Own, and Bono recounted his dad's life in show business, finishing with a fitting snippet of Tom Rush's No Regrets.

Love and Peace or Else, under red light, featured a duel of sorts between Bono and Larry. In the end, Bono, in a red, black, and white leather jacket and white bandana, pounded on Larry's marching drum. Sunday Bloody Sunday ushered in Bullet, in red, Bono staggering blindfolded onstage. The Hands that Built America and a lengthy When Johnny Comes Marching Home followed.

Running to Stand Still, with smoke pots and blue light, centered on Edge and Bono, the 1948 *Universal Declaration of Human Rights* scrolling on-screen. "He's back and he's blind," Bono said. I anticipated an appearance by McPhisto, but the Fly came up instead. "Everything you know is wrong."

The encore opened with Pride, accompanied by MLK's "I Have a Dream" speech. With a vision "as big as the world," African flags dropped into the curtained lights for Where the Streets Have No Name.

"San Diego turned out to be the best place to start this tour tonight," Bono said. Roar! Roar! "Thank you!" Roar! Roar! The band felt "blessed," he said, and acknowledged "our friends from Mexico." People are "more extraordinary when they act as One."

Yahweh—the promise of an energetic, joyful celebration—gentled, with "multi-instrumentalist" Larry jabbing at a small keyboard, Edge on acoustic guitar, Bono on rhythm. They "hadn't played (40) since 1983," Bono erroneously claimed.

And then it was done.

Wednesday, March 30, 2005

10:00 a.m. Sharon and Jane have nipped over to Tower Records and on to the box office in hopes of snagging tickets for tonight's second San Diego show. Late Monday afternoon, two-hundred were released.

Yesterday, we cruised the city with Old Town Trolley Tours,

challenging for the nerves, as the drivers fill any rising silence with constant chatter or recorded ditties linked to features in their monologues. The route covered seven or eight "points of interest," from Balboa Park and the San Diego Zoo to Old Town and Seaport Village. We crossed the Coronado Bridge in an icy wind, but having started out late, we had a mere twenty minutes on the Hotel Del Coronado's wide white sand-dune-barriered beach, before heading back to Old Town.

Monday night, with only two GA tickets, Jane and I dropped down to the pitch. Hoping to be together on the floor then, I gave my ticket and wristband to Jane, who walked them back into the stands for Sharon. I waited and waited and waited, nerve-wracked as venue security began a random ticket/wristband sweep. By great good fortune, they passed me by.

Though musically spot-on, with a balance of vintage, mega-hits, and new songs, this concert, from beginning to end, seemed somehow off. Perhaps the humanitarian agenda had become more prominent than the concert, obscuring the celebration, the joy, and the passion.

Post-concert, we dawdled at the backstage entrance until close to one o'clock. A great commotion rose up at one point, and Bono appeared, only to be instantly swallowed up by a horde of young Hispanic fans. We learned later that he'd asked that they form a line he could make his way down. When no one paid him the least bit of attention, he jumped into his waiting van and was swept away.

Passed the afternoon at Sea World today. Beautiful beasties. Unbearable crowds.

Thursday, March 31, 2005

A major ticket triumph yesterday! Sharon and Jane scarfed up three tickets on Adam's side, right beside the stage. They'd returned with dour faces. Things had not gone well. In fact, they'd only managed . . . row 2, seats 6, 7, and 8!

3:30 p.m. An hour ago, we pulled out of San Diego's rough and ready Greyhound bus station, all speckled fifties flooring and metal benches. We're off on a two hour/ninety-eight mile run up to Anaheim.

Traveling alongside the sea now, rolling green hills buried in housing estates and palm trees. Lush vegetation to our right, sun-splattered Pacific inlets to the left.

While I have time, I'll take on second San Diego last night. Here's the set-list: City of Blinding Lights; Vertigo/Stories for Boys; The Cry/Electric Co.; Gloria; Beautiful Day; With or Without You; New Year's Day; Miracle Drug; Sometimes You Can't Make It On Your Own; Love and Peace or Else; Sunday Bloody Sunday; Bullet/ The Hands that Built America/When Johnny Comes Marching Home; Running to Stand Still/Hallelujah; Zoo Station; The Fly; Elevation//Pride; Streets; One; All Because of You//Yahweh/40

Red and silver confetti fluttered down from the rafters for the City of Blinding Lights opening, and a bit of banter about Edge taking Spanish lessons came just before the "uno, dos, catorce" of Vertigo. Bono shouldered his microphone stand like a spear and chanted shaman-like to Edge for The Cry/Electric Co. A superb Gloria followed.

"It went pretty good last night?" Bono asked after With or Without You. "That was just a rehearsal—we're just getting to know the songs, getting to know each other onstage again, getting to know you." Did anyone speak Spanish? And up came a fan who did. "Tell them there's lots of love in Dublin," Bono directed, flashing peace signs for Love and Peace or Else. All the "men and women from Camp Pendleton" and other local military bases, were acknowledged for Running to Stand Still. "Our hearts are with you—welcome home."

The recitation of *The Declaration of Human Rights* fell a bit flat to me, though it's a nice moment. For Streets—with African flags and dropped-down light-bulb curtain—Bono asked for help. "Not for money," he said. "You've given us enough of that already." Instead, he suggested we sign the ONE petitions outside. For the 40 finale, Edge played off-key for some time before restarting. And then, once again, it was over.

7:45 p.m. In our room at Best Western Sportstown on East Katella in Anaheim. In and out of Oceanside in just short of twenty-five minutes. The drive further north on #5 grazed San Clemente, San Onofre, and San Juan Capistrano. We glided past reedy inland marshes, brushy hills, and pale bluish mountains.

Saturday, April 2, 2005

10:00 a.m. Sharon and I are heading north again on the train. About six o'clock this morning, we waved Jane off to the Ramada Inn, where she caught an LAX shuttle and so home to Leeds. (And then there were two.)

Surprisingly pleasant in atmosphere, Anaheim had nothing much in the way of activities to recommend it, beyond Disneyland and Knott's Berry Farm. Moreover, the hotel pool only offered up an unpleasant blanket of slime. We considered moving on to San Francisco. But the train took twelve hours and a flight cost upwards of five-hundred dollars apiece. So we've opted instead for a few days in Santa Barbara.

Yesterday morning, we pavement-sat from ten-thirty on, in hopes of Anaheim tickets. The queue mushroomed, scalpers in evidence. One of them snagged a ticket, stepped aside to change cap and t-shirt, and then rejoined the line. Sharon reported this to venue security, after which buyers were instructed to move well away from the ticket window after their purchases. But in the end, nothing much changed.

Here's the set-list for Anaheim: Love and Peace or Else; Sunday Bloody Sunday; Bullet; Running to Stand Still; Still Haven't Found; New Year's Day; Miracle Drug; Sometimes You Can't Make it on Your Own; Beautiful Day; Pride; Streets; One//Zoo Station; the Fly; Elevation; Mysterious Ways; City of Blinding Lights; Vertigo; All Because of You//Yahweh/40

Our seats were in a small alcove, half-way up the second tier, on the curve of the right side as you face the stage. With only two rows of five or six people a piece ahead of us, we had an outstanding view.

The show opened with Love and Peace or Else. Bono donned his head-band as a blindfold for Bullet and groped for the microphone, roaring jets on-screen. At the close, he dropped to his knees, a hostage or prisoner of war. One article of *The Declaration of Human Rights* concerns prisoners' rights and undue punishment. Bullet's miming pointedly reflected on the horrors coming out of Abu Ghraib Prison.

In Zoo Station, Bono alluded to his past penchant for ringing up the White House, which would never take his call. Now he speaks to the president himself, he said. During Elevation, McPhisto materialized in a look or a raspy cough. A young fan named Tiffany, completely at home onstage, decked out as Mac in huge platform shoes, strutted about with Bono for Mysterious ways, prancing and dancing and then sitting out City of Blinding Lights behind Larry's drum kit.

"Some people dress up to go out," Bono said. "And some people dress up to go out!"

For me, Miracle Drug is the highlight of these shows. Vertigo channeled Stories for Boys, and All Because of You became wildly raucous.

"Tonight we sing this for the Holy Father, a friend to the world's poor," Bono said, and launched into a pretty, acoustic version of Yahweh. (Such a papal assessment is open to debate. Pope John Paul II passed away just yesterday, so I may have found the second Anaheim show too "religiously" out of control for my taste.)

A shimmer of cell-phones glowed like stars for 40.

12:50 p.m. Chugging through Glendale on the *769 Surfline*—quiet, smooth, and comfortable, with footrests and cushions. We rolled into LA—brown smog and hazy mountains—all the disheveled dinginess there that we'd expected in Anaheim. Broken concrete this and that, and graffiti everywhere.

9:45 p.m. We reached Santa Barbara at three-twenty this afternoon and grabbed a taxi to the Best Western Beachside Inn on Cabrillo Boulevard. We're in room #208, with a small balcony.

Out of LA, we climbed into a California countryside of rolling foothills sprinkled with tan boulders. We coasted through two mountain tunnels, and emerged in Simi Valley, limey spring trees and dark oaks in the bottomlands, eucalyptus spread out on high ridges. None of the vibrant dampness of English or Irish fields, but still dustily pretty, slow and pastoral.

The valley broadened to crop fields and spacious orchards, and just before Ventura, we ran parallel to the ocean, the Channel Islands in mist off-shore. At Camarillon, the valley floor widened further. Workers and idled produce trucks dotted the fields, coastal hills in smoky blue to the west.

Under a whitening sky, we passed through Oxnard, a dilapidated little town scattered with rustic adobe taverns and monstrous produce warehouses. Housing estates of a rich retirement nature popped up on the outskirts of Ventura, mansions inching up grassy hillsides. The ocean, speckled with sailboats, danced in sunlight.

Sunday, April 3, 2005

9:00 a.m. on a coolish day. I'm out on the balcony. We face north, and across the street, toward the sea, a small park called Plaza del Mar is hosting a large group of men gathered at a sort of soup kitchen with a long line of tables. To the left, a forest of masts delineates the small harbor. We're due for a whale watching excursion over there at ten, provided two additional customers can be rustled up.

Last night, we strolled the harbor. A sea of masts bristled against the distant mountains, some of them belonging to recreational yachts—*The Serena U, Sí Sí, Windswept, Possible Dream, Sea Spray,* and *Summers Time.* Others were working boats, signs and plaques along the pier delineating aspects of the Pacific fishing industry.

After sea-food at Brophy Brothers—New England clam chowder, grilled yellow-fish with veggies, rice pilaf, and cole-slaw— we drifted over to Stearn's Wharf, a collection of souvenir shops and eateries. As the sun slipped behind dove-grey hills, the sea turned metallic silver, reflecting the sun's tangerine brilliance on the curl of each wave.

Noon. Our whale-watching boat—the *Sunset Kidd*—failed to garner the requisite customers for an early sailing, so we've re-booked for two o'clock this afternoon.

A scan of billboard advertisements for yacht sales, presented a forty-seven foot 1992 Bristol racer/cruiser, boasting a "north spinnaker stuffer" and "dual electric winches," which could be had for $449,000.

The owners of the *Sunset Kidd* featured here as well. Our skipper, Aynsley Dunbar, a session man and drummer from Liverpool back in the day, had worked with John Lennon, Jefferson Starship, Jeff Beck, Frank Zappa, and David Bowie, among many others. For four years he'd played with Journey. His "musical occupation" was listed as "Rock Star".

Passing time now on an empty stretch of beach between the harbor and the wharf. A dredger stands out to sea in front of us, boat trailers lie to our right, and, on a spit of land across the harbor, a flock of brown pelicans has gathered.

5:30 p.m. In from whale watching on the *Sunset Kidd*, a green-trimmed, "thirty foot stem-to-stern" ketch. What was a yacht? I asked a fellow passenger, himself a boatman. "A yacht is any boat I can't afford," he answered.

We were five, excluding our two-man crew. A couple with their young daughter hunkered in the cabin. Sharon and I perched on the prow, behind the bowsprit. We motored down the coast with the intention of sailing back. But with a thin wind, we only managed the jib and mizzen sails.

Brown pelicans, out fishing, shot into the sea like arrows, or skimmed the surface of the water, wing-tips a hair's breadth above the waves.

In the last half-hour of a two-hour excursion, we spotted two grey whales—cow and calf—grey-brown leviathans blanketed in barnacles. They dove beside us several times and, on the last dive, the baby raised a small fluke as if to wave.

8:00 p.m. In from mahi mahi and red snapper at the Breakwater Café.

Monday, April 4, 2005

1:30 p.m. Sitting by the pool. On our way back from State Street, we stopped for a halibut burger at the Minnow Café down on the pier. The thicket of harbor masts hummed and clanged and buzzed in a great wind that had cleared the coastal Santa Inez Mountains of smog and fog. Pelicans sailed high overhead, sand pipers prowled the shoreline, and wind-surfers dotted the churning seas.

10:00 p.m. In a chilly breeze, we ate supper on an upstairs balcony at Brophy Brothers, overlooking the harbor. Tomorrow it's the train to LA, hopeful of U2 tickets. Then back home to Tucson on Wednesday.

Tuesday, April 5, 2005

In perfect weather—a light breeze and sunshine—we're relaxing on the surf-board bench just north of the harbor. Clutches of sandpipers with long thin beaks, wait above the surf line, and then dash down as the water recedes, to dig up sand-crabs. A cloud of tiny shorebirds on stilted legs moves as one down to the wave-line and back again.

Two for Tuesday at the Minnow Café this morning. Zoo Station and Vertigo.

2:30 p.m. Left the Santa Barbara train station for LA at one-fifty-nine. Idling on a siding near Ventura now, awaiting the passage of a north-bound train. All the seats face backwards, so that the sea lies blue-green to our left, the Channel Islands on the horizon again, in dusty blue. To the right, gentle hills stacked like giant sand-dunes, are cloaked in low bush and flowering grasses.

Thursday, April 7, 2005

10:00 p.m. Home again, on a busy, busy day. Must squeeze in a short break for the LA show.

We arrived in central LA about five o'clock Tuesday afternoon, wending our way through an industrial sector filled with tattered, graffiti-covered warehouses. Our hotel, the Holiday Inn Los Angeles, situated about a hundred yards from the U2 venue—Staples Center—was an enormous building, all angled chunks of glass and metal cylinders.

We intended to queue for tickets at the box office, but a broker in the hotel lobby had two extraordinary seats at a hundred dollars over face value. In the loge area, second row up on Edge's side. We entered into a klatch of bars and restaurants, through VIP doors.

For this show—the best *Vertigo* thus far—Bono, positive and animated, smiled and laughed and danced all night, radiating a deep joy that touched audience and band members alike, especially Edge.

Here's the set-list: Love and Peace; Vertigo; Elevation; Cry/Electric Co; An Cat Dubh/Into the Heart; City of Blinding Lights; Beautiful Day; Miracle Drug; Sometimes You Can't Make It; New Year's Day; Sunday Bloody Sunday; Bullet; Running to Stand Still; Zoo Station; The Fly; Mysterious Ways; Pride; Streets; One//All Because of You; Yahweh; 40

Bono opened the night with "My name is Bono and I'm the singer in the loudest folk band in the world." Larry would sing, Bono promised. Adam only smiled back when mentioned.

The Into the Heart snippet in Electric Co. featured a young boy five or six years old, plucked from the barrier outside the point of the ellipse. "My name is Jack," the little boy managed after some coaxing. He and Bono strolled the ramp together, Jack looking up to a shower of red confetti spilling from the rafters for City of Blinding Lights. Little Jack sat out most of the song on the riser of Larry's drum kit. Bono crawled down the ramp to sing most of An Cat Dubh lying there on his back.

Miracle Drug was dedicated to "a very special person who came to see us today at sound-check." Bono hesitated here, as though weighing whether or not to name this person. Instead, he segued into how "nurses and doctors don't get paid enough," how "the world needs science," how "God uses science." We've speculated that the over-the-top exuberance of this show reflected some good news about Edge's daughter Sian, who's been battling leukemia.

Mysterious Ways set off this show for me. Bono called for a top-hat and someone tossed him a Fedora. With cowboy hats so prevalent, I was amazed that the stage wasn't inundated with headgear. After begging for handouts, Bono sent the fedora back out into the crowd.

What he loved most about LA, Bono said, was its imagination. Brad Pitt's name was dropped before One, and, while he may have been a guest, I've since learned that he'd contributed to a One-based anti-poverty TV ad that airs today. "This would be a good time to use your cell-phone," Bono suggested, and a sea of light glittered through the arena, as fans sought to raise the UNITE campaign to a million members.

Once again, Yahweh remained subdued, and, with 40, Bono draped his rosary on his microphone stand, gave it a kiss, and then, one-by-one, the lads left the stage.

We reached the airport by eight-thirty Wednesday morning and waited briefly in the International Terminal food-court, overlooking the Tahiti Nui Restaurant. In short order, I shuttled my way to the domestic terminal. (And then there was one.)

Friday, April 15, 2005
Mesquites have leafed out in the back yard, acacias vibrantly in bloom.

Without further ado, here's the set-list for the U2 show in Glendale last night: Love and Peace or Else; Vertigo; Elevation; Cry/Electric Co.; An Cat Dubh/Into the Heart; City of Blinding Lights; Beautiful Day; Miracle Drug; Sometimes You Can't Make it on Your Own; New Year's Day; Sunday Bloody Sunday; Bullet; Running to Stand Still; Pride; Streets; One//Zoo Station; The Fly; Mysterious Ways//All Because of You; Yahweh; 40.

Dan and I had seats on the left side as you face the stage, two-thirds up from the floor. The band arrived about nine-fifteen. Early on, a fan passed Bono an iris in honor of his mother. "Iris is here," Bono said. This same young woman walked behind us after the show, buoyed by the "eye contact with Bono" she'd had "for the rest of the show."

"Remember, Arizona, when there wasn't a Dr. King Day?" Bono asked at one point. "This is a better day." Dr. King's dream was "big enough to fit the whole world." During Mysterious Ways, he hauled a shirtless, tattooed fellow up onto the ramp and gave him a hug before the lad left the stage. Larry, late for Yahweh, raced down the ramp to his keyboard. And then—once again—it was over.

Just watched an *All Access* U2 special on *VH1*. "Suddenly everything is possible," the narrator said. This is the power and poignancy of U2. They almost always leave you more hopeful. Suddenly everything is possible.

Joining a band, Bono has said, was like signing up for the army or the priesthood. Even the color scheme of *How to Dismantle an Atomic Bomb*, reflects Maurice Stendal's 19th century novel, *The Red and the Black*, a tale of a young man's experiences in both of those powerful institutions. The Red and the Black—militarism and religion—have, unfortunately, defined and manipulated the world for eons.

I'm sensing more of a hopefulness than a celebration on this tour. In moments of intense possibility, faith's intolerance and a world filled with "wars and rumors of wars" should always be tested and questioned. Bush's arrogant politics. The ignorance and intolerance of so much of contemporary religion. At the same time, such powers must be addressed in order to achieve anything on a national or international level. Dancing with the devil really *can* cause Vertigo.

We put Mom and Dad's home on the market today. The house I grew up in. The *For Sale* sign went straight through my heart.

Tuesday, April 19, 2005

One Las Vegas U2 ticket arrived today. I'd gone in to the public sale Saturday morning at exactly ten o'clock and all the tickets had gone but one. Twice more, and I picked up two more singles.

Friday, May 19, 2005

5:00 p.m. Sitting in Victoria Park [Kitchener, Ontario, Canada], on a windy but bright blue day. Spring laciness in the trees has ripened to a full, lush canopy.

For years I've relished by-gone lives preserved in tea-colored photographs. Now I'm only dispirited. Too much time spent alone, sorting the house, sifting through two long lives.

Pensive feelings have tracked me back here to my hotel room. They're hunkered in the corners of the room, skulking just outside the door. I need an escape. I need to shift to hopefulness, a place where "suddenly everything is possible."

Sunday, June 12, 2005

9:00 a.m. In the Tucson airport awaiting a flight to Chicago and on to Manchester for the European leg of my *Vertigo Tour*. Nice to have this break. At the same time, I can't wait to get back home.

Monday, June 13, 2005

I'm in Piccadilly Station [Manchester, UK] with Debbi. Though the pilot had promised a smooth ride "with a few bumps," the Chicago flight was a rough one.

10:40 p.m. In our room at the Manchester Travelodge on Ancoates Road, after dinner at a crowded, clubby, basement restaurant called Velvet.

Tuesday, June 14, 2005

A wet grey day. Hoping for the *Vertigo* ellipse—affectionately called The Bomb Shelter—Sue, Debbi, and Julie left for the venue [The City of Manchester Stadium] earlier this morning. Able physically, psychologically I rebelled, especially with this cold rain.

Wednesday, June 15, 2005

11:00 a.m. A dull and overcast day, with another spit of rain. Last night's fine performance, under a splendid half-moon, left me with a creeping sense of religiosity. Spirituality is so easily consumed by *right*-tiousness. "Wherever two or more of you are gathered together in anyone's name, there's trouble."

We had an excellent spot on the pitch by the front barrier, at the end of the right stage wing. To our immediate left, the crowd surged menacingly. Vertigo opened—as it should—but the lads seemed to be somehow at odds with each other.

Here's the first Manchester set-list: Vertigo; I Will Follow; Cry/Electric Co.; Elevation; New Year's Day; Beautiful Day; City of Blinding Lights; Miracle Drug; Sometimes You Can't Make It On Your Own; Love and Peace or Else; Sunday Bloody Sunday; Bullet; Running to Stand Still; Pride; Streets; One//Zoo Station; The Fly; With or Without You//Yahweh; Vertigo

Thursday, June 16, 2005

Another grey day. I'm at Sharon's in York. We're booked for Royal Ascot this afternoon, a once-in-a-lifetime experience—at least for me. Sharon managed two free tickets at work.

We left Manchester last night after a second brilliant show—intimate and personal. We trudged to a downtown garage in a stream of fans and pulled into York just after two a.m.

We reached the venue mid-afternoon and still achieved great positon at the back of the Bomb Shelter, beside the walkway. Wristbands dispensed with, the first three-thousand people were allowed in.

Here's the set-list: Vertigo; I Will Follow; Cry/Electric Co.; Elevation; Still Haven't Found; All I Want is You; New Year's Day; Beautiful Day; City of Blinding Lights; Miracle Drug; Sometimes You Can't Make it on Your Own; Love and Peace or Else; Sunday Bloody Sunday; Bullet; Running to Stand Still; Streets; One//Zoo Station; The Fly; With or Without You//Yahweh; Vertigo

Two bands opened—Idlewild with some rocked-out James Taylor-styled tunes, and The Athletes, a Scottish group with grand-scale harmonies similar to Runrig's. With the concert advanced a half-hour, darker skies improved the lighting, though we did have a sprinkle of rain.

"Sorry, I forgot to start," Bono said, as Miracle Drug struck up. "I was enjoying myself. It's such a nice melody."

Sometimes You Can't Make it on Your Own spoke powerfully to me, given my Dad's recent death. Sunday Bloody Sunday emphasized "all sorts," redemption for the semi-dogma of the first night.

Friday, June 17, 2005

Yet another cool and cloudy day. Yesterday, early afternoon, Sharon and I hiked over to the York racetrack, crossing a Hob Moor finally dotted again with cattle, as it should be.

Royal Ascot's racing grounds down south are being refurbished this year, and the five-day event has been transferred north. Ladies' Day entailed heels and hats, at least until meadow walking and an enormous wind made both untenable.

We negotiated the railway underpass, emerging at the top of a lea where a stone cairn marked Tyburn, the site of York's past executions. Down a narrow banked wood then, to the turf track on Knavesmire.

We narrowly missed the entrance of Liz and Phil. They'd flown in from London by helicopter and had been carriaged to the Royal Enclosure. Footpaths directed us along the grassy racecourse to the locals' Rail Enclosure at the far end of the field.

Ascot has been an English tradition since 1711. "A unique event in the [British] summer sporting and social calendar," my flyer reads. Hats, hats, and more hats defined the day. Lady Somebody-or-Other had sported a massively flamboyant chapeau one year in the misty past, and the gauntlet had been cast. Hats abounded. Gargantuan hats. Plain and simple hats. Feathered hats and netted.

The Royal Enclosure specifies "formal dress with a hat" for women, "gentlemen in black or grey morning dress," with waistcoat and top-hat. I'd just recently read about the "sporting and social" season in Victorian and Edwardian England, eras of masterful pretense. These days anyone can finagle the Royal Enclosure if they can cough up the hefty fee. Row on row of tail-gating limos presented awnings and top-hats, linen table cloths, champagne, and tuxedoed chauffeurs.

At one point, I swam against the tide, worming my way trackside from The Rails. Stiletto heels pounded the metal walkway, advancing on me like a herd of shod horses. One top-hat-and-tails fellow flew at me with such a feverish pace that I had to step off the path in order to avoid being bowled over. A unique and potently English experience, Ascot.

Out of six races, I dropped a fiver on Indigo Cat to place in the *Hampton Court Stakes*. Came out two pounds richer. Indigo Cat was dead last "pacing off." As the thicket of horses passed the Rail Enclosure, I caught the blue silks of his jockey, third place on the inside, before he pulled ahead to win. The Queen ran a horse in the *Hampton Court Stakes*, too. Her Forward Move lost to my Indigo Cat, leaving Liz out a couple of bob. On my last bet—the *Buckingham Palace Stakes*—my horse, Millennium Force, went nowhere.

Every half-hour or so, between races, jockeys would mount and dismount, horse and rider would be described, and loading gates announced. A fine day at the track, with a picnic lunch and LL Bean chairs. Sharon's mother's bowling friends had collected in one corner of The Rails. One of them asked where in America I was from. "Arizona," I answered, and they sang me the whole of Ragtime Cowboy Joe.

3:30 p.m. A gorgeous day of sunshine, slow-moving grey-bottomed clouds, and blue sky. I'm on a backless bench off a Hob Moor bike path, the trees light and fragile with spring, the air filled with birdsongs, munching cattle, distant traffic, and the occasional passing train.

Humanity has crisscrossed this common in all seasons, in all weather, through all time, and, disoriented by deep fog or strange sounds, they've sometimes told tales of otherworldly beings. In truth there *is* something haunting about the place. I'd walked and walked and walked—the whole of the open area, I'd thought—and yet, as

I sit here next to Sharon's back gate, a fresh expanse of grass and buttercups moves away distantly to my left.

Saturday, June 18, 2005

On the train to London. We left York about ten-twenty this morning.

Sunday, June 19, 2005

Blazingly hot and humid. I'm in room #207 at the Travelodge in Kingston-Upon-Thames, a plain inn identical to Manchester's. I came in by bus from the Marriott on Bath Road by Heathrow, where Sharon, Jane, and I stayed last night. One pound twenty for this hour and a half ride, Heathrow to Kingston. A monstrous city, London. Like a giant amoeba, gobbling up everything in its path.

I got a kick out of traveling with the locals through the streets and villages of Greater London—Richmond, Twickenham, Teddington, Kingston. Klatches of elderly women climbed on board with carrier bags of groceries. A young girl of ten or twelve wore an unlikely "Wild Thing" jacket, and one scruffy fellow's t-shirt read "I don't get out of bed for less than a grand." He must get an awful lot of sleep.

Sharon and Jane have returned north, Sue and Julie off to Hampton Court. Been there. Done that. A time or two.

We left York for London on Saturday. A quick run through English fields and villages, into the bustle of the city. Paul, half of a young couple also on their way to London for U2, overheard my first name, factored in the U2 and Canadian tags on my luggage, and asked if I wasn't the author of *A Grand Madness*. I was chuffed. His girlfriend had given him a copy of the book for his birthday and he'd just re-read portions to get hyped up for the show. Had it worked? I asked. It had!

Arriving at King's Cross Station, we hopped the tube to Heathrow, and then took a cab to the Marriott. Additional buses brought us to Twickenham Football Stadium, affectionately called Twickers. Where the City of Manchester Stadium had been quite posh, with a design that featured high mast-like towers, Twickers, a cement-pillared venue with high fading green walls, seemed sketchy by comparison.

While the lads sounded-checked, we hunkered down at Gate G, in the meager shade of one stunted beech tree and a fading rose bush. Venturing inside about six o'clock, we sat through the two openers, Doves and Morrissey.

Here's the U2 set-list: Vertigo; I Will Follow; Cry/Electric Co.; Elevation; New Year's Day; Beautiful Day; Still Haven't Found; All I Want is You; Blinding Lights; Miracle Drug; Sometimes; Love and Peace; Sunday Bloody Sunday; Bullet; Running to Stand Still; Pride; Streets; One/Zooropa; The Fly; Mysterious Ways//Yahweh; Vertigo

Our seats, second row up in the second tier, were at the back of the stadium, to the right. With a bright sky that lingered even at the concert's close, most songs were performed without much visible stage lighting at all. At first, I blamed my ears for the dismal acoustics, or the echo from a wall of sound bouncing off the back of the stadium. But on occasion the vocals and the music just parted ways. Some of the apparent tension may have come from the fact that this show was to be broadcast live. Then again, Bono had been treated for pain in his back, which might equally have accounted for the literal stiffness. The high-point of the show came with Streets— fifty-thousand fans fist pumping, color and light everywhere.

We chanced the backstage entrance at Gate P afterwards, and Adam, Edge, and Larry all stepped out about half-midnight. Edge chatted his way down the entire fan line. Larry offered up a word or two, and when Adam asked Jane if she'd been to any other shows, she told him that she'd started her tour in America.

Monday, June 20, 2005

10:00 a.m. Finished packing to a rumble of thunder. At least the heat of the last few days may dissipate. We ate at Little Italy last night—penne pasta with blue cheese, gorgonzola, and mushrooms—then moseyed back to Twickenham on the bus. We had no tickets for the second London show, but from outside the main gate, the sound seemed much improved from Saturday night.

Fans milled everywhere, and as Bono crooned one tune or another, directly opposite him, a blackbird, on a nearby rooftop, trilled right along.

As the encore commenced, we trekked back to Gate P, and almost as the last note faded, a police contingent pulled in and someone shouted "here they come." Staff and security still sported walkie-talkies as a blacked-out decoy van sped away, escorted front and back, by motorcycles.

At twelve fifteen, a second departing van stopped, and Bono climbed out. Pandemonium ensued after that. Well out of the way as the swarming intensified, I could just make out his face, tense and pale, as he shook hands. Quite suddenly then, the crowd swooped and he disappeared altogether. A group of tall men, arms outstretched like the unfurled wings of vultures, swallowed him up.

This knot of mayhem inched to the far side of the car, and then up against the barrier. Very soon after that, Bono backed himself into the van and was whisked away. We learned later that a fan had asked Bono to kiss her daughter who was asleep against the fence and, of course, he had.

1:00 p.m. Three minutes short of Stansted, where we'll catch a flight to Glasgow. Mechanical problems in the approach tunnel have already delayed us twenty minutes.

6:20 p.m. In our room at the Travel Inn on Embank Gardens. A London train, Kingston to Vauxhall Station; the Victoria Line to Oxford Circus; Central Line to Liverpool Street Station; Stansted Express to the airport; and so here, to Glasgow.

Tuesday, June 21, 2005

The Full Strawberry Moon rises on Midsummer tonight.

My Glasgow ticket reached Carlisle [in the north of England] yesterday and was forwarded post haste to Dawn in Dumfries [Scotland]. With luck it will make it here in time for today's show.

We ate in the hotel restaurant last night—"goujons" (mushroom and haddock fingers)—for starters, and a main of steak and chips.

Joined Alan—Bono from the first-rate tribute band NU2—in the bar afterwards.

Just after 11:00 a.m. We'll soon set off for the venue [Hampden National Stadium].

Wednesday, June 22, 2005

Six-thirty p.m. and I'm seated on a white, wrought-iron bench outside Bewley's Ballsbridge, Dublin. The attractive yellow-brick building with red trim and small dormer windows was a Masonic Girls School from 1792 to 1881. In addition to an iron fence, a canopy of maples and chestnut trees separates Bewley's grounds from the busy thoroughfare out front.

Three a.m. before we got to bed this morning after a spectacular Glasgow concert. We'd gathered at reception by ten for a taxi to the railway station.

The 11:00 a.m. train brought us through the Scottish countryside to Prestwick Airport, where a thirty-five minute flight landed us in Dublin about 2:00 p.m. The elderly Irish nun beside me in Economy, had just visited her son in Arizona. "It was like going to hell," she said. An hour-long Air Coach from the airport carried us through Dublin City, and so here to Bewley's.

Meanwhile, Dawn had to depart Dumfries by twelve-thirty. My Glasgow ticket, shipped off to her from Carlisle by a friend of Sue's, was snatched from the postman at twelve-fifteen, before he even reached the door. By three that afternoon, I'd collected it from Dawn at the retail complex next to the venue.

Even with that complication, I found myself at the same pitch turnstile as the rest of our group, and they'd been in line from nine-thirty. Even managed a spot near the Bomb Shelter railing, half-way to the outside ramp, right of the B-stage, on Adam's side.

This Glasgow show was extraordinary, so full of fun, as Scottish shows often are. Here's the set-list: Vertigo; All Because of You; Electric Co.; Elevation; New Year's Day; Beautiful Day; Still Haven't Found; Wild Horses; City of Blinding Lights; Miracle Drug; Sometimes You Can't Make it on Your Own; Love and Peace or Else; Sunday Blood Sunday; Bullet; Running to Stand Still; Pride; Streets; One//Zoo Station; The Fly; With or Without You//Yahweh; Vertigo

Bono prowled the stage for Elevation, kissing the cheek of a photographer who pulled him down for a lip lock. "Dirty boy," he proclaimed afterwards. Running to Stand Still, for Aung San Suu Kyi, incorporated a rousing "Happy Birthday" sing-along for her sixtieth. There'd be a party, Bono said, when he returned to Scotland for the G8 Summit. And we were all invited. Special thanks went out to Scottish Chancellor Gordon Brown, for everything he'd done for the G8's anti-poverty campaign.

"Take this heart, this Glasgow heart, this great big heart and keep it safe," Bono said at the concert's close.

As a singer, Bono often soars into another dimension inside the music, taking the audience right along with him into the stratosphere, and the band expands into something larger than the sum of its parts. Glasgow was that kind of show.

In the misty rain afterwards, we had a devil of a time flagging down a taxi. Glasgow cabs of the blocky, black English variety are scarce, and in the end we hailed any car that passed, finally meeting with success.

Friday, June 24, 2005

12:30 a.m. Yesterday, we fancied the noon play at the Café Theatre in Bewley's on Grafton Street. We reached Landsdowne Station by a pleasant pathway along the River Dodder, shaded by summer trees. The river glided between stone walls, suffused with wildlife—and the occasional sack of garbage. On one roof-top, a great blue heron balanced on one long thin leg, while, directly behind, a one-legged mechanical crane—one of dozens in Dublin these days—punctured the skyline. Mallard ducks paddled the eddies, in concert with schools of grey mullet that churned the surface shallows with their fins and tails. They'd worked their way up from the sea to breed and would be flushed out again with the tide. Two magpies in black-and-white bobbed around in the treetops ahead of us.

The play, *Casanova's Limp*, was well-written and wel-performed. The cast included an actress from the *BBC TV* series *Ballykissangel*. The gist of the piece concerned two ex-lovers of Casanova who were working to help him "get it up," so to speak, on his deathbed. In consequence, the hour was heavy with bawdy, ribald, often sophomoric humor.

What a great concept this theatre is. Hour-long performances at one in the afternoon, fourteen Euros for soup and a sandwich. I ordered Italian vegetable, with smoked salmon on a bagel. The venue measures about thirty feet square, with a smattering of tables and chairs, the stage in one corner, a serving window in back.

The Pierce Station Dart brought us back to Lansdowne and we returned to Bewley's along the Dodder. A heron fished in the shallows, mallards slept on rocks among snapdragons and wild orchids, one female puddling about with a clutch of frizzy babes. The mullet still swarmed, and moor-hens with bright red beaks poked about in the mud with their young—black fuzz-balls on stilted legs, with giant, black-spider feet.

About four-thirty, we called a taxi to Ken and Elizabeth's in Dun Laoghaire. Moni, the East Indian neighbor who'd purchased #10 next door—the flat we'd rented so often in times past—dropped by with his wife, Anna. Seven-year-old Max, the cat, sprawled on the dining room table. His great friend, Moni's puppy Bobo, a rescued black Lab, joined us too, his thin, short tail spinning with excitement. (*Bobo and Max* would make a great title for a short story.)

La Strada for supper then, where we met up with Chris, who'd flown in from Germany for the Dublin shows. We parted company with her at Lansdowne, and sped home on the dart, the sea a luminous powder-blue, melting with the sky. No line at all on the eastern horizon. A single ferry, sparkling with lights against a deep blue twilight, glided on the mirrored water below Howth.

Once again, we followed the River Dodder back to Bewley's. At nearly ten-thirty, mallards still puttered in the stream and a heron flew up-river for some late night fishing. Just short of the bridge, Sue and I had paused to admire the foliage on the lofty sycamores lining the walkway, when Debbi let out a sudden shout of "Rats!" Two enormous sewer rats charged us before vanishing again into the bushes.

Saturday, June 25, 2005

Just after 10:00 a.m., with a sprinkle of rain from blank white skies. I'll head over to Croke Park about six o'clock for the second Dublin show.

Yesterday, in a fine mist that lingered all night, we arrived at the first Dublin Concert just short of seven. The opening band, Snow Patrol, was excellent. Our seats, in a crowd of 87,000, in the lower tier to the left as you face the stage, were about a dozen rows up from a packed pitch. Sue, Julie, and Debbi all had *U2.com* seats and found themselves four rows from the very top of the stadium, where the sound was abysmal. A Garda [Irish police officer] who accompanied us on the long hike to the bus-stop after the show, said he'd heard many similar complaints.

Balloons often bounce around the larger venues before a U2 show. At the second Manchester performance, I'd batted away one that drifted into the Bomb Shelter. It struck a fellow a few feet to my left and spilled his beer. Here in Croke Park, we had inflatable leprechauns.

This first Dublin show became my third favorite of this leg of *Vertigo*, after Glasgow and second Manchester. The lads had a grand time. Here's the set-list: Vertigo; I Will Follow; Electric Co.; Elevation; New Year's Day; Beautiful Day; Wild Horses; Blinding Lights; Miracle Drug; Sometimes You Can't Make it on Your Own; Love and Peace; Sunday Bloody Sunday; Bullet; Running to Stand Still; Pride; Streets; One//Zoo Station; The Fly; With or Without You// All Because of you; Yahweh; Vertigo

Bono sports a cowboy hat in recent Vertigo videos, and head gear of that ilk has sprung up in audiences and souvenir stalls, all shades and fabrics, from glittery pink felt and tri-colored straw, to green leather and red velvet.

All Because of You, performed under green and orange on-screen lights, seemed more than appropriate. All because of Dublin, they are. In swirling Irish mist, the emotion and celebration of this tune were unmatched. One lit up the stands, cell-phones twinkling like fireflies, and a snatch of the Beatles Rain closed the show.

At the backstage entrance, two blacked-out ambulances, separated in time, pulled out into the roadway, where each broke out in flashing lights. A novel escape route for the band, we thought.

In a damp cold, we ambled to O'Connell Street, escorted by the aforementioned Garda, and hopped the #7 bus to Ballsbridge. Just as we reached our stop, the young woman behind me hurled into the center aisle. When the fellow in the seat in front of me stood up and began to gag, I mercifully stepped out into fresh air.

Larry came out to fans last night, Sue said. Signed and smiled and talked. Larry! Signing! Smiling! Talking!

Sunday, June 26, 2005

10:00 p.m. A beautiful day. I'm in my room—#123—at the Crowne Plaza Manchester Airport Hotel.

Sharon and Jane left for home so early this morning that I had to say goodbye to them after last night's show. Debbi set off at six this morning. Someone had charged a breakfast to her room, an issue easily remedied by comparing signatures. Sue, Julie, and I took the Airport Shuttle about ten o'clock, passing the oh-so-Irishly named pub, Waxie Duggel's. Sandwiches at the airport, seething with travelers, and then Sue and Julie moved on to their respective gates.

My three-thirty Manchester flight, delayed an hour, plied its short and gentle way across the Irish Sea, smoke stacks and the broad arc of Dublin's harbor receding in pale dusty blue. I sat with two seriously under-bathed Malaysian novice nuns. Earlier, a pod of lanky, malodorous, brusque and bossy German men had cut me off in line. As Dave Berry would say, *Waxie Duggel and the Whiffy Germans* would make an excellent name for a rock band.

Monday, June 27, 2005

9:00 a.m. Not a cloud in the sky this morning. I'm in the Manchester Airport for a flight that leaves for Chicago at eleven. When my carry-on luggage was searched in Dublin, security quizzed me about Arizona. Very hot this time of year, I said. But we were looking forward to the start of our wonderful summer storms. "What do you mean by a storm being wonderful?" the agent asked.

4:10 p.m. Dead-knackered. On a hot and humid day, with smudgy grey skies, I'm awaiting my flight to Tucson out of Chicago. Four more hours to go yet. While I have time, I'll wrap up the second Dublin show.

Sharon, Jane, and I wandered the docklands until four o'clock, when I left for the Gresham Hotel on O'Connell Street. We hardly recognized that area anymore, it's so full of high-rise glass and metal. I rather missed "dirty old (Dublin) town."

For this second show, I stood midway up the stands on the right side, half-way along the pitch. "We're going to have a party," Bono promised. And we did.

Here's the set-list: Vertigo; Out of Control; Electric Co.; Elevation; New Year's Day; Beautiful Day; Still Haven't Found; All I Want is You; Blinding Lights; Miracle Drug; Sometimes You Can't Make It; Love and Peace; Sunday Bloody Sunday; Bullet; Running; Pride; Streets; One//Zoo Station; The Fly; Mysterious Ways; Party Girl//All Because of You; Yahweh; Vertigo

There was early mention of "stealing Edge from Wales" and delivering him to the G8, and of U2 being simultaneously "the worst wedding band" and "the best rock and roll band." Though they were getting older, they were still "a band of the future," Bono said.

Brad from Canada, with an orange sign none of us could read, hopped onstage to play guitar. "It pays to advertise," Bono declared, displaying Brad's hand-painted sign which, still, none of us could make out. Did he want to play guitar or sing? Bono asked. Play guitar, Brad answered. And play he did. Afterwards, arms draped across each other's shoulders, they ambled down the ramp, before Brad dropped back into the crowd.

After idling at the backstage entrance briefly after the show, we heard later that Bono had left in a van, with a clipped wave to fans. Edge and Larry pulled away in a second vehicle. Adam, with his mom and dad, left in a third. I never saw a hair of any of them.

Mechanical problems have delayed my Tucson flight another hour.

Thursday, August 4, 2005

Finished *Bono in Conversation with Michka Assayas* [Riverhead Books/Penquin Group; 2005] Bono, a long-time friend of the French journalist, has written the book's foreword. Much of the contents pertain to *DATA*, though there are one or two more personal bits. As a child, for example, Bono was a fan of the Beatles, Bob Dylan, and Neil Diamond. "No artist alive or dead" has meant more to him than Bob Dylan.

He isn't really trying to "figure things out" anymore, Bono says. He just needs the silence in which he can rediscover things. U2's music is often "shot through with light," which fans have understood for a very long time. We know him better than his best friends do, Bono says. Because he "sings through his fans' headphones directly into their ears."

Ostensibly, he's adopted the disturbing trait of respecting people who "stay true to their convictions," people who believe passionately in something. This sounds admirable, until you realize that Adolph Hitler and Idi Amin, [Vladimir Putin, and Kim Jong-un] would be among them.

Heaven "looks like this present life without this present evil," Bono says. I could live with that. "Christ teaches that God is love— and as much as I respond in allowing myself to be transformed by that love and acting in that love, that's my religion."

The Pei-designed Rock & Roll Hall of Fame, Cleveland, Ohio – August 14, 2003

San Diego Sports Arena, Opening of the *Vertigo Tour* – March 28, 2005

Hotel Del Coronado, San Diego, California – March 29, 2005

San Diego, California – March 30, 2005

The Sunset Kidd, Santa Barbara, California – April 2, 2005

The Santa Inez Mountains, Santa Barbara – April 2, 2005

The Staples Center, Los Angeles – April 5, 2005

The author with the band, Los Angeles – April 5, 2005 (Sharon Harton)

The Royal Enclosure, Royal Ascot, York, UK – June 16, 2005

The author on Ladies Day at Royal Ascot –
June 16, 2005 (Sharon Harton)

Edge signs autographs at
Twickinham, London –
June 18, 2005 (Sue Fell)

Larry signs autographs at
Twickers, London – June 18,
2005 (Sue Fell)

Adam signs autographs
at Twickers, London –
June 18, 2005 (Sue Fell)

Croke Park, Dublin – June 25, 2005

Banknorth Garden, Boston, Massachusetts – October 3, 2005

Banknorth Garden – October 3, 2005

Edge at Banknorth Garden – October 4, 2005

Bono on-stage at Banknorth Garden – October 4, 2005 (Sue Fell)

Adam at Banknorth Garden – October 4, 2005

Bono balances
Adam on his head,
Banknorth Garden
– October 4, 2005
(Sue Fell)

Where everybody knows your name. Cheers restaurant, Boston –
October 5, 2005

Bono at the MGM Grand Garden Arena, Las Vegas – November 5, 2005

American Airlines Arena, Miami, Florida – November 13, 2005

Outside AA Arena, Miami – November 14, 2005

Outside AA Arena, Miami – November 14, 2005

Star Island mansion used for *Scarface*. Harbor cruise, Miami – November 16, 2005

Thrush's Glen, the Wicklow Mountains, Ireland – May 17, 2006

Adam at HQ – May 8, 2007

Bono at HQ – May 8, 2007

Dublin and the River Liffey from the Penthouse at the Clarence Hotel, Dublin – May 10, 2007

Monday, August 29, 2005

Hurricane Katrina slammed into the Gulf Coast this morning. Came ashore just west of New Orleans, with a twenty-five foot tidal-surge and category five winds. The city escaped the brunt of it, though there's increasing fear that levees will break.

Thursday, September 15, 2005

U2 closed out Toronto last night with Bad!

An inspiring story in the newspaper this morning. A Kenyan man, at eighty-three the world's oldest grade-school student, promotes the value of education and wants to be a veterinarian.

Monday, October 3, 2005

6:00 p.m. I'm in our room—#201—in the Bullfinch Clarion Hotel on Merrimac Street in Boston. Set off for the airport at quarter to nine yesterday morning. My Tucson to Chicago flight left on time, but as we neared O'Hare, the captain reported two thunderheads parked directly over the city. We would have to hit a holding pattern for half an hour or more, possibly being diverted to Milwaukee.

Water, water everywhere, when we finally made landfall. The storms lasted a mere ten minutes, but my five-seventeen Boston connection was delayed two hours. At seven o'clock, after driving around the tarmac for an hour or so, the engines quite suddenly shut off. "Usually a bad sign," our pilot admitted.

A second line of thunderstorms advancing on the city had again forced the closure of our runway. So we sat for yet another hour and finally, at quarter to ten, the flight took off. We reached Boston close to midnight, and I hopped a shuttle to the Bullfinch. I have no idea where in the city I am, other than the North End.

Boston has a comfortable, old Dublin atmosphere to it that I quite like. A little ragged at the edges. Yesterday, a five minute walk brought us to the U2 venue—TD Banknorth Garden, formerly The Fleet Center, where Sue and Julie collected lime-green wristbands for the pitch. Every tenth person would be fingered for the Bomb

Shelter. I myself am pretty much behind the stage for both Boston shows.

We lunched at the Anthem Restaurant on Portland—a lettuce wedge with blue cheese and bacon bits—and headed back to the venue about two o'clock. The crowd thickened and the heat rose and the caterer's lobsters arrived. Thank God!

At quarter to five, the lads pulled in, Adam first—four heads in a blacked-out van. An entourage of similar vehicles and flashing police motorcycles, sirens blaring, followed. Staring straight ahead, Bono, riding shot-gun, offered up one half-hearted wave.

Tuesday, October 4, 2005

One a.m. In from an awesome show. Here's the first Boston set-list: City of Blinding Lights; Vertigo; Elevation; Cry/Electric Co; The Ocean; Still Haven't Found; Beautiful Day/Many Rivers to Cross; Miracle Drug; Sometimes; Love and Peace; Sunday Bloody Sunday; Bullet; Miss Sarajevo; Pride; Streets; One//For the First Time; Wild Horses; With or Without You//All Because of You; Yahweh; 40

On Adam's side, in line with Bono's front mike and the entrance to The Bomb Shelter, my row had only three seats, mine right beside a railing. The opener, Keane, was well received and U2 arrived at ten to nine. Miss Sarajevo came as a welcome surprise, Bono's aria stunning, though it took a lot out of him. Eighteen-thousand strong, the audience delivered much of the follow-up, Pride.

"See John Kerry right in front of you," Bono sang in Beautiful Day. If Kerry hadn't existed, "you'd have had to invent him," the Massachusetts senator had done so much for AIDS and other causes. Tom Brady, quarterback for the New England Patriots, was also in attendance.

Sometimes You Can't Make it on Your Own had a slice of The Black Hills of Dakota, a favorite tune of Bob Hewson's, and the Smashing Pumpkins Bullet with Butterfly Wings snippet—"despite all my rage, I am still just a rat in a cage"—came with Electric Co. One fan passed Bono a Boston Red Sox t-shirt, which he donned briefly before dangling it on his microphone stand. For With or Without You, he danced with a slim young woman, long hair gathered into a loose ponytail. She planted one hand firmly on Bono's butt. A pregnant woman who carried a sign that read "Baby in my belly wants to dance with Bono," got her wish, and Miracle Drug was dedicated to two AIDS specialists, Paul Farmer and Joia Mukherjee.

When the second and final encore finished, the lads left the stage, with the promise of a timely return. They'd been honored with some UK award, the presentation and acceptance of which would be filmed. "Help us out," Bono asked, but when they reappeared, we couldn't make out a single word of anything he said. Larry donned the Red Sox t-shirt before leaving the stage, eliciting great applause.

A handful of fans gathered afterwards by the backstage entrance at the bottom of a lengthy ramp sloping up to the second floor. We'd hung around a mere half-hour, when a departing van stopped and we were asked if we'd like to "say hello to Larry." Well, of course we would. So out Larry came. As courteous and soft-spoken as ever, he moved along our short line—we were seven—shaking each hand with a quiet "how are you?", a little non-plused that no one had anything for him to sign. So Julie dug up her album and Larry waited patiently while the rest of us rustled something up.

6:15 p.m. We re-convened at the backstage ramp just after three o'clock this afternoon. Larry, in a blacked-out car, drove straight into the venue, and fifteen minutes later, Edge did the same. Adam's van pulled half-way up the incline and then backed down again. Handsome and silver-haired, in a plum-colored t-shirt and dark pants, he stepped out to waiting fans.

"How are you?" he asked as he signed my *ATYCLB* booklet.

"Fine," I answered, and told him that Jane from Leeds was getting married in March. Would he sign her wedding card? "Do you remember Jane?" I asked, reaching for her photo.

"Of course I do," he answered, and took up the entire left side of the card with his message: "Congrats, Jane. Love, Adam C."

"Bless you," I said. "Jane will be thrilled," as indeed she will be. [And indeed she was!]

A minute or two later, Edge stepped out from the bowels of the venue, wearing dark pants, leather jacket, and his ubiquitous woolen cap. He signed for everyone and then sauntered up the ramp, turning a time or two to wave.

Bono arrived last, riding shot-gun in a black van. In dark shirt, denim jacket, and charcoal trousers, thick-soled slip-on sandals, and a pale straw cowboy hat, he moved stiffly as if in pain. Directly across the driveway from us, stood a fan with his two or three-year-old son, both in green Boston Celtic t-shirts. Bono had just hoisted the little boy up for a photo when a *Duck Tours* amphibian bus pulled up. He dropped his laid-back Zen demeanor for little boy smiles and waves.

Around he came to our side of the entranceway, and had just signed for Sue when he looked up and made an odd clicking sound together with a wink of surprise. "How is everyone?" he asked. "You picked the right weather."

"Would you be playing Bad tonight?" I ventured as he signed my *HTDAAB* booklet.

"I don't know," he answered. "We haven't decided yet." We all thought this unlikely.

After he'd gone, we drifted over to the Onyx Hotel's cozy Ruby Room, a half-moon bar in deep burgundy with fuchsia-flowered chandeliers, red leather couches, and tea-lights on all the tables. [I know you'll all want to know that I had a scrumptious grilled chicken sandwich with fries, washed down with a sangria cocktail.]

Wednesday, October 5, 2005

12:35 a.m. The second Boston show ended up a hair shorter than the first, the set the same, with the addition of a rather touch-and-go Crumbs from Your Table; Stuck in a Moment in place of Wild Horses; and no Yahweh. Added bits were tacked on here and there: Behind Blue Eyes with Electric Co., Old Man River (for New Orleans), and Sometimes I Feel Like a Motherless Child. Edge wore a green Celtics t-shirt and Larry's drummer arms were wrapped in some sort of brace. A plethora of young women claimed to be pregnant at this show.

In an amazing coincidence—I'd purchased my Boston tickets at different times and in different places—my seat was one row down and one seat over from the first night.

2:00 p.m. We're in Boston Public Gardens Park on a sunny blue day, joggers, walkers, starlings, robins, and fat grey squirrels everywhere, hints of autumn stealing into the trees. We ate a delicious New England clam chowder at Cheers, the pub—two bars and tiffany lamps—whose image features in the sit-com of the same name.

I do like this city, homey and comfortable, with a "common-man" feel.

3:00 p.m. I'm people-watching outside the Prudential Center on Newbury Street while the others shop. Just popped into the convenience store next door, and as I entered, a young fellow leaving said 'hi', to which I responded, before realizing he was talking on his cell-phone.

9:40 p.m. We climbed up to the Sky Walk in the Prudential Building this afternoon for a view of the city—the off-shore islands, the rivers, bridges, bays, and distant suburbs. Back Bay, below, with its long lines of stone row-houses in greenery, is an especially attractive area. The Top of the Hub Restaurant then, about seven, for an exceptional last meal.

Thursday, October 6, 2005

On a grey and cloudy day, I'm in the Boston airport for my flight back to Tucson. Though they were both emotional and polished, I felt a distance in these Boston shows that I can't put my finger on. Maybe it just comes down to something Bob Dylan once said about what happens when you've "arrived" and are no longer "becoming."

Thursday, November 3, 2005

8:35 p.m. We're on the 4th floor of the MGM Grand Hotel in Las Vegas, room #218. The colors and flash of The Strip blaze just outside the window, intense and frenetic. Dan and I set off for the airport about five-thirty this afternoon, collecting Danielle at her apartment on route.

Friday, November 4, 2005

We had a room service meal last night. Nothing to write home about, but the employee who delivered it brought along some personal Las Vegas tales.

A super-rich gambler given "The Mansion", a suite at the top of the hotel—fifteen-thousand square feet stocked with custom-made Armani suits—once dropped a $125,000 tip on a waitress, $80,000 on a bartender. 'Lil Buddy,' as said gambler, a Texan, dubbed him, laid a ten dollar bet that he could mix a drink the gambler couldn't down in one gulp. Lil Buddy won with a bottle of Coca Cola. He'd once been assigned to host a do for Loretta Lynn and Dolly Parton. When they'd insisted that he tuck in with their guests, he explained that he wasn't allowed to. So Dolly rang up the hotel manager. Lil Buddy "will be eating with us," she said. And then Loretta rustled him up a plateful.

U2 had just taken possession of one of the upstairs penthouses, Lil Buddy told us.

3:30 p.m. After a pricey brunch in the hotel's Studio Café—five dollars for one single slice of ham!—we lounged by the pool an hour or so, U2 tunes playing much of the day—All Because of You, In God's Country, Acrobat, One Tree Hill, Van Dieman's Land. When the pool lapsed into a bit of a bore, we rode the monorail around town, and then mingled with millions on The Strip for lunch at Wallensky's.

Sunday, November 6, 2005

Five-thirty in the afternoon and we're ready for take-off after a hefty continental breakfast at the MGM. A shuttle, rumored to appear every fifteen minutes, never materialized and so, like Sammy [O'Sullivan], who was also in the shuttle line, we opted for a taxi.

A long queue had formed at the airport for electronic ticketing, and, a half-hour from departure, Danielle was pronounced "restricted." Resolving that issue, we hit another snag at security, so that our Tucson gate closed, and we had to slip into yet a third line at Customer Service, to update our flight. One snitty fellow chewed up a half-hour with a demand for a first-class ticket. And then a fight broke out between two other travelers. One woman, on her cell-phone, expounded at great length on an endless variety of personally upsetting familial glitches. The woman next to her sniffed that we were *not*, in fact, awaiting a *Jerry Springer Show*. Things went downhill from there.

5:40 p.m. Off at last on our fifty-one minute flight back to Tucson. Time to jot down some specifics from the Vegas show.

The massive MGM Grand, with shops, theatres, pools, sixteen restaurants, and U2's venue—the sixteen-thousand seat Grand Garden Arena—gave the impression of a small village. High-rise accommodations towered in green lights, and a vast sweep of electronic bleeps burbled from the casino where we'd gambled away forty dollars the night before, coming away with sixty.

Here's the set-list for the show: City of Blinding Lights; Vertigo; Elevation; Mysterious Ways; End of the World; Still Haven't Found; Beautiful Day; Miracle Drug; Sometimes You Can't Make It; Love and Peace; Sunday Bloody Sunday; Bullet; Miss Sarajevo; Pride; Streets; One//Zoo Station; The Fly; With or Without You//All Because of You; In a Little While; BAD!!!

City of Blinding Lights opened with a shower of metallic red and silver confetti. Mary J. Blige pulled off a so-so duet with Bono on One. Brandon Flowers, singer with Las Vegas band The Killers, came onstage for In a Little While. And Dennis Sheehan, who'd been with U2 for twenty-three years, received a peppy "Happy Birthday" sing-along from the audience. This may be his last tour, we hear.

Our seats were unbeatable—four rows up from the floor, just where the ramp meets the stage. Edge performed all of Zoo Station there.

Closing the show with Bad was, of course, the high-point for me. The second encore launched with All Because of You, and I'd resigned myself to perhaps never hearing Bad live again. And then those familiar opening notes broke out!

Saturday, November 12, 2005

Eleven in the morning and I'm at Gate 9, in the Tucson airport, for a flight through Houston to Miami for the last of my *Vertigo* shows. Sharon will fly into Miami from Chicago. We rounded out our down time in Tucson with a Rotunda Room tour of Kartchner Caverns [Southern Arizona] and a couple of days at the cabin in the Chiricahua Mountains. A doe with spotted twins dropped by, alternating with our resident javalina herd.

Wednesday night we ate at the Rodeo Tavern [Rodeo, New Mexico]. Amazingly, a woman from Whitby [England], a coastal town forty miles from Sharon's home in York, sat at the next table. She'd been visiting her son, who owns a ranch in Cave Creek, and had honed in on Sharon's Yorkshire accent.

Midnight. The Tucson flight suffered a bump or two easing into Texas, as we passed through high black clouds. I reached the Holiday Inn Port of Miami Downtown close to nine-thirty. My short Houston-Miami flight grazed the Mississippi delta in Louisiana. A mass of rivulets branched out like tree roots in the pale smoke-blue of evening. Post Katrina, the river looked drowned. Sprinkles of light winked amid great swathes of water. Ribbons of land snaked along the banks, backed by more great swathes of water, and roadways would emerge from the sea and dissolve again. A lonely, sad, desolate landscape.

Sunday, November 13, 2005

2:00 p.m. We're at the pier of the Port of Miami on a humid, noisy, salsa-driven day. Out across the water, a line of cruise ships is hunkered down like multi-storied floating villages. We'll have a wander over to the venue soon—American Airlines Arena, at the north end of downtown.

A huge city, Miami. Over Biscayne Bay two long bridges, left and right, span army-green water thick with garbage at the shoreline. Miami Beach stretches beyond distant hotels, the water in-between choked with moored touring boats, sleek yachts, and soaring black seabirds. The atmosphere hums with Cuban dancers and salsa bands, Panama hats, big blousy shirts, spicy Cuban food, and Spanish, Spanish everywhere. Generations born and raised without a drop of English.

Flashy clubbing sorts must get off on such a big-haired, bling-bling city. Not remotely my kind of place, even with the tropical seas. Aspen, Palm Springs, the French Riviera, South Beach Miami—they're all venues for the super-wealthy to mingle with their own.

7:30 p.m. We drifted over to Snapper's for an evening meal of blackened grouper and shrimp served by a surly waiter. With tips automatically appended to bills, there's not always any incentive to be civil. The city seethes with people, with rushing traffic and canned music. An occasional snippet of U2—Stay, Stuck in a Moment, One—vanished mid-sentence under salsa rhythms.

Afterwards, we people-watched by the bay, a broad boardwalk running north and south, lined with sport-fishing boats advertising the hunting prospects for sailfish, shark, swordfish and—sadly—dolphin.

Too many people. Too much noise.

Monday, November 14, 2005

We're lazing by the hotel pool on a humid blue day, smudgy clouds drifting overhead.

For the show last night—one of the best of this tour—Bono's voice had much improved over Las Vegas. All the intimacy lacking in some recent *Vertigo* shows almost made up for the omission of Bad.

Here's the set-list: City of Blinding Lights; Vertigo; Elevation; Mysterious Ways; End of the World; Still Haven't Found What I'm Looking For; Beautiful Day; Miracle Drug; Sometimes You Can't Make It; Love and Peace; Sunday Bloody Sunday; Bullet; Miss Sarajevo; Pride; Streets; One//Stuck in a Moment; Wild Horses; With or Without You//All Because of You; Yahweh; 40

We had an excellent spot on Edge's side, right beside the

ramp—row thirteen, seats nineteen and twenty. "Since we opened the last tour, we've had a special relationship with Miami," Bono said. The city had given them a big kiss. "We're giving it back."

Before Miracle Drug, he told the tale he'd shared in Boston about Edge hailing from another planet. The other band members were standing on a Dublin street corner when a bright light heralded the arrival of a space ship from which Edge emerged.

"Who are you?" they asked.

"I am The Edge."

"Where are you from?"

"The future."

"And what's it like?"

"It's better. Gas is thirty-nine dollars a gallon. But it's much better."

Adam just grinned and shook his head.

Among fans from all over the world was a hundred-strong crew from the Netherlands, Bono said. "Where's section 105?" he asked, eliciting a massive cheer. The band loved America. Not only the country, but the idea of the country. "Hold on to it."

A woman with long dark hair took the stage for a With or Without You dance and a boy with eye-glasses popped up for Sunday Bloody Sunday. All of Bono's attempts to have the lad sit on a stage prop failed. In the end, he patted his own behind, tapped the seat, and the little fellow finally sat down.

Every morning for twenty years, the first thing Bono's father said to him was to "take off those fucking sunglasses." So, as it was his dad's birthday, he did. Out came Phil Docherty then, Bono's guitar tech, who shared the birthday date, and we all sang him a hardy Happy Birthday. At the band's exit, Bono tossed kisses to the audience and Adam passed notes to friends.

3:00 p.m. Outside the venue for sound-check. Waiting. Waiting. Waiting.

7:30 p.m. Just in from supper at Latin American Cuban Cuisine in the Bayside Marketplace. After we'd been an hour at the backstage entrance earlier, a poised young woman hoisting a TV camera on her shoulder conferred with a plethora of venue security. "There's about thirty or forty," one of the men mumbled into his walkie-talkie. And then, "they're on their way."

Within minutes, a massive entourage advanced. Paired motorcycle cops, lights flashing, lead the procession. Four black vehicles followed, twinned motorcyclists stationed between them. Bono, in a straw cowboy hat, poked out one back window, filming the fan gathering. The car stopped and he climbed out.

Edge, already out with a bullhorn, opened a "Bo-no" chant, and the bourgeoning crowd joined in. Moving down the row of fans, several bodies deep now, he shook hands. I stood alone against the barrier, ten or twelve feet to the right of the crowd. And Edge, bless him, walked over. "Nice to see you," he said.

One fellow emerged from the chaos in tears. "I just shook Edge's hand," he stuttered. "I can't believe it. My hands are still shaking."

Sharon had remarked the night before that whenever Edge and Adam were on a roll with fans, Bono would steal their thunder. He did just that when he stepped over with his video camera. "Who do you like best?" he asked. "Does anyone have anything nice to say about Edge?"

"I like Edge," an older woman gushed. "But I really love *you*, Bono."

As Bono moved down the line, the crowd clumped up behind him. People screamed and shoved and jostled, and more than one fan sprinted from one end of the line to the other and back again. Bono filmed back down the queue, passed through the opened gates, jumped in a golf cart, and arrived all over again. Photo ops with the police escort commenced then, before Edge and Bono went inside.

Tuesday, November 15, 2005

Relaxing by the pool, soon to step out for supper. Here's the set-list for the second Miami show last night: Blinding Lights; Vertigo; Elevation; I Will Follow; Electric Co.; Still Haven't Found What I'm

Looking For; Beautiful Day; Original of the Species; Sometimes; Love and Peace; Sunday Bloody Sunday; Bullet; Miss Sarajevo// Pride; Streets; One//End of the World; The Fly; With or Without You//All Because of You; Walk On/BAD!!

Our seats, on Adam's side, a third of the way up from the floor, conjoined a section just ahead of the Bomb Shelter.

Having eaten "lots of pasta on South Beach," Bono would have no trouble with Miss Sarajevo's aria, he claimed. We had snatches of Rock the Casbah and Sergeant Pepper's Lonely Hearts Club Band, and at the end of the main set, Old Man River for Katrina's victims and the cleanup crews.

"No wonder they call it American Airlines Arena," Bono said at one point. The audience sounded "like a fucking 747." One joined "the casino and the church—the preacher and the rock star."

A huddled consultation then commenced. Something along the lines of, "Dianne, Sharon, and Lyn are in town for the show. How about giving them Bad?" And there it was. An incomparable finish to my *Vertigo* tour.

8:00 p.m. Dinner outside at Bubba Gump's. Overly spiced New England clam chowder, but a delicious mahi-mahi with shrimp. Key lime pie for dessert.

Wednesday, November 16, 2005

1:20 p.m. Breakfast this morning at the Cuban Cuisine section of the Latin American Cafeteria. Dawn and Lucy, a mother/daughter duo we'd met earlier in the week, were eating there as well. Lucy has been a U2 fan since *before* birth, Dawn having been pregnant with her during *The Joshua Tree Tour*.

At eleven o'clock, we chugged off on the *Island Queen* for an hour and a half cruise of the harbor. We sailed in the care of Santiago, captain and guide. Life preservers would be sold "for forty-five dollars cash," he said, and it wasn't true that the captain went down with his ship.

A long bowed bridge sweeps up from downtown Miami to the first of the Florida Keys, Virginia Key, a squat tree-fringed island beside better-known Key Biscayne. Lines of stacked containers, monstrous cranes, and rusting off-shore dredgers on pontoons crowded the port, the *Seabound Intrepid* from Panama at anchor. Fisher Island up next, strung out with private yachts, celebrity mansions, and pricey condominiums, among them Oprah Winfrey's, Tom Cruise's, and Brittany Spears'. In the 1920s, Carl Fisher had sold the copious off-shore islands he owned to the City of Miami. He then bolted with his winnings—some eighty-million dollars—to New York City, where he promptly lost everything in the Crash of 1929.

We steamed across to South Beach, where the marina was jammed with yachts—*Kisses, Rasselas, Charade*—and then on to Star Island, all balconied mansions, swimming pools, turrets, gardens, guesthouses, wide immaculate lawns, and scores of palm trees. One long mediocre white house had served as the setting for *Scarface*. The palatial yellow stucco next door could be had for a mere twenty-three-million dollars, a nearby vacant lot for six point five.

The most spacious home on the island belonged to a pharmaceutical magnate named Dr. Frost. He'd constructed the pile for fifty-million dollars, excluding a twelve-million dollar adjacent garden plot. Most Star Island homes shriveled by comparison, some to the size of Dalkey mansions, others to the beachfront homes of Santa Barbara. Al Capone's quarters appeared puddly, comparable to an office building.

Neither dolphin nor manatee plied the waters of the fuel-spilled harbor. Aluminum cans and glass bottles bobbed at the harbor's edge, among coconuts and mats of floating grass.

7:10 p.m. Another great meal at Bubba Gump's Shrimp Company, a tray of crab-stuffed shrimp in garlic-butter sauce.

Such a salsa-driven city, Miami. Big hair, big earrings, big rhythms, bright colors, short skirts, bare midriffs, Panama hats, Cuban shirts. Store clerks shout and barter like border vendors, catering to Spanish speakers. In English-accented Spanish, I made an attempt to set aside a few items I'd accumulated while browsing a shop. Not a flicker of understanding, feigned or otherwise. In the end, I just abandoned the lot.

U2 delivered an outstanding Wanderer for a *Johnny Cash Special* on *CBS*.

Thursday, November 17, 2005

Off to Houston again. Anticipating long lines, we set off at eight o'clock this morning, snacked and chatted until Sharon boarded her plane for the UK. (And then there was one.) A rough take-off for me soon after. Bumps and dips and shakes and shudders, as we shot through towering storm-clouds. Miami spread out below, the deep blues of the bay wrapped in high-rises and causeways.

My *Vertigo Tour* is over! It couldn't have ended better than with Bad.

Monday, November 21, 2005

The band will tour Mexico, South America, Australia, New Zealand, and Japan next year. In a short interview on *60 Minutes* [*CBS* news program] Bono asserted that, even with his activism and politics, the music still matters most.

Saturday, May 13, 2006

Six o'clock in the evening and I'm awaiting a flight to Dublin from Chicago's O'Hare. Danielle dropped me at the Tucson airport this morning.

I skimmed a couple of Dublin guide books in preparation for this trip. In one—*Dublin, a Portrait* [HarperCollins, June 1967]—V. S. Pritchett says: "You begin to think that your large early Victorian room in Dublin has only three walls to it; and that where the fourth wall should be, there is rain, air, space, whispering, and the chaos of myth." How Irish is that!

Sunday, May 14, 2006

6:15 p.m. In my room at St. John's Wood on Castle Avenue in Clontarf, the stillness broken only by singing blackbirds. We have a three-bedroom two-storied unit near Clontarf Castle.

My Dublin flight yesterday took seven hours. I sat by the

window beside an Irishman who desperately wanted to talk, as the Irish so often do. I held him off until we landed. He then commented on an article I'd been reading about Dan Brown's *The Da Vinci Code* [Doubleday, New York; 2003]. A bona fide Opus Dei man himself, he'd been vastly offended by their portrayal in both the book and the Tom Hanks movie.

"Now that's the Ireland I know," he said, as we touched the ground in a pea-soup fog. "Cold and wet. It's been raining since September."

Monday, May 15, 2006

A dreary bleary day, with a light rain and a blank sky. Yesterday, we prowled the churchyard of St. John the Baptist next door. Ivy-covered stone walls rose up in its midst. The Irish must abandon such ruins when they've become too costly to remove or repair, but they do flesh out the atmosphere.

"Til the day break and the shadows flee away," read one of the old stone markers. Another—to Maureen O'Leary—pronounced her a "Super Trooper." And a third said of its occupant, "Her surpassing excellence as wife, mother and friend has rarely been equaled."

A Dublin spring is awash in purple lilacs and creamy, spike-bloomed chestnut trees. We stopped on Killiney Hill for a view of the bay and then had High Tea at the cozy Fitzpatrick Hotel—crust-less sandwiches and bon-bons served on a teetering lop-sided silver dish that seemed quintessentially Irish. The lounge, in pale wood with windows to the sea, had a painting on the wall of a young woman in the frocks and petticoats of some distant era. Her stance, hunched up against the wind, suggested a chat on her cell-phone.

2:45 p.m. In Jury's on the quays, sunlight poking through high, smudgy clouds. The view to Principle Management is a little glum these days. The orange-brick façade has been swallowed up by multi-storied glass and steel. The three-masted schooner *Jeanine Johnson* stood at anchor on the river.

We've come from *Exit Cuckoo*, the current play at Bewley's, a short cliché-ridden piece about nannies and working mothers. To the very end, I held out hope for just one reasonably accomplished woman, one reasonably adjusted child, one reasonably well-treated nanny.

Snapped photos at the studio cement bench, but didn't stay long. Bono is in London editing a newspaper for *DATA* and will fly to Africa on Wednesday.

10:30 p.m. In from an exceptional meal at O'Connell's in Bewley's Ballsbridge—fish cake starter, Irish wild salmon with scalloped potatoes, and Bewley's signature carrot and parsnip mash.

On a swing through the docklands afterwards, we discovered that Dockers Pub has gone, completely boarded up, the pub itself relocated to near The Point. Killiney's Court Hotel has vanished too, replaced with a parking-garage-inspired apartment building. Principle Management remains out of danger for the moment. The carved water-spirit heads on the exterior wall, rescued from the old O'Connell Bridge, are protected.

Lofty glass buildings have crept right up to Kilsaram Concrete, opposite Hanover, and Misery Hill has disappeared altogether. Years ago, I thought Sue and Jane had invented that name. But Misery Hill marked the spot in the docklands where lepers gathered in the past to be ferried downriver to a church where they could receive Holy Communion through a peep hole.

Thankfully, Dublin's brightly-colored doors live on. One story I've heard in regard to this tradition involved some drunken sot making his way home from the local to find his wife in bed with another man whom he promptly killed. He'd actually entered the wrong house. Hence the continuation of techno-color entrances.

We wended our way back to Clontarf—which is, by the way, where Brian Boru defeated the Vikings—at least those that weren't his retainers—and have been listening to the alternate *HTDAAB*.

"What are we drinking?" Sue asked.

"I was drinking wine," Bono replied.

Tuesday, May 16, 2006

4:30 p.m. A quick visit with George [former Principle gateman] this afternoon, at his flat, a narrow three-story row-house near the Ferryman. He's had great difficulty with his leg again, requiring hospital visits twice a week. Sadly, one sister and two brothers passed away at the end of last year.

Wednesday, May 17, 2006

Off to the Wicklows in a light rain, mist on the hilltops, flowering bushes everywhere—lavender lilacs and buttery-yellow laburnum.

8:00 p.m. Driving into Shankhill now and so back to Dublin. Still raining from a blank grey sky. We stopped above Ashford at the twenty-acre Mount Usher Gardens and warmed ourselves in the tearoom. Our server, a lad from Miami, has exiled himself from America until Bush is gone. "Better times ahead," he said.

The rich soils of Mount Usher, laid out around an old mill on a tributary of the River Vartry, are fed by a multitude of waterways. The mill's original grist stone still stands on the grounds. Founded by the Walpole family in 1868, and maintained by them until 1980, the exquisite gardens feature over four-thousand flowers, trees, and shrubs. Paths lined with wild garlic wander the riverside, there are meadows of bluebells and wild grasses, and azaleas bloom in cerise, orange, and scarlet, pink, cream, and lavender. Blissfully, the rain kept the crowds at bay. In a quiet corner of the woods, in a small dog cemetery Shem, Cain, Tam, George, Digger, Precious, Jolly, Darling Scampi, and Top Dog Muffin all rest in peace.

We'd planned for Brittas Bay afterwards, but finding the strand too soggy for beach-combing, we circled back into the mountains where Glenmasole Valley (Thrush's Glen) ends in a gorgeous River Dodder waterfall that drains the highlands above. Sally Gap (Gap of the Willows) and Glen Cree unfolded in the mist, with ragged black-heather moorland, overgrown glens and vivid green dales whitened by falling streams. Peat bogs, golden gorse on the hillsides, tree tunnels edging the bottomlands, stone walls, track-ways in a sheet of rain, and black water pooling everywhere.

Wild Wicklow! I loved it all!

Thursday, May 18, 2006

Yesterday, ensnared in traffic and so fifteen minutes late to the theatre, we opted for a drink at Jury's instead, and then moved on to Clontarf Castle, now a renovated hotel. We settled in a small candle-lit alcove in the old keep.

4:00 p.m. In from Jury's Il Barista bar near Christ Church Cathedral. Earlier today, the Dart carried us to Connolly Station, where we hopped the Luas Tram to Four Courts. ('Luas' is Irish Gaelic for 'speed'). Walked over to St. Audoen's, founded by the Normans in 1190. Though the present church is quite new, St. Audoen's is the very one to which the lepers of Misery Hill were ferried.

Dublinia, a tourist mecca connected to Christ Church Cathedral by a Medieval footbridge, proved too noisy and Disneyesque for my taste, though its attempt to make Irish history vibrant and accessible is admirable. The cathedral passage had been blocked off. Refugees from Afghanistan are on a hunger strike in the cathedral at present. Some have already been transferred to the hospital.

We also hiked up the tower of St. Michael's church, affording us an imposing view of Dublin City and the nearby Dublin Mountains.

Nearly midnight. After excellent sweet and sour chicken, roast duck, and refried rice at Fan's Cantonese Restaurant on Dame Street, we set off for our Musical Pub Crawl. Featuring a formidable fiddler named Andy—a taller, lankier Edge—the band opened up in the Oliver St. John Gogarty Pub and moved on to the Ha' Penny Bridge Inn, one of only two authentic pubs still in Temple Bar. Sitting opposite us here, the bleach-blonde girlfriend of an Oscar Wilde look-alike rubbed his face with hers so incessantly that, between sets, we expected her to purr.

Our third and last pub, The Exchequer, was empty out front, but we were escorted into the back room for more fiddling, story-telling, and lots of laughs.

"What do black goats sing?"

"Clip-clop." [Groan]

Saturday, May 20, 2006

At gate B31 at the Dublin Airport, making my way back home.

We dropped into Kilmainham Gaol yesterday, the guide's recitation punctuated rather excessively with "it changed the course of Irish history." Interesting specifics, though few countries fall short in the 'martyrs for freedom' department. As a rule, they transform themselves rather quickly into the dominant culture, inflicting their own mistreatment on others. It all depends on where you stand in the process of 'nation building.' Both sides too often adopt a penchant for dropping the enemy in a dungeon and forgetting he's there.

We met Declan at the Clontarf Hotel last night, before going into Dun Laoghaire for a last meal at La Strada. After sea bass in marinara sauce with a goat cheese salad, La Strada's management graciously offered us each a complimentary glass of an anise liqueur called sambuco. Coffee beans floated on top, the drink served with a blue flame of burning alcohol. A tad too strong for us, Sue discreetly off-loaded hers in a fake potted plant, and I topped off my water glass.

We have lift-off, over patchy green fields, into a thick bank of grey clouds.

5:30 p.m. In Chicago. Claimed and rechecked my luggage. While waiting to board, I became aware of a miniature beagle snuffling at my carry-on.

"Do you have any fruit?" a security woman asked.

I'd had an apple, eaten hours earlier, I said.

Nevertheless, Spidey placed a paw repeatedly on my bag and I was hauled off for x-rays.

In Terminal 3 now, for a flight to Tucson at seven-thirty. Home by nine. A few short weeks and Dan and I will be off again, to Prague and Langue D'Oc.

Tuesday, May 23, 2006

Bono will be reporting to *NBC World News* on his humanitarian tour of Africa.

Monday, September 25, 2006

U2 and Green Day reopened the Super Dome in New Orleans on *Monday Night Football* with Beautiful Day and a raucous The Saints are Coming. They're raising funds for Edge's post-Katrina *Music Rising*.

Friday, May 4, 2007

On my way to Dublin via Phoenix. Dan drove me to the airport at seven-thirty this morning. I've a window seat and an aisle seat, so lots of room.

Saturday, May 5, 2007

7:00 p.m. In the sitting-room of our rental, Seaview, on Strand Street in Sandymount. Beyond a low stone wall across the road, lies Sandymount's broad low-tide mudflats. We landed at eight-thirty this morning in a blanket of mist.

Our corner home on Strand and Lea Avenue, with stuccoed yellow exterior walls and doors framed in white, is the far left of three apartments in the building. We have two bedrooms, a kitchen/ sitting room, and a tiny walled garden. We park on Lea Avenue beside a carpet of brilliant green vines over-flowing a high stone wall. Poolbeg Power Station at Ringsend—the red and white twin towers that define Dublin—marks the entrance to the Liffey, just beyond the strand.

Sunday, May 6, 2007

4:30 p.m. Picnicked on Killiney Beach in a sprinkle of rain. The slate-colored water of the bay shattered on the shoreline in wide white arcs. Shredded clouds raced overhead, the Wicklows pale-grey to the south.

I love this time of year in Dublin, with lilacs in creamy white or purple, pale pinkish flower-spikes on the chestnuts trees, yellow laburnum and wild irises tucked into the corners of intersections.

Monday, May 7, 2007

1:00 a.m. We rode the Dart from Sandymount to the Tara Station last night and crossed the O'Connell Street Bridge to reach the Winding Stair Restaurant. On the second floor, looking down on the gentle arc of the Ha'penny Bridge, the room's thirty square feet of fearsome noise, held eight to ten tables, a bar at one end slung with an array of wine glasses. My starter, a chicken liver pate with sweet tomato and fruit chutney on toasted French bread, was very tasty. Not so much the Portobello mushroom/spinach main.

12:30 p.m. Off to the Wicklows on a quintessentially Irish day, low black-bottomed clouds in a soft blue sky. Into hills of deep forest green, with flowering gorse and glistening trees. The sea stretches flat and blue to our left as the countryside turns ever more pastoral, dotted with cattle and sheep.

5:00 p.m. Back at the flat. On our way to Brittas Bay Beach, we stopped on the grounds of Blainroe Golf Club. Bushes of yellow gorse and pale-blue butterfly weed framed the sea. Then on to Brittas, empty but for one distant surf fisherman, a young lad flying a lime green kite, a hand-holding couple or two, and a family at work on a sand castle. A gorgeous field of indigo blue-bells spread out in a low sloping meadow, trees in a roiling wind, gleaming with sunlight.

I loved being on Brittas. We made our way to the water on a path that sliced through grass-anchored sand-dunes. At Killiney I'd collected smooth, oval stones in a kaleidoscope of color, along with one heart-shaped "holey" stone. Brittas offered up lustrous shells and bits of shells, sleek and pearly and pale gold.

We drove south to Arklow afterwards, a small town seething with cars and pedestrians, though only one or two shops appeared to be open. We did our best to get out of town. In a thoroughly Irish way, not one directional sign could be found, but we eventually made our way to Avoca Valley.

10:45 p.m. Sevenish, we dropped in for an agreeable visit with

Ken and Elizabeth. Their neighbor Anna, whose son goes to school with Bono's daughters, joined us before we headed off to La Strada for supper.

Tuesday, May 8, 2007

Outside HQ on a bright and sunny day, the canal blackened with come and go clouds. Inside Kilsaram Concrete's padlocked gate, heaps of rusting iron bars and barriers lie scattered. Few trucks arrive or depart, the company sign swings lop-sided on the wall, and the cement bench has been hauled away.

We alternate fifteen or twenty minutes of 'guard-duty' apiece. Sammy made his way to the Spar a short time ago, returning with a carrier bag, and Dallas [Dallas Schoo, Edge's guitar tech] left and came back with two coffees.

What else? Who else? Who knows? Who cares?

The docklands change almost daily, with ever more upscale apartments and office complexes in glass and metal. Low and battered, dusty and disheveled, the studio survives, a humble reminder of Dublin's past. Echos of long-gone Windmill Lane graffiti embellish Kilsaram walls, a stenciled Joshua tree on the side-walk.

5:00 p.m. Tea at the Fitzpatrick, looking out on a blossoming chestnut tree.

Our studio wait met with great good fortune. A silver Mercedes pulled into the garage about two o'clock and Adam stepped out, fit and trim, in a skull-and-crossbones t-shirt and a resplendent shock of white hair. Where was I from again? he asked.

"Canada," I told him, "But I live in Tucson."

"Oh, yes, right," he said. That he'd remembered is doubtful, but it was gracious of him to say.

A second car arrived, and within minutes, Bono lounged in the studio doorway. "Hello," he said quietly and we all drifted over.

Debbi suggested a cell-phone video, but he declined, and went on at some length about how the internet had "ruined things that way." Hardly possible any longer to spend time with "people you enjoy". How difficult it had become to have any "intimate moments." Here he leaned forward. "And we've had many," he added.

What had we been doing? he asked. We were in town for a week, Debbi answered, and I said we'd been out to the Wicklows. "We were walking on Brittas Beach."

"That's one of my favorite places," he said. What else were we doing?

Now we'd made specific plans and many. And yet we couldn't come up with a single one.

"You're just making this up as you go along, aren't you?" Bono said.

"Should we tell him?" Debbi asked.

"Tell me what?"

"Yes, go on then," Sue advised, and Debbi explained that we'd booked ourselves into the Penthouse at the Clarence Hotel on Thursday night.

"You dirty girls." He laughed. "You dirty, dirty girls." (We're trusting that this was a judgement on the poshness and expense of the place.) We'd have "a wonderful time," he assured us.

Was it a special occasion? It was.

"What special occasion?" A birthday.

"Whose birthday?" Dianne's. (My mid-June birthday was the first thing that popped into Sue's head.)

What was *he* doing for *his* birthday, Debbi asked. Well, he'd forgotten all about it. He usually stayed in the penthouse. "We beat you to it," Debbi said, and suggested he stop by for a drink.

"That would be nice." (Yeah, right!)

We thanked him for being so generous with his time, and as he stepped back into the studio he turned and waved. "Happy Birthday, Dianne," he said. And he was gone.

As we prepared to head home, a fellow in a City of Dublin truck jumped out to check the drains. He'd been working down the road one day, he told us, when a car pulled over and someone said "hi." Bono climbed out to shake his hand. That's just the sort of man he is.

11:00 p.m. Seven-thirty, we called a taxi to the Abbey Theatre for the Billy Roche play *The Cavalcaders*. A bit disjointed and the ending fell flat, but a good production nonetheless.

Wednesday, May 9, 2007

4:00 p.m. Sipping tea in Jury's Inn Customs House, on a dull grey day. We swung by the studio earlier, in any icy wind, with a bottle of wine for Bono's birthday. Adam arrived and chatted briefly, but Larry and Edge wisely got out of the cold. We gave our Cabernet Sauvignon to Sammy, who said he'd pass it on.

9:00 p.m. In slashing down rain and a wind that upended our umbrellas, we walked over to Fan's Chinese in Temple Bar for spring rolls, roast duck, sweet and sour chicken, and beef chow mien. Irish weather all around today, gusty winds, and torrents of rain.

Thursday, May 10, 2007

6:30 p.m. Sitting on the first floor balcony of the Clarence Hotel penthouse, looking down on the River Liffey and the Ha'Penny Bridge. The domed and turreted city rushes and hums below, and distant hills darken with the setting sun. Construction cranes loom everywhere. We've roused a wave or two from pedestrians, celebrities that (they think) we are.

Our chauffeur, Keith, fetched us from Seaview in a white stretch limo with black leather upholstery and a wet bar along the right-hand side. He popped a bottle of Belnor Sparkling Perry Medium and poured us each a glass. Two TV screens above the bar played Debbi's *U2 Go Home* [the band's Slane Castle concert from the *Elevation Tour*]. Keith's only contribution in the way of music would have been a Nora Jones CD, which he played for weddings, "to calm everyone down."

For an hour then, we stalked the streets of Dublin. Most people ignored us completely. Some tried not to look but did. And a few were actively curious. We cruised along the River Liffey, passed the O'Connell Street Bridge, and on our arrival at the Clarence, the staff remarked that we had certainly "come in style." Was it a special occasion? It was.

Following a short tour of the hotel, we were escorted, in a private key-operated elevator, to the penthouse, suite 505. We passed through a set of pinewood double-doors and came in at the base of a staircase that curved up to a second floor.

The apartment's green suede sitting area, to the right of the entrance, had a couch and comfy chairs pockmarked with cigarette burns. An ice bucket with champagne and four wine glasses would be deposited on the long table here while we sipped Cosmopolitans upstairs.

Outside the south wall, potted plants lined a narrow balcony, off which a bathroom adjoined a master bedroom. A balconied dining room, a tiny blue kitchen with wet bar and non-functioning electric stove, and two additional bathrooms—the larger one adjacent a twin bedroom—rounded off the first floor.

An off-white spiral staircase lead to the large second floor 'party' room, the west end fitted with champagne-colored carpeting, a large screen TV, and an enormous L-shaped beige sofa. The CDs in the shelf below the TV included *When Will the Loganberries Be Ripe*, *The Big Band Selection*, and *CD to be Played in the Mornings Only*.

At the opposite (east) end of the upper room stood a black grand piano, together with a second bar and a small squared outside deck with jacuzzi. Perhaps Bono would stop by later to "tickle our ivories," Debbi said.

Not a trash bin or a clock in sight, upstairs or down.

Friday, May 11, 2007

12:30 a.m. Jacob, of the hotel's overnight staff, has arrived to coax the DVD player into giving us *Rattle and Hum*.

At eight o'clock this evening, we swept into the Tea Room downstairs in all our finery—"You're looking beautiful tonight ladies"—and were seated at a window table below the upper deck. At once, a waiter handed Debbi a note that had been propped up unnoticed in the center of the table. She would say, by way of a joke, I thought, that Bono had left a birthday note.

But he had! (Or at least the staff had been instructed to.)

'Happy Birthday, Love Bono', typed on a sheet of Clarence Hotel stationary. And then along came a bottle of champagne from The Man himself.

Long moments passed, as we all stared off into space.

The meal was exceptional, as usual—fillet with mushrooms and pea pods and small roasted potatoes, foie gras for my starter, and orange crème brulee for dessert. When we check out later today, we'll drop a thankyou note at reception.

5:30 a.m. The potted bay-laurel bush beside me here on the balcony exudes a subtle fragrance. I've already tucked a leaf into my journal. A pale orange light in the east promises imminent sunrise. Thick purple clouds stretch along the horizon, and rose tinges the southeastern sky where a half-moon still hangs. The city lightens by degrees, one Liffey bridge illuminated in orange and green.

At one point during the night, we exchanged views on birthdays. Thus far, the best time of my life is always the one I'm in. But deep inside I hover somewhere around thirty-five. I can identify with Dame Judi Dench. Asked how she felt about seeing herself as frumpy Queen Victoria in *Her Majesty, Mrs. Brown*, she said that she was unfamiliar with that woman. She thinks of herself as "a tall, willowy blonde of indeterminate years."

I also aspire to the life philosophy of one of Dan's patients. At eighty-seven, she was adamant about not going into a nursing home. They were only "full of old people."

6:00 a.m. Russet clouds puddled with gold now.

10:30 a.m. On the deck once again, after a tea and toast breakfast downstairs in the Tea Room. What a difference a day makes! Last night, one of my rings snapped and, almost before it could hit the floor, a waiter snatched up the pieces. Workers cast furtive glances our way, curious as to how we so obviously older women related to Bono.

Breakfast, rather neglectfully served, was a whole other crop of hay. Entertaining to be a VIP for a short time, but not any way I'd choose to live life in the long-term.

7:00 p.m. Back in the real world again. We returned to Sandymount by taxi just after noon, gob-smacked at check-out to find that our drinks last night had been paid for by Bono! Complimentary on Bono's instructions, we assume. Had we known, we'd have managed a couple more bottles of Domaine de la Janasse 2005, Châteauneuf du Pape.

Saturday, May 12, 2007

Nine-thirty in the morning. We dined at Bewley's yesterday, after handing off a thank you note for Bono at HQ. Dallas answered the buzzer and Debbi asked if we might leave Bono a message.

"Who are you?" Dallas asked.

"We're the girls who were in the penthouse last night," Debbi said, and Dallas promised to pass our note along.

When Debbi thanked him by name, he added gallantly, "I like the tint in your hair."

Monday, May 14, 2007

Here we are, Dan and I, at the cabin [Chiricahua Mountains, Southern Arizona]. I flew to Tucson last Saturday night, the end of a twenty-four hour trip. Eight hours of sleep Friday night, after thirty plus awake in the penthouse. A surreal and privileged way to celebrate not only my birthday, but twenty years a U2 fan, my first concert being the opener of *The Joshua Tree Tour* in April of 1987.

In Chicago, a fellow traveler from Dublin asked her friends, "So what was your best part then, guys?"

Well—she didn't ask me.

Wednesday, May 30, 2007

Finished *U2 by U2* [HarperCollins, 2006]. Chuffed to see an alternate to Adam's studio photo collage at the back of the book. *A Grand Madness* is prominent again—at least to me—on the studio shelves.

Monday, November 26, 2007

Sue and Debbi had an opportunity to thank Bono in person for his thoughtfulness and generosity at the Clarence Hotel in May.

"Did you stay up late?" he asked. We'd stayed up all night. "Yes!" he said.

They'd booked themselves into the Clarence once again, they told him, though not in the penthouse. "I should think not," Bono said. "What do you think you are, bleedin' rock stars?"

Monday, January 28, 2008

Dan and I checked out *U23D* at the Arizona Mills Mall Saturday. I loved it! If only you could get as participatory in a theatre as you can in a concert. Hard to toss love back to the stage during Pride, or fist-pump for Beautiful Day.

That will just have to wait for the next tour.

3.
The 360 Tour

"Live is where we live."
—Bono

Thursday, June 12, 2008

U2 are a week out from wrapping up their new album, as per Edge, a tour to open in Las Vegas in March of next year. Brian Eno, one of several producers, numbers one of the tracks among the best he's ever done with the band.

Sunday, September 21, 2008

1:30 a.m. In our Dublin flat on St. Margaret's—The Pines ("The Poines," to our taxi driver). Back from a celebration of Sue's retirement at the Clarence Hotel's Tea Room. The bar manager came through to let us know our Cosmos were waiting in the study. He'd mixed them himself.

The meal—mousse bouché, tuna starter, and "Female Duck" with green beans, roasted potatoes, and carrots—was first-rate. Debbi had arranged a custom-made chocolate cake for the occasion and had only to catch a waiter's eye, nod, and the cake arrived. The pastry chef had "made it personally."

A hefty fellow stationed himself left of the lobby's front door as we left. To our right, a second hulk in a black suit, arms across his chest, blocked the entrance to a darkened Study.

"It's Edge," Debbi whispered as we walked past.

Tuesday, September 23, 2008

Bono, speaking at the UN in New York tomorrow, returns to Ireland Thursday. He'll then meet with McCain and Palin [John McCain, US senator from Arizona, and Sarah Palin, the Governor of

Alaska, made up the Republican ticket in the 2008 US presidential election]. What a tremendous step forward for the country to have Barack Obama, such an eminently qualified person, heading the Democratic ticket.

Friday, September 26, 2008

The band has remained in Ireland because the Irish are "our people." They function more easily here, which is no doubt true. But Ireland's tax laws recently changed and they spirited their business side off to Holland, where artists pay no taxes.

An Irish woman passed us outside HQ yesterday. "Are you waiting for U2?" she asked. "That Bono's the pits."

Sarah Palin declined to meet with Bono. Gave him "a quick phone call." He was not impressed.

Home to Tucson tomorrow.

Thursday, November 6, 2008

Barack Obama has won the presidency! Such a positive hopefulness for the country.

Friday, February 5, 2009

I've finally seen the video for U2's new single, Get on Your Boots, from their upcoming album, *No Line on the Horizon*. Colorful, creative, and energetic, it extols women. Men continue to "fuck things up," Edge says. Why not give women a chance.

Amen!

Sunday, February 7, 2009

U2's tour revs up in Europe, ending my five-year streak of tour openers.

Tuesday, February 9, 2009

In a recent *Q Magazine* interview, Larry claims the band intends to work up left-over material from their new album. Significantly, in ten years, he says, he'll be able to "do all the things (he's) missing now." Hopefully that leaves at least two more tours out there.

Monday, March 2, 2009

U2's new album 'officially leaked' in Australia, so *U2.com* streamed it.

Friday, March 6, 2009

In San Francisco for a meeting. We idled on the runway in Phoenix for over an hour. Something about a loose rivet. I could have jogged over to Ace Hardware faster than maintenance delivered one.

I've just had a run-through of the new U2 album, *No Line on the Horizon*, which I picked up at a local HMV. I literally couldn't face the music for some time. What if I didn't like it? How far would I go to convince myself that I did? Or would it be so outstanding that the hype would overwhelm?

Now that I've had a listen, it's a winning compilation, though Bono's claim of learning to write in the third person seems exaggerated, with the exception of White as Snow and Cedars of Lebanon, which still reflect his mindset. The "traffic cop" of the title track is very much Bono's story. He's wrestled with spiritual angst, with love and death, faith and doubt, all of his life.

For the most part, the album—Bono's very own *Book of Psalms*—probes song-writing and performance as his calling. With hymns of praise and singing the blues, *No Line on the Horizon* could have just as easily been titled *Make a Joyful Noise*. It's teeming with Biblical references: "c'mon ye people," "cease to speak that I may speak," "magnify the magnificent." Reconciling a hunger for an unfettered faith with the realities of the world has been one of Bono's life-long struggles, at the heart of many a U2 album. That's how he lives, making *No Line on the Horizon* another spiritual journey.

Here's the blow by blow.

NO LINE ON THE HORIZON – With Larry's driving drums and some crack harmonies, this number has great potential. In Bono's *Book of Psalms*, this would be the ideal, much as Where the Streets Have No Name is the ideal of *The Joshua Tree*. A place where there are no divisions or boundaries, where we're all spiraling upward to the light or God or the Universe. Everything is One and time does not exit. ("Time is irrelevant; not linear.")

In this scenario, Ali might be the girl who has everything sussed out. She doesn't ask questions. Bono strives to be there, but it's just not in him. He's too much a moving part of the physical world, aware of his own physical presence, scheming and plotting and hatching plans, straining to be the traffic cop. He craves a *reason* for being, a worldly purpose. For him, it's singing.

MAGNIFICENT – Magnificent is simply magnificent! The opening pulse-like beat and the powerful musical build-up remind me of Miracle Drug. As with so many other U2 songs, I Still Haven't Found What I'm Looking For, for example, spiritual uncertainty is at the core of this tune. Magnificent expresses Bono's reason for being, his calling. Singing justifies and explains his earthly existence.

"I was born to be with you in this time and place. After that and ever after, I haven't had a clue."

MOMENT OF SURRENDER – Moment of Surrender, soulful and bluesy, in spirit more than in sound, coalesces around Adam's solid bass line. I like the ethereal opening and Edge's lyrical guitar. The "oh oh"s give the song something of a gospel feel. Live, with swaying arms and fired up cell-phones, this one will be a winner, though the tune itself has the hint of a dirge about it.

Bono has tied himself in knots trying to figure things out. Here, he bows to the notion that his calling is to sing and his gifts are his songs. When you've looked everywhere for the answer, sometimes it's better to surrender. He may never know why he was 'chosen' for this life role. Maybe it's best to just accept that singing is what he does and The Singer is who he is.

UNKNOWN CALLER – Musically, this song sounds very Eno-esque—the birdsong, Edge's keyboard, an ambience similar to Three Sunrises or Bass Trap. The ending swells to a joyful noise that ends up just a bit too churchy for my taste. Unknown caller is the place/being/power from which Bono's call to sing comes. The Biblical "Hear me; cease to speak that I may speak," suggests that he stop thinking about it so much and accept this as his life's purpose.

I'LL GO CRAZY IF I DON'T GO CRAZY TONIGHT – I love everything about this song—Edge's guitar line, the rousing chorus, Bono's lyrics. A song made for a sing-along, both in spirit and in substance. "Slowly" reminds me of the "slow down my beating heart" of In a Little While from *All That You Can't Leave Behind*. The same sense of trying to reach a balance in life.

Like most of us, Bono lives so fully on the present physical plain that he can't stay in any 'peaceful life' for too long. Philosophically, you can know the deeper value of a spiritual life, but you still need balance. Be a little wild and frivolous now and again, get your feet wet and your hands dirty.

GET ON YOUR BOOTS – Boots represents some of that craziness. You can't focus on serious issues—"wars between nations"—all of the time. This song is exactly where it should be in the track sequence. With its driving beat, it would make a fabulous opener, as Vertigo and Elevation did. Bono's Roy Orbison Pretty Woman growl echoes in Edge's guitar.

STAND UP COMEDY – A rocked-out Stand Up Comedy, with its industrial buzz, reflects the negative side of surrender, the down-side of allowing something or someone else to direct your life. People who do that often end up so certain of their own spiritual vision, so self-righteous and judgmental, that they're constantly trying to "help God across the road like a little old lady." Bono makes this personal with "Napoleon is in high-heeled shoes," and "Josephine be careful of small men with big ideas."

FEZ/BEING BORN – Eno-esque again, with an ethereal keyboard and some scratchy vinyl, Fez/Being Born sounds like journal jottings, a vignette of impressions in the vein of New York, Miami, or October. Fez paints a picture of the physical place in which this album was recorded, and of Bono's arrival there. It's a snapshot that bring us back to the real world, a world in which people sing the blues much more often than they rejoice.

The reality of a Moroccan market allows the writer to be born again into the reality of our violent world, expressed with marching drums and White as Snow. An echo of the escapism of Boots comes with its haunting "Let me in the sound" refrain.

WHITE AS SNOW – With yet another otherworldly Eno-esque intro, White as Snow addresses the wars between nations that Bono didn't want to talk about in Get On Your Boots. A variation on the hymn Oh Come, Oh Come Emmanuel, White as Snow is basically a heart-wrenching Middle Eastern folk-song about someone who's lost their faith. The only thing this search for God—Emmanuel, the lamb, some hint of Divinity—has turned up is poppies in barren ground and the violence of a war supported by drug revenue. Muslims probably don't often see the gentleness and purity of the Christian lamb in what has so frequently been done to them.

BREATHE – Larry has some fantastic drumming in Breathe, Bono's last gasp at accepting a divine calling to sing. "The songs are in our eyes, gonna wear them like a crown. Walk out into the sunburst streets. Sing your heart out. Sing my heart out."

In a lot of cultures breathing and singing are the same. In my earlier U2 memoir, *A Grand Madness, Ten Years on the Road with U2*, I quoted from Clarissa Pinkola Estes book *Women Who Run with the Wolves* [Balantine Books, New York, 1992] where she writes that "To sing means to use the soul voice . . . to say on the breath the truth of one's power and one's need . . . to breathe soul over the thing that is ailing and in need of restoration." This song is a reminder to take a deep breath and affirm that your (Bono's) calling is to sing.

CEDARS OF LEBANON – This second third-person song after White as Snow, allows Bono one more opportunity to see the flip side of 'joyfulness' and question his faith. Ambient, ethereal, and Eno-esque, like Fez/Being Born, Cedars of Lebanon has the same scratchiness of an old LP and the same marching drums that are the undercurrent to so much of the world. You may not want to talk about wars between nations but you can't ignore them.

Like the best of U2, Cedars of Lebanon poses a question.

"Where are You in the Cedars of Lebanon?" Where is God in our violent world? Where is Divinity in the morass that is the Middle East? Returning the call to home connects back to the Unknown Caller. Will anyone ever answer?

The concept of many paths up the mountain is a popular image that symbolizes the variety of spiritual quests in our world. "It's not a hill, it's a mountain," Bono writes in Crazy. "As you start out the climb, do you believe me or are you doubting? We're gonna make it all the way to the light."

U2's next album may well be titled *Songs from the Ascent,* Bono has suggested, a continuation of the struggle to reach that place in life where there's *No Line on the Horizon.*

Monday, March 9, 2009

The *360 Tour* opens in Barcelona June 30. I just can't manage that. British shows, however, are do-able. London, Glasgow, Sheffield, and Cardiff, all in mid-August. And I may take in Dublin. The U.S. leg opens in Chicago on September 12.

Just stepped out for Guinness soup and a fish and chip lunch at Johnny Foley's on O'Farrell Street [San Francisco]. "Honest Food, Stiff Drinks, No Blarney." Irish portraits adorned the walls, Oscar Wilde, Richard Harris, and Michael Collins in our section. By the main entrance, hung a beautifully executed oil painting of Bono.

Friday, March 27, 2009

My U2 *360 Tour* is taking shape. Sue has first Dublin tickets and I'll pick up first London at the Wembley box office on the day. We lost out on the second Dublin show, but we may try for the third. Sharon came through with second Wembley. We also have Glasgow. And Sharon, Jane, Youssef, and I will take in Sheffield.

Meanwhile, I've tickets for both Chicago shows and will try for Phoenix when they're released.

Tuesday, June 30, 2009

The U2 *360 Tour* opened in Barcelona today.

Thursday, July 23, 2009

8:05 p.m. Overcast, in the mid-sixties. I'm at Bewley's Ballsbridge in Dublin. Hard to part with Dan at Toronto International this morning, as he heads back to Tucson.

My Newark, New Jersey flight departed at six p.m. and we reached Dublin in less than six hours, landing fifteen minutes early. With only three seats to a side, the plane was packed to the gills, seething with small children. I gave up my seat to an Hispanic family—the dad in a *Vertigo 06* t-shirt—so they could travel together. The L.A. couple beside me then was also headed to the Dublin shows.

Not a peek out the window the entire flight, but for a stretch of green fields as we banked for landing. The airport shuttle, teaming with U2 fans, off-loaded a couple of us at Bewley's, and though check-in was two in the afternoon, the staff, bless them, found me a room as soon as I arrived at eleven o'clock this morning. I've just had fresh grilled Irish salmon for lunch downstairs.

Saturday, July 25, 2009

The others came in yesterday and we set off for our flat at 61 Landsdowne Village, right behind Landsdowne Stadium. Unfortunately, U2 *360* shows are at Croke Park this time around. A transport bus from Bewley's, due at six p.m., breezed in a half-hour late, and we rambled to Croke Park through congested Dublin streets.

Here's the set-list for last night's first Dublin show: Breathe; No Line on the Horizon; Get on Your Boots; Magnificent; Beautiful Day/Blackbird/Auld Triangle; Elevation; Desire; Stuck in a Moment; One; End of the World; Unforgettable Fire; City of Blinding Lights; Vertigo; I'll Go Crazy Remix; Sunday Bloody Sunday; Pride; MLK; Walk On/You'll Never Walk Alone; Streets; Bad//Ultraviolet; With or Without You; Moment of Surrender.

A massive three-legged presence christened "The Crab" enclosed the main stage. Rather like a space ship or a giant spider, this monstrosity held video screens and much of the lighting. A separate walkway, with two movable metal bridges, nearly surrounded the main stage, providing for a bona fide 360° experience.

Larry's exemplary Breathe drums opened the show, followed by a superb Crazy, which featured band members' pulsating heads on-screen, and a wild sound to which they strutted down the walkway, Larry pounding on a bongo. Sunday Bloody Sunday, surprisingly vibrant, with veiled Muslim women and scrolling Arabic, had Rock the Casbah tacked on the end.

At one point, Bono pulled up an Irish flag from the pitch, and draped it on a camera. Volunteers from One and Amnesty, rather like a Greek chorus, strolled out for Walk On, holding masks of Aung San Suu Kyi. Desmond Tutu flashed up on-screen afterwards to extoll the goodness of the Irish people and all they'd done for human rights. The high-point, of course, came with Bad, at the end of a frenetic and communal red-lit Streets.

With ticking clocks and much more, the passage of time formed an obvious theme of the staging. A snatch of Ronnie Drew's Royal Canal came as a welcome surprise. Edge would sashay over a bridge to the outer walkway and then sashay back. Sometimes he would hesitate, and then, with an apparent 'what the hell, I'm going over again,' over he came. A lot of talk about Ireland and the Irish infused this show, touching on all the visitors in town. A Dublin show meant the very best from U2.

The first encore opened with Ultraviolet, the upper part of the claw ablaze, while below Bono all but disappeared, his suit of lights morphed into red-speared Freddy Kruger fingernails. A giant radio microphone, dropped down from the rafters, became the magnetic focal point of both Ultraviolet and With or Without You, a mesmerized Bono, the celebrity, stalking after an addiction.

By three this morning, we were back at our flat. Pizza and garlic bread, and to bed by five a.m.

Monday, July 27, 2009

Four o'clock in the morning. After Chinese last night, we popped in to the Octagon Bar at the Clarence Hotel. They spun some of the oddest music. Weird, monotonous, thudding dance beats, one comprised completely of choral inserts. Another, underscored by a deep drone, resolved to a dust buster in use behind the bar.

Debbi set off to the airport this afternoon, after an excellent carvery lunch at Dun Laoghaire's Royal Marina Hotel.

Tuesday, July 28, 2009

After making our way along the River Dodder last evening, we caught the Bewley bus—a hot, stuffy, sweaty experience—for our second Dublin show. We cooled off on a park bench before heading into the venue.

Here's the set-list: Breathe; No Line on the Horizon; Boots; Magnificent; Beautiful Day/My Hometown; New Year's Day; Still Haven't Found What I'm Looking For; Stay; Unknown Caller; Unforgettable Fire; Blinding Lights; Vertigo; Crazy Remix; Sunday Bloody Sunday; Pride; MLK; Walk On/Never Walk Alone; Streets; One; Bad//Ultraviolet; With or Without You; Surrender

Though Friday's show unfolded with more emotion and intimacy, I enjoyed this one ever so much more, being less jet-lagged. We had superior seats Friday night as well, fifteen rows back on Edge's side. Last night found us half-way up the stands just right of the main stage. Crazy, Vertigo, and Boots, were high-points, and bars of silver and red flashed on-screen before Blinding Lights, mimicking the streamers of the *Vertigo Tour*. We also relished a second amazing performance of Bad.

"Hands up" if you're not Irish Bono commanded, and a sizable percentage of the stadium responded. Ireland was "rising up" out of darkness into the light, he said. Someone tossed up a red and white Polish flag which Bono slung on a piece of sound equipment, and With or Without You was dedicated to Adam's parents, Jo and Brian Clayton.

The band's intent with this monstrous staging was to establish the audience as a fifth member of the band, Bono explained. (Perhaps, we all thought, inviting a fan to the stage would have accomplished that far better.)

Last night's encore improved over Friday's, with the mirror ball rotating *beneath* the lowered screens instead of at the top of the claw's center spike. This allowed bits of light to swirl around the stadium, while a greyish stage minimized the Freddy Krueger vibe.

We suffered a spattering of high-tier stadium annoyances last night as well. Rafts of people who *never* stand up. Beer drinkers coming and going ad nauseum. In and out. In and out. In and out. The last time one of them squeezed past me, I had to steel myself to keep from shoving him down the bleachers.

11:30 p.m. In from supper at the Clarence Hotel. Mushroom-and-seafood-tart starter, with chicken. Blissfully, we're into the countryside tomorrow.

Wednesday, July 29, 2009

We're sitting in Devil's Glen, a woodsy spot some twenty-five miles south of the city. A cool breeze rustles in high trees flanked with ivy. We've just picnicked in a grove of silver birch. The glen accommodates a collection of sculptures, the one next to us a blasé pillar topped with spikes. But in the woods just over the hill is an amazing piece called *Chrysalis,* carved in Irish bog oak.

11:30 p.m. In from a visit with Ken and Elizabeth. Rain slashed down as we walked in the door. Lots of laughs, great conversation, and Elizabeth's usual scrumptious meal.

Thursday, July 30, 2009

Here we are on Killiney Beach. The silver-blue bay is heaving, and a scattering of fishermen, strollers, and beach combers dot the strand. I've a collection of water-smooth stones in all hues, one or two 'holey' stones, and three black 'line on the horizon' pebbles, each with a single white stripe of quartz in gray basalt.

11:00 p.m. In from the Town Bar and Grill, my current favorite Dublin restaurant—soft lighting, geometric black-and-white art pieces on the wall, and consistently superior food. My rack of lamb—two chops and a bit of shoulder served with carrots, squash, and roast potatoes—followed a monkfish cheek starter served on a bed of risotto, with shrimp and saffron. A whiff of camembert from my dessert cheese and crackers plate arrived long before the dish. "Wafting over like old socks," Sue said.

The restaurant called a taxi for us about ten o'clock. As we waited, nearly forty others cruised by. Sixteen-thousand cabbies ply Dublin's streets these days, they say, more than any other city in the world, outnumbering private cars three to one.

Friday, July 31, 2009

Sue asked this morning, in her pleasing Cumbrian accent, "Have you seen Anayan?" Well, I thought she meant some pastoral little Irish village out in the wilds of Donegal, or such. She was actually after a clothes iron.

The glossy, glassy dockland buildings so prevalent on my last Dublin visit stand empty now, bankrupt developers unable to finish them up. The Irish government bought up those loans, just as the U.S. government took on the toxic mortgage assets of American banks. Such is the fall of the *Celtic Tiger* since those heady days of the *Vertigo Tour*.

360 concerts have altered in a sense, too. The spectacle's the thing. But then what else can a band of U2's magnitude and fame do? A dozen arena shows per tour-stop would be unthinkable.

Saturday, August 1, 2009

I'm at Sue's new digs on the edge of Carlisle for the next few days. Our forty minute flight from Dublin arrived in Manchester yesterday on an overcast, dribbling day. As we drove north, the clouds broke, the bare-topped Pennines rolling off to one side, the misty heights of the Lake District to the other. A dazzling landscape. Green pastures glowed in intermittent sunlight, tea-colored becks emptied the moorlands into wide brown rivers and on to the sea. Everywhere, ancient stone walls mounted through bracken and heather.

We ate fish and chips in a cozy pub called Table Table.

Sunday, August 2, 2009

3:00 p.m. We're off to fetch Max and Pepsi at Ravenside Lodge kennel/cattery in the village of Wreay. We rambled a bit on Warnell

Fell, where heather, brown grasses, and buttercups swirled in a hefty wind, newly sheared sheep planted about on high fells that look down on the Cumbrian countryside.

Noontime, we stopped at Caldbeck village and sauntered along the creek, passing white-stone cottages convulsed in summer gardens. St. Kentigern's Parish lies along the waterway, and below the church stands the holy well of St. Mungo. Even today, wedding couples pause at St. Mungo's for a blessing after their chapel ceremonies.

The earliest church here dates near to CE [Common Era] 600. Mungo, meaning "dear one," was St. Kentigern's nickname. The well floods from a small spring bubbling in from the creek bank. Naturally, I added to the coins resting in the silty bottom, and then took a quick turn around the churchyard where one gnarly old stone read poetically, "Until the day break and the shadows flee away."

In the company of bicyclists, hill walkers, and a young couple reading tea leaves, we snacked on scones and tea at the Watermill Café, where a slice of the sepia burn gurgled over an old wooden water-wheel. A further stroll brought us to the village pond, where we fed the ducks

11:00 p.m. When we came back from Caldbeck about three this afternoon, Sue whipped up an awesome dinner of green beans from her garden, peas, boiled potatoes, and wild salmon fresh from the River Eden.

I spoke with Sharon briefly and she asked about biking into town [York] next week.

Biking?! Into town?! Moi?!

Monday, August 3, 2009

5:30 p.m. Off for the Lake District at eleven o'clock this morning, the drive stunning, but for the southern edge of Whitehaven. We followed the coastline westward, distant mountains in a misty haze.

Our objective—Wastwater—the farthest and the most remote of the lakes—has been designated one of the most picturesque views in England, a wild beauty with rounded and layered hills climbing up from crystal water. Pale pink stones lie just beneath the surface and scree slopes in red, beige, grey, and black drop down from great heights to the water's edge, bracken bogs and craggy outcrops lining the near shore. A narrow path, a mere scratch on the scree, circles the entire lake, moving through a wild and primal serenity.

We returned to Carlisle by a quicker but less scenic route, and stopped for supper at the Lowther Arms Country Inn in Cumwhinton. The old country pub's entrance bloomed with myriad potted plants, and depictions of the North Country covered the deep-green walls.

Tuesday, August 4, 2009

6:00 p.m. Off to Scotland this morning, on an overcast, gray day, headed for Samye-Ling Monastery. Almost as we crossed the border, Scottish mist dipped down out of the Cheviot Hills. We followed the River Esk into Eskdale. The wide green valley from which it flows is the wettest spot in the UK, and often the coldest. At its broadest, the Esk stretches five or six-hundred feet, divided into two rapid-laden channels.

We carried on through Langholm, down skinny black roads, to the village of Bentpath, where 'Rumble Strips' [speed bumps] created washboard patches in the roadway. (*The Rumblestrips of Bentpath*— another fab short story title.) All about us the countryside glowed with an expansive Scottishness—whale-backed treeless hills, heavy rain clouds, and lonely farmsteads, their grey-stone houses crouched down against the wind.

Round about Bilholm Forest, fields of wild fuchsia-colored fireweed reached into the misted hills. The upper reaches of the Esk River, a mere fifteen feet or so across now, paralleled the road. The profusion of moldering grey walls at Eskdalemuir, the village nearest the monastery, perfectly matched their surroundings, just as Caldbeck's cottages had matched theirs.

In the rain, the Samye-Ling Monastery, the first and largest Tibetan monastery in Europe, struck me as a tad disheveled. Tibetan prayer flags flapped everywhere. Brass Buddha statues, Oriental gateways, and a stupa completed the grounds.

We joined a worship service in the temple, admiring an incredible collection of Buddhas, geometric patterned walls in a profusion of color, depictions of scenes from Buddha's life, drums and bells, symbols and horns. The central figure, a robed Buddha with two standing Buddhas below, had the misfortune to have a face identical to the puppet in the movie *Magic*.

Workers outside contributed hammered blows on occasion, a percussion that melted right into the drumming, chanting, clapping, bell ringing, and cymbals, as though part of the liturgy, and recitations droned on like readings from the Koran or the 'rocking' monotone of Jewish worshippers at the Wailing Wall. One of the three monks in charge, flipped through a large rolodex on a stand in front of him, scanning his recipe file for a quick and easy tea.

A browse in the gift shop and a pot of mint tea in the café, and we set off for home, the heavy rain through Eskdale easing as we slipped out of Scotland.

Wednesday, August 5, 2009

7:00 p.m. At ten this morning we headed for the spa at Oxley's at Underscar, situated in a grey-stone hotel by the village of Underscar near Applethwaite, out of Keswick. Gracing the slopes of Skiddaw Mountain, the central tower has an Italianesque facade, tall and squared, with a turreted top. Our treatment consisted of a stint in the pool, lunch, a massage, and a facial.

From the hotel, the view reflected a gentler version of the one from the terrace of the Banff Hotel in Alberta, a placid lake in place of Banff's glacial river. Beyond a field of grazing cattle and a fringe of forest, Derwentwater lay in the valley below, the pale-blue humps of Lakeland mountains behind. The green-velvet lawns of the hotel, designated red-squirrel habitat, had protected rodent homes planted in hedges and garden plots. Red squirrels are declining, threatened everywhere by greys and blacks moving into their territories.

We turned back to Carlisle on a back road Sue had not traveled before. High in a broad grassy valley, with an occasional stone farm in the lower reaches, up and up we drove, topping out on Caldbeck

Common, wild with buff grasses and rocky outcrops. Sheared black sheep and miniature fell ponies roamed freely over the moors here, the ponies, stocky little things, munching on brown grass. They snuffled in our pockets for treats, one scarfing up a tissue that whipped out of the car when I went in after my journal.

The ponies have plenty of forage, but there are track-way signs everywhere, indicating trails that veer off into the valley or rise further into the highlands. Several parked cars suggested their occupants had trekked up one path or another, most of which were under a mile. Accustomed to handouts from hill walkers, ponies moseyed in from the moorland, a couple picking their way through broken walls. When we returned to the car, a pony to each side pressed a nose up against the windows, and they all stared forlornly after us, as we drove away.

Thursday, August 6, 2009

8:00 p.m. In from another adventurous day. We crossed over to Dumfries and Galloway at eleven o'clock this morning. Solway Firth pushes farthest inland here, and the outgoing tide had left behind an expanse of sand and rivulets. In short order, we came upon The Devil's Porridge in Gretna.

During World War I, it became something of a scandal that British forces could only return one bullet for every ten fired by the Germans. With only enough ammunition for an hour's worth of pitched battle, a munitions factory was conceived for Gretna. Three mountain ranges would protect the enterprise from German zeppelins, though one did eventually get through. Memorabilia, memoirs, and photographs in the museum honored the thousands of women who'd mixed the munitions concoction known as "the devil's porridge."

From here we continued north to Dumfries for a pleasant lunch and a showing of a *Jonathan Ross* U2 interview at Dawn's.

Next, in a broad cow pasture field near Holywood, we encountered The Twelve Apostles stone circle. Eleven of a dozen monoliths remain, many recumbent. One of these had a grouping of what are purported to be man-man cup-markings. The circle, the largest in Scotland, dates to the Late Neolithic/Early Bronze Age. Erected between 3000 and 1500 BCE [Before the Common Era], it may have formed part of a later Druidical sacred forest, giving rise to the area's name.

From Holywood, the road to the Solway coast bypasses the major landmark of the area, the rounded headland of Criffel Mountain, which can occasionally be seen all the way from Carlisle.

Nearby, in the small, pretty village of New Abbey, we visited the ruins of Sweetheart Abbey, constructed of red sandstone brought from across the River Nith. Established in CE 1273 by Devorgilla, Lady of Galloway, Sweetheart memorializes her Norman husband, John Balliol of Barnard Castle. Cistercian monks from nearby Dundrennan Abbey cleared the land of granite boulders with which they raised their precinct wall, much of which remains intact. Red sandstone grave slabs, originally in the adjacent churchyard, have been inserted into the abbey's walls.

Devorgilla was born about 1218, one of the three daughters of Alan, Lord of Galloway, one of Great Britain's last pre-Norman Celtic princes. She died in 1289, and was buried by the high altar, holding in her hand a small casket that contained the embalmed heart of her husband, which she'd kept with her all her life. She and John co-founded Balliol College in Oxford. Their son, also John of Balliol, became the rather hapless King John of Scotland.

After tea and cake at the Abbey Cottage, we puttered about the white-washed village, admiring gardens ablaze with summer flowers, and on the return to Carlisle, we stopped at the Café Royal for fish and chips in Annon. The River Nith flows under a regal bridge at Annon, where sandstone facades echo the ancient abbey just down the road.

Saturday, August 8, 2009

Happy Birthday, Edge! Sitting in Sharon's east patio in York, on a bright blue day, her English garden a riot of color.

Monday, August 10, 2009

4:00 p.m. Breezy and overcast, with a light rain. Two o'clock this afternoon, we drove over to Bishopthorpe, a village so close to York I hardly knew we'd left town. We ordered a Yorkshire pudding lunch at The Ship Inn, a pub beside the River Ouse, with leather chairs and wood-paneled walls.

Dropped by the Bishop's Palace [the residence of the Archbishop of York] afterwards, where we discovered the melting remnants of a small chapel and an overgrown churchyard. Though the Doomsday Book records a parish here in 1086, these moldering remains—low red-brick walls outlining a priory—belonged to 13th Century St. Andrews church. The entrance, comprised of a soft pale-gold limestone which the brush of a finger could diffuse, had stone-carved heads on turret edges and door frames. Grave stones in the cemetery date to the mid-1800s. One commemorated a former minister who had spent most of his life tending the ruins.

The archbishop was "in residence," and as we approached the reception office, an employee returning from lunch complained that it just "wasn't right" to wander about the place while his archbishopness was on site. We did, however, catch a glimpse of the estate, a cloister-like expanse of bright green lawns and flower-beds, concrete walkways and iron benches.

Tuesday, August 11, 2009

At ten o'clock this morning, we escaped to the moors on a search for the Stones of Snilesworth. We rolled into the village of Osmotherly in the Cleveland Hills by eleven. Like all the hamlets on the Bilsdale side of the River Rye, Osmotherly was neat and flowered, constructed of a soft pale-brown stone.

Two miles out of the village, on Osmotherly Moor, the Square Corner Car Park sat at right angles to an ancient moorland trackway, the Cleveland Way, which follows much of the coast. The forward portion strikes up and over the balding bulge of Black Hambleton. We crossed the creek several times as the road wound toward Hawnby, bracken on the hillsides, blooming heather purpled in sunlight, and mountain ash hanging heavy with red berries.

Our map proved a challenge, and we'd been stung by nettles and stymied by plausible stone constructions, when Sharon glanced back up the hill and there, silhouetted against the blue sky, stood a tight intact circle of four stones, one broken in two and one half buried. Three of them had iron gate-hangers pounded into them. The beck of Cringle Ing Stack tumbled out of the moor here, cold and clear and choked with bracken.

Eleven-thirty, we pushed east toward Ramsdale near Robin Hood's Bay, breaking for tea in Hawnby, where the bulk of Black Hambleton hunkered once again. The small village, a tad on the shabby side, was constructed of the same pale-brown stone as Osmotherly. We had tea and a lavender scone at the Hawnby Tea Room, looking toward the gurgling but unseen River Rye.

Down into the valley then, we followed the River Rye, reduced now to a narrow brown stream banked with bracken. In the near distance loomed the North Yorkshire Moors, their purple heather cast in shadow.

At the bottom of the moor, the Rye Valley sheltered gold-stone Helmsley castle near Rievaulx. Rows of new-mown hay lay drying in the sun or stacked in hay bales on the valley floor.

Failing to find the stone row purported to be near Ramsdale, we carried on toward Whitby, the sea calm and blue on the horizon, Whitby Abbey's dark remains high on a bluff to the right. Down off Blue Bank into the grey village of Ugglesbarnby.

Robin's Hood Bay was seething with holiday makers when we arrived. They'd packed themselves along incoming roadways, clogged the beach, and crammed their vehicles on crooked village streets. We left at once for Rudston, arriving just as the church bell chimed four o'clock.

"Prehistoric Monolith in Churchyard," read the sign that brought us to the Rudston Monolith in the Parish Church of All Saints. The smoothly tapered giant, at twenty-six feet the tallest standing stone in Britain, is capped with metal to protect against erosion. A slab of moor grit conglomerate, Rudston had been hauled up from Cayton Bay, Comelian Bay, or perhaps the Cleveland Hills to the north. The stone weighs upwards of forty tons. Erected between 1600 and 2000 BCE, Rudston is probably buried as far underground as it soars above. A sprinkling of coins lay at its base along with a small lit glass-enclosed candle.

Wednesday, August 12, 2009

Early this afternoon, we took in a performance of *The Railway Children* at the National Railway Museum in York. Something akin to *To Kill a Mockingbird* permeated the tale, told from a child's point of view, though the story is not so profound. Adapted from a book written in 1903 [*The Railroad Children*, Edith Nesbit, 1906], the play tells the story of an imprisoned Englishman falsely accused of espionage, his wife and three children relocate to Yorkshire.

Platforms on railway tracks were shifted about for various scenes. Trains would arrive with click-clacks from loud-speakers, flashing lights, and steam puffing along the tracks. At the close, a real steam engine chugged in. Narration moved seamlessly into dialog. For example, as a railroad executive doled out medals for bravery, one of the children described his speech. "It was . . . ," she said, and the railroad man jumped in oratorically with "boring . . . long . . . long . . . boring."

Off to Leeds afterwards, for supper with Jane and Youssef. Youssef had prepared an outstanding meal of home-made pita bread, Moroccan hot salad (tomatoes, red peppers, onion, garlic, and hot peppers on a bed of Bibb lettuce), chicken tagine, and zucchini and raison couscous. Moroccan mint tea, strawberries, and marshmallows in chocolate fondue for dessert.

Thursday, August 13, 2009

This afternoon I took a closer look at the National Railway Museum. Sleek engines, railed stagecoaches, mining trams, and Royal Tour trains kept company with the retired *Flying Scotsman*. The warehouse, filled with model trains, railroad signs, furniture, switches, and more, would have fascinated my Dad, and I pictured him at every turn.

We walked into town over the River Ouse afterwards, via the single-spanned Lendal Bridge, and had sandwich wraps— Wensleydale cheese with grapes, and cranberry with brie—at Stickleback's River Café, a small boat at anchor off the riverside path, Dame Judy Dench Walk.

All Saints Pavement church nearby had a cluster of black plaques with a list of 17th century parishioners who had bequeathed loaves of bread or small amounts of cash to Yorkshire widows and the poor. One of these donors had financed the education of a handful of needy children.

Our last stop of the day was A Taste of Tuscany, a café whose outdoor tables bordered a public garden with stone seats, a gazebo, and a line of benches in alcoves of the old city wall.

Friday, August 14, 2009

In Wembley [London] on the bottom floor of Mullanes B&B on Wembley Hill Road. Our train left York at nine-thirty this morning, and by noon we'd made King's Cross Station, where we caught the Circle Line to Baker Street, Bakerloo to Wembley Central. Despite picking up U2's sound check from our flat—one of the two metal arches of the new Wembley Stadium is visible from our back garden—I'm feeling no impending U2 excitement as yet.

We collected our tickets, handing off three to Julie, and then drifted around the stadium. Friends who'd queued in the GA line at eight o'clock this morning, were seated comfortably in folding chairs.

Saturday, August 15, 2009

2:00 a.m. We were to the stadium by seven o'clock last night. No one mans the turnstiles in this state-of-the-art facility, and we simply scanned our own ticket by punching the bar code in a slot.

Here's the set-list for the first London *360*: Breathe; No Line on the Horizon; Get on Your Boots; Magnificent; Beautiful Day/ Blackbird; Elevation; Still Haven't Found What I'm Looking For;

Stuck in a Moment; Unknown Caller; Unforgettable Fire; City of Blinding Lights; Vertigo; Crazy; Sunday Bloody Sunday; Pride; MLK; Walk On/Never Walk Alone; Streets; One; Mysterious Ways// Ultraviolet; With or Without You; Moment of Surrender.

Beautiful Day, with its "we love you" intro, ended with Blackbird, and Sunday Bloody Sunday, all in red, excelled, old chestnut that it is. Moment of Surrender, dedicated to "national treasure" Brian Eno, incorporated a snippet of London Calling. The sound was skewed for many of the tunes, and I blamed my ears at first. But everyone else remarked on it too.

Opening about eight-thirty, the show concluded at eleven, and we convened in a cold wind at the West Service Entrance to await the band's departure. The young couple we'd met on the train to London on the *Vertigo* tour—they'd re-read *A Grand Madness* pre-tour—were there as well. We call them the Huddlesfields, as that's the Yorkshire town from which they hail. Had I written another book? the lad asked. I had. A novel called *Power's Garden*. "Does it have Bono in it?" he asked.

Sunday, August 16, 2009

8:30 a.m. Tea on High Street yesterday before trooping over to Wembley to pick up our Red Zone tickets, wrist-bands, and instructions. As though she'd arranged it, Sharon, who'd planned to meet us at the West Service Entrance at three-thirty, clocked in just as a blacked-out van pulled into the stadium.

We were just a handful, twenty or so, when Bono appeared, and moved down the line, shaking hands and chatting. In our small group, Sue declared last night's concert had been "great." Bono's voice "spot-on." He'd thought so too, he said. How was the sound? He asked. Though I couldn't answer, others did.

Here's the set-list for the second London show: Breathe; No Line; Boots; Magnificent; Beautiful Day; End of the World; New Year's Day; Still Haven't Found/Stand by Me; Unknown caller; Unforgettable Fire; Blinding Lights; Vertigo; Crazy; Sunday Bloody Sunday; Pride; MLK; Walk On; Streets//One; BAD!!//Ultraviolet;

With or Without You; Moment of Surrender.

I thought at first my soaringly favorable assessment of this concert sprang from being in the Red Zone. But Sharon had a seat in the nose-bleed section, at the very back of the stadium, and she'd felt the same.

We'd settled into the Red Zone by six o'clock, on Edge's side, a third of the way down the inside barrier. Even by seven, the enclosure had not reached full capacity. The Hours played a fine set, followed by Glasvegas. The stadium roof had been lowered, which improved the acoustics, but, beyond that, this concert was so just emotional, Bono chatty, relaxed, and funny. Friday night he'd promised the band would "make something special happen." They'd put on a good show—they always do—but nothing particularly 'special' had happened. Last night, they succeeded.

Streets ended the main set with an explosive celebration, and the Ultraviolet/With or Without You encore was spectacular. More and more I appreciate Moment of Surrender as the closer, meshing, as it does, addiction and struggle with an acute awareness of the passage of time. Sometimes you have to give up the fight and accept your life's purpose, should you be lucky enough to know what that is.

Sunday Bloody Sunday saw Edge racing on the walkway. Bono lost track of him for a time, and peered out, hide and seek fashion, from one of the bridges. Larry pounded his bongo drum right in front of us for Crazy, and Adam strutted and posed with all his "dangly bits," as Sue has tagged his sparkly guitar strap, the beaded fringes of his white trousers, and his glittery shirt. "It's been a long time since we rock and rolled," Bono sang.

At one point, security rushed to the far side of the walkway where a woman had scrambled up onto one of the bridges. We learned too that Joe O'Herlihy had come earlier to see the new Wembley under construction and had placed one of Edge's plectrums in the foundation stone. So a bit of The Edge will always be with London.

I see the concert story as expressing the reality of living "in this space and time." Our destiny is to live the life we're given, to stop the struggle and surrender. We all live circular lives, with the ticking clock of time. New Year's Day follows the End of the World. No here and now; no now and then. The sky blends with the sea. No Line on the Horizon.

With flashing lights on-screen as spacey as the sequence in *Close Encounters of the Third Kind*, this is perhaps ultimately the sense of the powerful W.H. Auden poem, *Funeral Blues* or *Stop all the Clocks* [*Funeral Blues* from *Collected Poems*, Random House, New York, 1976] which opens Blinding Lights. A life lost and a world suspended.

Here is the realization of mortality, with a deeply spiritual dimension. We all think that things and people will last forever, and of course, they don't. Perhaps Bono has emerged from an overly 'Christian' sense of spirit into something more profound and inclusive—the living in the now of spirituality, rather than the living for the hereafter of Christianity. This life and whatever comes next are aspects of the same matrix. No line on the horizon.

Or maybe, as Sue says, he's just feeling fifty.

Monday, August 17, 2009

6:00 p.m. In our fifth-floor flat in the Central Glasgow Apartments on Oswald Street. We left Wembley Park Station about eleven yesterday morning, taking the Westminster Tube to Liverpool Street Station. A forty-five minute ride on the Stansted Express to Stanstead Airport, and so on to Glasgow.

We have two bedrooms and a large living-room/dining room area, with a kitchen running along the inner wall. We look down on Glasgow's Central Train Station. Round about seven o'clock, we fetched in groceries from Tesco's for our after-show U2 celebration, and then popped out for Chinese at the Ho Wong Restaurant on York Street.

Wednesday, August 19, 2009

12:35 p.m. I'm waiting on Platform 11, Waverly Station, Edinburgh, for the 1300 to King's Cross London, calling at York.

I'm due to arrive at 3:33—"when the numbers (fall) off the clock face."

1:00 p.m. On my York train on an overcast day. Yesterday morning, ten-thirty, Dawn arrived from Dumfries, and we headed out to the Glasgow venue, Hampden Park—Glasgow Central to the Mount Florida Station, a ride of about twenty minutes. The sky threw down a steady spray of rain all day—except for U2.

We huddled at the backstage entrance in spits of rain and strong gusts of wind, and when the doors opened at five, we managed the barrier in Red Zone 1—Edge's side—further forward than in London. We had a full view of the main stage, instead of the occasional headless band members we had to settle for in Wembley. Hampden holds about thirty-five-thousand people to Wembley's eighty. The stands at either end of the stadium were painted with one massive blue-and-white Cross of St. Andrew.

Though not quite as over-the-top as second Wembley, I did love this show. Here's the set-list: Breathe; No Line; Boots; Magnificent; Beautiful Day/Here Comes the Sun; Elevation; Still Haven't Found/Stand by Me; Stuck in a Moment; Unknown Caller; Unforgettable Fire; City of Blinding Lights; Vertigo; Crazy; Sunday Bloody Sunday; Pride; MLK; Walk On; Streets; One//Ultraviolet; With or Without You; Moment of Surrender. Flower of Scotland came very close to the beginning.

I've found that a high-point of *360* shows is Edge's Unknown Caller guitar work. I almost prefer the song as an instrumental. At the start of MLK, a deep growl blasted from the sound system, worsening by degrees. By Walk On, the sound collapsed altogether and fans picked up the slack. Bono and Edge exchanged woeful glances but soldiered on. A football game had been scheduled for the stadium earlier in the afternoon, and the lads, held up on their way in from London, had missed sound check.

"Let's hope you don't plan a match on the same night," Bono said at the concert's close. "We might have better luck."

Mist swirled everywhere after the show, and a long, long queue formed for the train, supervised by mounted Glaswegian policemen. We were home by twelve-thirty, up until five with a champagne and buffet supper.

Saturday, August 22, 2009

3:30 p.m. On a nine-hour flight to Denver. Tea and toast this morning, and then the two-hour York to Manchester train, followed by a half-hour flight to Heathrow.

Lasagna for lunch at Jane and Youssef's Thursday, and then over to Oulton Hall where Youssef had arranged a fantastic tea of cakes and scones before we headed off for the U2 show in Sheffield's Don Valley Stadium.

Here's the set-list: Breathe; No Line on the Horizon; Boots; Magnificent; Beautiful Day/Blackbird; Elevation; Still/Movin' on Up; Happy Birthday; Stuck in a Moment; Unknown Caller; Unforgettable Fire; Blinding Lights; Vertigo; Crazy; Sunday Bloody Sunday; Pride; MLK: Walk On/Never Walk Alone; Streets; One; Mysterious Ways//Ultraviolet; With or Without You; Moment of Surrender.

Lots of banter and good fun this time around, and the sound and the encore were the best of this leg of the tour. Bono shared the fact that Sheffield University had an on-campus spot called The Edge, so that people could drink on The Edge, lay on The Edge and so forth.

It was that time of year too when people received their "A-level results". Some would do better than expected. Others would be disappointed. But everyone would exceed the foursome onstage.

What had Adam gotten? Six—eight?

"What did you get Edge?"

"More than you," Edge answered.

"That was hurtful," Bono sighed.

Sheffield was birthday-boy and light man Willy Williams' home town, so we all sang him a happy one as he beamed and waved on-screen.

What a dreadful time we had getting home from this show, which wrapped up about ten-thirty. We didn't even get out of the parking lot until after 1:00 a.m. We inched our way to the M1, and on to Jane's in Leeds. Sharon and I finally pulled into York about two-thirty.

After a lazy morning, we set off yesterday for the spa in Harrogate, wending our way through the sleepy little village of Blubberhouses, where tourists must go when they get homesick.

In Harrogate, we had smoked halibut fish-cakes for lunch in a pretty little café called Quantro's, before heading to the spa, one of only seven in the country originating as a 19th century Turkish Bath. The exterior was quite grand, the interior all cluttered hallways and peeling paint. Our treatments—body massage, facial, and manicure—were excellent, but for one unsettling moment when Charlotte slathered a mineral mask on my face, and stepped out. Judging from the length of time she was gone, apparently for lunch.

8:25 p.m. Through to Denver in fine fettle, and then the off-load belt from my London flight failed and I missed my seven-thirty Tucson connection. British Airways had printed "US Airways" on my ticket, so I hiked over to find that desk deserted. No one at United either, United being my original carrier.

A Frontier flight, due to depart at nine-thirty, popped up on the board, and the Frontier agent scrambled to find me a seat. We board in twenty minutes and I'll be home by ten.

Friday, September 11, 2009

In our room, #607, at the Doubletree Rosemont O'Hare [Chicago]. Sharon flew in noonish yesterday and I arrived about 6:00 p.m. No indication anywhere as to which hotel shuttle departed from which arrival door. But in good time, my van pulled up.

A blistering hot and humid today. We hopped the CTA [Chicago Transit Authority] Blue Line O'Hare down to Jackson Street in the Loop and hiked over to Navy Pier, more or less a lakeside mall with tour boats. The lakeshore has little walled niches of garden here and there, but otherwise huge lanes of traffic on both

Michigan Avenue and Lake Shore Drive barrel by, the shore-line thick with yachts and cabin cruisers.

Our Travelodge on Michigan Avenue is within walking distance of the U2 venue, Soldier Field, a half mile as the crow flies. The crow, however, does not have to negotiate six-lane highways. Still, close is good.

Saturday, September 12, 2009

The CTA Blue Line carried us to Clark Street from where we walked over to the Travelodge. Too early to check in, we left our luggage and caught a water taxi to Navy Pier, where we had a coconut shrimp lunch in a noisy Bubba Gump's.

Another water taxi brought us back down along the lake-front, dotted with white sails, to the Museum Campus terminal, with its gardens and wide green lawns, statuary, and rows of stately maples. Skyscrapers towered over the water. Yachts, cabin cruisers, police and coast guard boats crisscrossed the harbor.

Two concrete staircases lead up to the Field Museum of Natural History, the Shedd Aquarium, and the Adler Planetarium. We could just make out the oval of Soldier Field in a heat haze beyond.

Sunday, September 13, 2009

Last night's show was extraordinary, on a par with second Wembley. Possibly the best U2 show I've ever seen! [OMG! Not again!] Our seats, in section 106 on Adam's side, fifteen rows up, gave us an incomparable view of the main stage. Unfortunately, an upper tier of glaring neon lights, and food and drink stands, jutted out overhead, blocking the entire Crab but for the feet.

We tested the sound behind the stage before realizing that the couple in the row ahead of us had come and gone. Sharon tracked them to the very first row of our section. They'd paid a thousand dollars for their tickets, the fellow told her, and had flown in from Philly [Philadelphia]. Subsequently, he'd complained about the dismal seating and had been upgraded.

So off we went, up steep flights of stairs, advising attendants along the way of our "obstructed view." At the top of the steps, in a huge room, we were handed first row 'complimentary' tickets on Edge's side, where Bono would deliver at least half of the night's performance. Our spirits soared.

Here's the set-list: Breathe; No Line on the Horizon; Boots; Magnificent; Beautiful Day/Blackbird; Elevation; Still Haven't Found/Stand by me; Stuck in a Moment; Unknown Caller; Unforgettable Fire; City of Blinding Lights; Vertigo; Crazy; Sunday Bloody Sunday/Oliver's Army; Pride; MLK; Walk On/Never Walk Alone; One; Bad(!)/40//Ultraviolet; With or Without You//Moment of Surrender.

With Beautiful Day, after Bono's "I thought I found three friends," he pronounced Edge a man "who makes Mr. Spock look like Dr. Ruth," whatever that means, Adam, "well-endowed both physically and mentally," and Larry, a man who'd "given us our first job." Back at his drum kit, Larry lip-synced every word.

"I just have a few things to say about myself," Bono added. "But you might want to sit down." The end went something along the lines of "how can you be modest when you front a band like this."

The Irish thought they'd built Chicago, Bono said—the South Side, Grant Park, Lake Shore Drive. In large measure they had. How proud Bono was to have been a part of the inauguration of President Obama. A colossal step forward for the country and for the world.

Breathe and Crazy were both strong, with lots of pogo-ing from Edge. Bono sang the high-point, Bad, on our side, waving and throwing up his arms with "wide awake." With less smoke pot interference, Ultraviolet's light suit, the entire scene, in fact, shifted well beyond Freddy Krueger's fingernails. The only major change in the set came with the replacement of Auden's poem with a sort of prose plea for the earth, at least that's how I heard it.

A superb show in every way.

Monday, September 14, 2009

Yesterday morning, about ten o'clock, we stepped out of the

summer heat into the Field Museum. I found the exhibits much as I remembered them from old Chicago days, especially those two Tsavo man-eating lions who'd killed over a hundred Kenyon railway workers back in 1898. *The Ghost and the Darkness* recounts their story.

Two in the afternoon, we returned to the hotel to rest up and prep for the second U2 show. Here's the set-list: Breathe; No Line on the Horizon; Boots; Magnificent; Beautiful Day; Still Haven't Found; Elevation; Your Blue Room; Unknown Caller; End of the World; Stay; Unforgettable Fire; Blinding Lights; Vertigo; Crazy; Sunday Bloody Sunday; MLK; Walk On; One; Streets//Ultraviolet; With or Without You; Moment of Surrender.

We found a place at the back of Red Zone 1, on Edge's side, toward the front of the stage, sitting comfortably on the floor by the back railing. By far the best opening band the lads have had, Snow Patrol gave us great music played well. The singer, Gary Lightbody, was clearly chuffed to be onstage with U2 again. He would later join the volunteers for Walk On.

I headed for the loo about eight o'clock. I don't know what some women do in there, but with only three portables, a venue worker eventually prompted speed with "Let's go, ladies. This isn't a spa." Twenty-five minutes I waited for the six people ahead of me to finish up.

Willie Williams rushed past during that time, and we'd already caught a glimpse of Sammy propped up outside the Zone. He too tore off, no doubt in an effort to let the band know that we were in the house again.

They would play "old songs and new songs," Bono said. "And some never played before." Chicago friends and acquaintances were acknowledged with smiles and waves. For Beautiful Day, Bono tossed in a bit of King of Pain [The Police] for what had been a blisteringly hot day. "There's a little black spot on the sun today."

"Next in a long line of U2 accessories," Bono said, in reference to The Crab. They really *had* built it "to get closer to you, our audience." For City of Blinding Lights, he invited a small boy seven or eight-years-old to the stage, and they raced around the walkway hand in hand.

"Sing your soul," Bono asked for I Still Haven't Found What I'm Looking For. "Use your Sunday voice." Amazing Grace was sweetly sung for Grace, a *ONE* campaigner, and the premiere of Your Blue Room, which unfortunately garnered little attention, featured a Russian Cosmonaut reciting Adam's lines.

9:00 p.m. We're in a pretty white and blue room in The Castle B&B in Sabula, Iowa, on the Mississippi River, opposite Savanna, Illinois. We rode out to the airport on the CTA Blue Line, picked up our car, a navy blue Hyundai, and left town on #90. After a construction snafu near Rockford, we sailed down to Sabula through Byron on the Rock River.

Sabula, a pretty little clapboard town, sits at the head of Spring Lake, which is actually part of the river. The mighty Mississippi rolls by lined with grassy embankments, a few village benches, and the occasional tree.

Tuesday, September 15, 2009

On the front porch of our Sabula B&B on a bright blue, cloudless, hot, hot day. The Mississippi slips by at the bottom of a short levee across River Road. Poor little Savannah, across the water, once boasted twenty-five passenger trains a day. Now only freight trains rumble over the railway bridge to our right. In spring, bald eagles fish in the wildlife preserve beyond the tracks and the wooded river banks. I can see them now with their rods and reels and tackleboxes, lining the inner shore in their hip-waders.

An elderly, retired sailor we happened on in the Island City Café last night, left a note on our windshield suggesting we make a stop in Palisades State Park back in Illinois. We'll head there after breakfast.

11:00 a.m. At Lookout Point in Palisades. Ticks are prolific, we hear, but we have an incredibly panoramic view out over the Mississippi. Snowy ibis are fishing in a shallow expanse of green-algae marsh dotted with brushy islands, beyond which a paddle wheeler advances. Vultures soar above and oak trees drop leaves and acorns everywhere. Blue jays call and cicadas buzz.

5:00 p.m. Sitting on the deck of Le Fevre Inn Resort south of Galena, Illinois. We drove the Great River Road up from Savannah through a landscape of high rolling hills, soft hollows, lightly colored autumn trees, and fall wildflowers, mostly goldenrod and wild asters. From the porch here, we look west to the pale-blue forested bluffs of the Mississippi. Neat little farmsteads on low green hills accent the near distance and shadows stretch out with the setting sun.

Wednesday, September 16, 2009

After a continental breakfast in Le Fevre's lobby, we drove up Blackjack Road to the Casper Bluff conservation area beside the river, passing a herd of llamas, who trotted over en masse to see what we might have in the way of nibbles.

The highest point of Casper Bluff, a privately owned eighty-five acre plot of oak savanna and hill prairie, overlooks the Mississippi as it rolls south. Native American burial mounds are featured on the grounds, one on the edge of an oak-ringed field. The site map calls this a *Thunderbird Effigy Mound*. A second pamphlet identifies it as a peregrine falcon. The area had been mowed, but we could just make out a beaked head, a wing to either side, and a fan-shaped tail.

We continued north to Dubuque, Iowa. After tea in Café Manna Java just up from the harbor, we rode "the world's steepest, shortest scenic railway," two-hundred ninety-six feet up the bluff from Fourth Street to Fenelon Place, where we looked across to Illinois and Wisconsin. In the late 1970s, Dan and I had ridden the very same tram with Danielle and Dustin. Same squared trolley cars. Same green wooden benches.

An excellent Italian supper then, at Fried Green Tomatoes in Galena, in an old stone-walled restaurant on Main Street. Linguini with rosemary shrimp and scallops. Afterwards, a one-man Mark Twain show down the road shared lots of laughs and intriguing stories about Old Man River. But somehow the fellow just didn't have his heart in it, hurrying us along at intermission so he could "get this over with."

Thursday, September 17, 2009

3:30 p.m. A gorgeous day, in the low seventies. Not much of a summer in these parts, we hear, before this massive heat-wave dropped down.

This morning, after shopping on Main Street, we had tea outside at the De Soto Hotel. President Lincoln spoke from the balcony here—though not while we were eating.

We drove up Council Hill Road through a pastoral landscape of gentle vales, rolling grassland, woodsy copses, small squat farmsteads, and the occasional herd of cattle. Winding our way to Apple River, a tiny village near the Wisconsin border, we stopped at Apple River State Park, where two narrow brown branches of the Apple River meet in a picturesque stretch of deep-lobed oak forest and overgrown lime-stone cliffs.

We backtracked to Galena along Eagle Ridge. North and south, the land undulated in gentle folds, dirt roads the remnants of pre-industrial river paths or Native American trails.

Friday, September 18, 2009

6:00 p.m. At gate K9, in Chicago's O'Hare. We set off for the airport after breakfast this morning. Sharon flew out of K15 a half-hour ago. (And then there was one.) I'll set off at six-forty-five.

Saturday, September 26, 2009

U2.com reports that the *360 Tour* will pick up again in Europe in August of next year. I'm off to Raleigh [North Carolina] for U2 on Friday. Seventeen years since the Zoo Crew road-tripped for the *Zoo TV Tour,* though I did see Meri in Boston, and Lyn and Kim in Miami for *Elevation.*

Friday, October 2, 2009

9:00 p.m. In room #104 of the Marriott Residence Inn in Crabtree Valley, Raleigh. We have two en-suite bedrooms, a full kitchen/dining room, and a sitting area with fireplace. U2 tomorrow night and then I'm back home on Sunday.

Sunday, October 4, 2009

3:00 a.m. Back from the concert. Lyn and Kim arrived one o'clock yesterday morning, Meri about nine-thirty. We left for the venue, Carter Finley Stadium, at four, but with supper at Chilies, we hit a massive traffic jam and I hopped out and headed for the stadium alone. I'd hook up with the others at Gate 7 after the show.

The opener, Muse, came up at seven. With lavish orchestration, they were solid and commendable. (Kim, Meri, and Lyn limped into the stadium just as David Bowie's Space Oddity struck up, five minutes before U2.)

Here's the set-list: Breathe; Get on Your Boots; Mysterious Ways; Beautiful Day; No Line on the Horizon; Magnificent; Elevation; In a Little While; New Year's Day; Still Haven't Found; Stuck in a Moment; Unforgettable Fire; City of Blinding Lights; Vertigo; Crazy; Sunday Bloody Sunday; MLK; Walk On; One; Streets//Ultraviolet; With or Without You; Moment of Surrender.

As challenging as the stadium was to get to, it was pleasant enough inside, with no gates to speak of, only tape barriers to guide people in. The main floor, scattered with food, drink, and merchandise kiosks, had loos all long the back wall, and stairs at each entrance led to an upper tier and down to the lower levels. From my backless bench in section two, on Adam's side, I had a fine view, in direct line with Bono's front mike.

In the course of the evening, Bono acknowledged the U2 Academic Conference in town for the weekend. [Grateful to the Conference for selecting *A Grand Madness, Ten Years on the Road with U2* for its U2 Studies Bibliography.] With a rendition of Amazing Grace, he also wished a "Happy Birthday" to Agnes Nyamayarwo, a Ugandan AIDS activist. Dik Evans, Edge's brother, was also in the audience.

An awkward silence met Bono's suggestion that a U2 concert might be the sole venue for Jessie Helms and John Edwards [North

Carolina's two US senators] to be together. Both are wildly unpopular and some fans, including a man two rows ahead of me, said so.

With Sunday Bloody Sunday, Bono plucked a flag from the audience that read "People Get Ready" and included the song's chords. "Be cool now," he said, and passed the flag fellow his microphone. The bloke sang a verse of the Curtis Mayfield tune—largely off-key—but no one really minded.

For Blinding Lights, Bono brought up a little boy about the age of his eldest son, John, and they sauntered together down the walkway. At Beautiful Day's "the traffic's stuck and you're not moving anywhere," Bono acknowledged the stadium gridlock. Perhaps the band had experienced it themselves. Post-concert, I found the others at Gate 7.

A Full Hunter's Moon had beamed down throughout the concert, so fitting for the search for our lost car. No one could quite remember where we'd parked. We wandered through a forest of widely-spaced trees under which cars idled, headlights blazing, motors purring, pointed in all directions. The occupants of still darkened vehicles sat eating and drinking at portable tables.

From the field next a major thoroughfare, Kim located the car with her alarm, and off we went, reaching the Marriott by one. Meri leaves at eight, Kim and Lyn at eleven, and I'm to the airport by noon.

Thursday, October 8, 2009

The *360 Tour* moves to Mexico City May 30 next year. South America to follow, US shows to pick up again in July. Dustin will go with me to Denver.

Friday, October 23, 2009

Bono and sons, John and Eli, visited NASA's Mission Control in Houston a week ago. What an amazing experience.

Last Tuesday's show in Glendale [the University of Phoenix Stadium] was first-rate. Dan found his seat in section ten, and Danielle and I went down to Red Zone 2, Adam's side. The few benches had already filled, but we procured a spot at the back of the enclosure near the entrance. All of the Black-Eyed Peas, who'd opened the show, trooped in, obliviously clumped up right in front of us, and we had to shift to less favorable ground. No three-sixty audience here, as a huge black curtain blocked the stage end of the building.

Here's the set-list: Breathe; Get on Your Boots; Magnificent; Mysterious Ways; Beautiful Day; Still Haven't Found; Stuck in a Moment; No Line on the Horizon; Elevation; In a Little While; Unknown Caller; End of the World; Unforgettable Fire; City of Blinding Lights; Vertigo; Crazy; Sunday Bloody Sunday; MLK; Walk On; One; Streets//Ultraviolet; With or Without You; Moment of Surrender.

Adam spent a good deal of time on the bridge on our side, smiling and nodding and posing. Bono, however, rarely came over. The three blonde sisters he called to the stage from the Bomb Shelter of the last tour, perched by the drum kit, before he danced with each of them in turn. The presidential campaign was also referenced. Both Obama and McCain support Bono's African initiatives. McCain and family were in the audience, along with Mohammed Ali.

This entire concert emanated a joyful vibe, though I still feel the walkway is underutilized, The Crab somewhat obstructive. Visibility over vision. Bono sounded almost apologetic about fashioning a "space-ship to get closer to you." But again, how else to accommodate U2's legions of fans?

The lads played Las Vegas last night. The Rose Bowl in Anaheim on Sunday will be streamed live on YouTube, as well as filmed for DVD release.

Saturday, October 31, 2009

More U2 dates up. The Rose Bowl was fantastic!

Friday, November 6, 2009

U2 appeared at the Brandenburg Gate in Berlin yesterday as part of the *MTV Europe Awards*. A masterful and stirring performance. Can it really be twenty years since the Berlin Wall came down?

The 360 Tour, Croke Park, Dublin – July 24, 2009

Cottage on the Dodder River, Dublin – July 26, 2009

The author at Wastwater, the Lake District, Cumbria, UK – August 3, 2009 (Sue Fell)

Caldbeck Common, Cumbria – August 5, 2009

Sweetheart Abbey, New Abbey, Cumbria, UK – August 6, 2009

The author at the Stones of Snilesworth, Osmotherly Moor, Yorkshire, UK – August 11, 2009 (Sharon Harton)

Wembley Stadium, Wembley, London – August 14, 2009

MacPhisto in the GA queue, Wembley – August 14, 2009

Bono on-stage , Wembley – August 15, 2009

Bono at sound check, Wembley – August 15, 2009

Adam on-stage , Wembley – August 14, 2009

Band on-stage , Hampden Park, Glasgow – August 18, 2009

Bono at Hampden Park – August 18, 2009

The Crab at Don Valley Stadium, Sheffield, UK – August 20, 2009

Soldier Field, Chicago, Illinois – September 13, 2009

City of Blinding Lights, Soldier Field, Chicago – September 13, 2009

The Mississippi River at Sabula, Iowa – September 15, 2009

Rural Illinois from Le Fevre Inn Resort, Galena, Illinois – September 15, 2009

Bono on-stage ,
University of Phoenix
Stadium, Glendale,
Arizona – October
20, 2009

University of Phoenix Stadium – October 20, 2009

Invesco Field at Mile High, Denver, Colorado – May 21, 2011

The Dwight D. Eisenhower Highway at Echo, Utah – May 23, 2011

Antelope Island in the Great Salt Lake, Utah – May 24, 2011

Reverend Camping's Judgement Day billboard, Salt Lake City, Utah – May 24, 2011

Hold Me Thrill Me Kiss Me Kill Me, Rice Eccles Stadium, Salt Lake City Utah – May 24, 2011

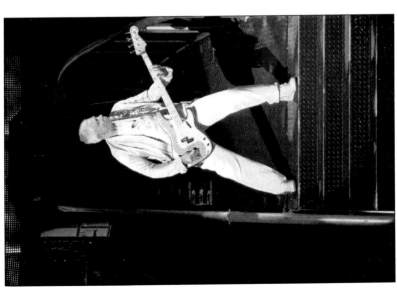

Adam on-stage, Rice Eccles – May 24, 2011

Bono at sound check, Rice Eccles Stadium, SLC – May 24, 2011 (Sharon Harron)

Hippodrome of
Montreal, Quebec
– July 8, 2011

The Crab at the Hippodrome – July 9, 2011

Get on Your Boots, the Hippodrome, Montreal – July 9, 2011

360 Restaurant in the CN Tower, Toronto, Ontario – July 12, 2011

The CN Tower
from The Crab,
Rogers Centre,
Toronto – July
11, 2011

Rogers Centre and the CN Tower from Toronto harbor cruise – July 12,
2011

Bono and uber-fan Lyn McCann (1959-2014) taken in the late 1980s (Photographer unknown)

Thursday, November 26, 2009

Only one UK/Ireland concert next year: Glastonbury Festival's Fortieth Anniversary in August.

Saturday, December 12, 2009

Watched Elvis Costello's *Spectacle* season opener [*CTV* Canada], Bono and Edge his guests. They delivered Stuck in a Moment, Stay, Two Shots of Happy, and Get on Your Boots, the last melded with Costello's own Pump it Up.

Friday, January 8, 2010

Gabrielle Giffords, one of Tucson's US State Representatives, narrowly escaped assassination today! She was speaking at a town hall on the west side, in the parking lot of the Safeway at Ina Road and Oracle. The six murder victims included Christina Taylor-Green, a little girl who'd been born September 11, 2001. We were at an eastside carwash on Kolb Road when *CNN* covered the incident. Surreal.

Saturday, January 16, 2010

A terrible loss of life from an earthquake in Haiti!

Sunday, January 24, 2010

Watched the *Concert for Haiti* today. A good cause, I know, but tedious. Divas all singing the same song. Bono joined Jay Z and Rhianna for some supremely forgettable tune. Wyclef Jean closed with a Haitian number, which, along with Justin Timberlake's take on Leonard Cohen's Hallelujah, was the highlight of an otherwise rather vapid evening. Still, celebrities manning a phone bank have thus far raised more than fifty-seven-million dollars.

Monday, May 10, 2010

Happy Birthday, Bono! The big five-o!

"Ireland has had a long-standing fondness for yew, too," I've put in my new book *Spirit Stones, Unraveling the Megalithic Mysteries of Western Europe's Prehistoric Monuments* [Five Star Publications; 2011], out next year. Couldn't help myself.

Tuesday, May 25, 2010

Bono was admitted to Ludwig Maximilian University Hospital in Munich, Germany, last week, for emergency surgery on his back. In pain for some time, he'd been more recently experiencing numbness in his legs. Eight weeks of recuperation will cancel the band's Glastonbury appearance. The North American leg of the *360 Tour* has also been postponed. On-line photos of Bono show him looking quite frail, as is to be expected.

Saturday, June 26, 2010

The return European leg of *360* opens in Turin [Italy] August 6.

Wednesday, June 30, 2010

Edge, accompanied by Muse, played a red-lit Streets for Glastonbury's 40th .

Tuesday, July 13, 2010

U2's North American *360* return has been rescheduled for next year. Sharon and I will take in Denver—with Dustin—and Salt Lake City.

Monday, August 15, 2010

Having spewed for weeks, British Petroleum's oil spill in the Gulf of Mexico has been capped. The oil, sinking in gooey globs to the bottom of the sea, has hardly "disappeared," as BP claims. But out of sight, out of mind, I guess.

On a positive note, U2 *360* revved up again in Turin two weeks ago. All went well. Sue, Debbi, and Julie flew over for German shows in Frankfurt and Hannover. Loved them both. Bono was funny and "little boyish," Sue said. He had *"Made in Germany"* stamped on his arse, he said, and introduced the band in an alien voice, as *Star Wars* characters. Larry was Darth Vader, Adam, Princess Leah, Edge, R2D2. He—Bono—was "the hairy one" [Chewbacca].

Saturday, October 9, 2010

The second European leg of *360* closed in Rome last night. The lads are off to OZ [Australia].

Saturday, November 13, 2010

Aung San Suu Kyi has been released from house arrest in Myanmar [Burma].

Wednesday, November 24, 2010

On the brink of bankruptcy, Ireland negotiated a gigantic loan from the International Monetary Fund and the European Union. The Celtic Tiger has nearly expired.

Monday, December 27, 2010

Bono, out busking on Christmas Eve on Grafton Street, played One, War is Over if You Want It, and I'm Dreaming of a White Christmas. "I'm not dreaming of a white Christmas," he sang. "I am so sick of fucking snow." With far too many Canadian winters under my belt, I can identify.

Friday, February 18, 2011

Adam's French girlfriend gave birth to a baby boy last year and *360* arrives in Cape Town, South Africa, tonight.

Sunday, March 13, 2011

An eight-point-nine earthquake and tsunami struck Japan Friday. Thousands dead!

Wednesday, March 16, 2011

The Japanese earthquake has been upgraded to 9.0. On Saturday, a thousand bodies washed up on shore! Workers struggling to contain the radiation at the damaged Fukushima reactor have released radioactive steam to lessen pressure and prevent an explosion. How terrifying for anyone, especially people whose psyches suffered the unforgettable fires of Hiroshima and Nagasaki.

Friday, March 25, 2011

The crop of uprisings in the Middle East against dictators and the ruling elite has been dubbed *The Arab Spring*. Could things really improve in that tormented region? No one's holding their breath.

As per Edge, the North American U2 *360 Tour* will close in Monkton, New Brunswick. That's Monkton! New Brunswick!

Wednesday, May 18, 2011

In celebration of his May 10 birthday, Bono brought cake and champagne to fans waiting outside the Mexico City venue on the eleventh.

Mark Kelly, the commander of the space shuttle Endeavor, woke up to U2's Beautiful Day. A musical wake-up call is a tradition aboard the shuttle and Kelly's wife, Gabby Giffords, battling back from an assassination attempt in early January, made the request.

Thursday, May 19, 2011

9:30 p.m. At the Days Inn Denver on Tower Road, on a dreary, bleary, soggy, foggy, shitty day. My flight was delayed several hours due to tornadoes in the Denver area. Sharon's Chicago plane was late as well, with both mechanical and weather issues.

Friday, May 20, 2011

Settled in the circular Hotel VQ, beside Invesco Stadium at Mile High. Had lunch in the 14th floor VQ Grill. Directly below, GA fans had gathered with fold-out chairs and coolers. A couple of women chatted about a private U2 gig scheduled for tonight for about two-thousand special guests—of a Coors nature, I assume. A dress rehearsal of sorts, the lads having just wound up Central and South America.

8:00 p.m. Dustin came in from Golden four-thirty or so, and we drove out to Sloan's Lake for fish and chips at GBs—motto *In Cod we Trust*. Thomas Sloan created the lake in the 1860s, when the well he was digging struck an aquifer that bubbled up to flood a large portion of his farm. Sloan's Leak became Sloan's Lake, an oasis of spring trees, walking and bike paths, green lawns, and lots of birdlife—Canada geese, red-winged blackbirds, mergansers, robins, mallard ducks, and white pelicans. Black-bottomed storm clouds passed to the southeast, silhouetting the Denver skyline.

Saturday, May 21, 2011

10:30 a.m. We ate a rather pricey buffet breakfast this morning on the fourteenth floor. A klatch of older women there had met the band before the gig last night.

1:00 p.m. A pleasantly cool day. I'm on a bench on the bike path in South Platte Greenbelt Park, across I-25 from Invesco. The wide brown river slips by in front of me, the songs of robins and red-winged blackbirds intermingled with hair-raising screams from the carnival rides next door.

7:00 p.m. I wandered down to a second bridge in the park, where I watched kayakers prepare to challenge a short stretch of white water, and then made my way back to the hotel on the Invesco side. A young fellow in the elevator, carrying a collapsible red chair, said he'd been queued up in the GA line for three days. What was he doing in the elevator, I thought?

Sunday, May 22, 2011

8:00 p.m. Off to the Denver airport this morning to fetch our rental car. We cruised over to Dustin's digs at the base of grassy South Table Mountain, in Golden, and then followed him north to Estes Park, through mountains capped with snow. In Nederland we had to yield for a mama elk ambling across the road to join her wooly brown babe in a small herd that dozed under a pine tree in someone's front yard.

A quick sushi lunch in Estes Park and a drift through the Stanley Hotel. The red and white beauty overlooks the Estes Valley and was the inspiration for Stephen King's *The Shining*. Dustin headed back to Golden then, and Sharon and I continued east to I-25 and so north into Wyoming. The Big Thompson River, headed for the South Platte, ran full and frothy by the roadside in the tree-lined bottomlands before the freeway.

Near Cheyenne, Wyoming, the mountains receded to a pencil-thin line on the left horizon, and then trees disappeared altogether as we merged with the High Plains. Cheyenne spread out in the grass. Westward on #60, the land began to roll again, bare-limbed trees in open draws, and slanted pools of water that resolved to remnants of snow drifts.

We reached the Fairfield Inn and Suites in Laramie about an hour ago, just as a silvery 'god-shot' sunset streamed bands of light to the horizon from a creamy cloud bank. We had an excellent supper at the Iron Skillet truck stop across the way.

The Denver concert last night was grand. Here's the set-list: Even Better than the Real Thing; I Will Follow; Get on Your Boots; Magnificent; Mysterious Ways; Elevation; End of the World; All I Want is You; Stay; Beautiful Day/Here Comes the Sun; Pride; Miss Sarajevo; Zooropa; City of Blinding Lights; Vertigo; Crazy/Discotheque; Sunday Bloody Sunday; Scarlet; Walk On/You'll Never Walk Alone//One/Will You Still Love me Tomorrow; Streets//Hold Me Thrill Me; With or Without You; Moment of Surrender.

We walked over to the venue about seven-thirty. Our seats, six rows up on Edge's side, put the Red zone right beside us. The opening band, The Fray, roused the sixty-seven-thousand strong crowd with ease. Better Than the Real Thing made for a lively intro, the band arriving just as Larry's drums erupted. Mysterious Ways featured undulating silhouettes on The Crab's screens.

The Reverend Harold Camping, previously of *Family Life Radio* in California, had predicted that Judgment Day would occur several hours earlier, at six o'clock, and so Bono dedicated End of the World to this fundamentalist flake. He'd apparently made similar predictions in the past, and each and every time they failed, he claimed to have "miscalculated."

"To be taken up to the air sounds like fun to me," Bono said, referencing Christian fundamentalism's Rapture. "Just as long as Larry Mullen is with me," though the Edge would probably "be the only one to go . . . . I'll get to stay here with you," he added, which drew 'rapturous' applause.

To me, the flow faltered with Zooropa, as the band vanished behind lowered screens. Though this suits the sense and concept of the song—a caged exhibit at the zoo, and such—it felt more like a commercial break, all sound and flash and sparkle.

For City of Blinding Lights, band members sauntered out in overkill suits of lights. An excellent Vertigo and Crazy followed, along with an energetic Sunday Bloody Sunday. Bono spoke about Aung San Suu Kyi's recent release from house arrest, about how Amnesty campaigns really did work. And then Amnesty and One volunteers filed onto the ramp for Walk On, holding up to their faces Amnesty logo lanterns, which they left behind.

When Walk On closed the main set, Bono promised a special surprise, and Aung San Suu Kyi came on-screen to praise U2 fans for their efforts on behalf of Amnesty. Seven billion people on the planet, Aung San said. And yet all it took was One.

"That old guy over there," Dustin dead-panned.

The second encore opened with a space baby "what time is it in the world" speech. Astronauts on the Mir Space Station flashed on-screen, apt and terse phrases scrolling below, my favorite being "My feet are killing me." One year ago today, Bono said, he was "in a very bad way in Germany . . . . Thank God and the Germans." He had *Made in Germany* stamped on his bottom. Not only was he "fixed," but he was "better."

"Where's my three sisters?" Bono asked, and, not finding them, chose a young girl in a *Larry Mullen Band* t-shirt who recited a Susie Kerin poem *The Garden**, about the American west. I love this idea and I hope it continues, though that seems unlikely. Not rock 'n' roll enough.

*[The Garden
by Susie Kerin (1870-1952)

Near the mountains is a lovely garden,
Denver beauteous, haven of the West;
Through her welcome arch the tired tourist
Finds an oasis of peace and rest.

In this garden there is always sunshine,
Happiness, good will, and blessings rare;
Rising in a cloud of benediction
To descend in fragrance through the air.

May all those who wander through this garden
Breathe this air from yonder snow-capped crest,
And enjoy each happy, restful hour
As the sun sinks in the golden west.]

At One, Bono spoke about being in Berlin [for the *Auchtung Baby* Sessions]. A wall was coming down, he said. Another one going up in the band. "But we're still together." And then he thanked fans for their patience and the band for letting him carry on. "Some of you were two years younger when you bought your tickets."

In Bono's band intro, he remarked on specific changes that had occurred during this tour, such as Adam becoming a father "for the first time." Larry was dubbed "the terminator," the most anxious to call it quits, we assume. Bitten by a spider, Edge—"superhero meets scientist meets artist"—had been transformed into a nerd. (Bono and Edge composed the score for *Spiderman*, now running on Broadway.)

A McPhisto-tinged Bono sashayed out in his suit of lights to sing Hold Me Thrill Me into a spinning red radio mike, which cooled to blue for With or Without You. Bono hooked his jacket on the mike and waved it off into the bowels of The Crab.

In a sense, he became one of us then, singing along with the audience. Moment of Surrender—dedicated to the Green family, ended a great show. [Joshua Green, a local One Campaign worker had died in 2009]. So infrequently had Bono graced our side of the venue, that Dustin pronounced the evening more of a *180 Tour*.

Monday, May 23, 2011

7:00 p.m. We're in the Best Western Holiday Hills, in Coalville, Utah. We'd heard much about the dismal nature of southern Wyoming, but I found it quite pleasant, especially the stretch between Laramie and Rawlins—vast vistas of buff-colored grasses dotted with Black Angus cattle and backed by snow-covered mountains. A big-sky country of wide storm-filled atmospherics. The landscape took on a moorish appearance on occasion, with sage in place of heather. Low hills of cloud-blackened brush would now and again alternate with patches of snow, latticed brown snow-fences, and natural-gas wells. Compact ranches sprawled on broad grasslands sprinkled with cattle or pronghorn antelope, and rare winter trees in gullies ran back from the road. The long ridge near Arlington carried lofty white windmills, and snow-melt puddled in the lowlands.

Where a hulk of tortured rock—Elk Mountain—climbed up out of the desert floor streaked with snow, brownish-grey foothills rose up in front, a herd of pronghorn antelope grazing on the open prairie. We crossed the Bow River as it snaked north and south, delineated only by a fringe of winter trees. The Platte River—a brown swath between low, dusty banks—had flooded. Sinclair, where we'd hoped to have lunch, materialized as just a small company town for Sinclair Oil. The refinery huffed and puffed in the midst of housing units.

At noon, we drove through Rawlins and the land went flat again, grey-green sagebrush, tan-colored short-grass, Black Angus, and a second group of pronghorn in tan and white.

1:05 p.m. All the way to Rock Springs, dramatic storms, lightning forking in their underbellies, would melt away on the horizon. Again we planned to eat at Red Desert, only to find a shallow pool of silty red water and an adult video store promising "Erotic Toys." Our next lunch fizzled out at Table Rock, which had been reduced to an abandoned gas station and an eerie and vacant housing development squatting on a bluff. Somewhere in all this flatness, we crossed the Continental Divide.

Fifteen miles east of Rock Springs, short cliffs built up on the right, and a three-minute shower left behind the sweet, pungent scent of sage. A span of ancient, eroded sand dunes came next, covered in powdery-green sagebrush and pock-marked with caves and crevices. And then—*poof*—everything went flat again.

Just as a tremendous thunderstorm unleashed itself, we pulled into Rock Springs, riding out the deluge in Applebee's with mini fajitas and a chicken Thai salad. Melting hailstones had layered the base of the car windows by the time we left.

"For Lyman's sake" [Lyman Beecham is a character in my 2009 novel, *Power's Garden*], we took the first turnoff to Lyman, Wyoming, just as ACDC's Highway to Hell burst from the car stereo. But the town was quite serene. Seven miles in, along wide Creek River, a slow-winding high-plains stream, brown and shallow, and four miles back to the highway, past far-flung ranches. Cattle stood munching or knee-deep in flooded fields.

At five-thirty, we cut across a series of lush valleys into Utah— the red-orange sandstone cliffs of the Dwight D. Eisenhower Highway flecked with jade-colored junipers, an undergrowth of dusty green sage, and bright lime grasses in the bottom-lands.

At Echo, we turned off at the junction of #80—which goes south to Salt Lake City—and #87—which heads north to Ogden. Most inconveniently, the Echo Information Center was closed, but we stopped to overlook the highway we'd just traveled as it passed through the canyon. In the parking lot, hundreds of prairie dogs scampered about, chirping in the bushes and chewing the grass. Echo presented one single row of dilapidated clap-boards, not a soul in sight. And so here we are in Coalville.

Wednesday, May 25, 2011

10:00 a.m. I'm on my flight back home. We dropped the car at the SLC airport at eight o'clock this morning.

Yesterday, in a light, cold rain, we left Coalville at ten and traversed a tranquil stretch of Coalville Valley. Dairy cattle bunched up in mushy fields, and creeks and rivers overflowed their banks. At Kimball Junction, flocks of Canada geese browsed beside swollen creeks or floated in water meadows. Thirty-nine degrees [Fahrenheit] outside by then.

On the downside of Porley's Summit, roadside crags and purple-sage hills faded under falling snow. In the near distance snow-crested peaks rose up, lacy with spring trees at their base.

We arrived in Salt Lake City at ten-thirty, too early to check in at the Marriott University Park on Wakara Way, a mile from the U2 venue, Rice Eccles Stadium.

Instead, we motored out to the Great Salt Lake, stopping at Saltair State Marina. Only a portion of the original resort building here, Saltair Pavillion, remains, with a small shop and a museum inside. A model of the palatial 1950s spa, in gleaming white with bright-red onion turrets, was the primary exhibit. The Marina, modest in both appearance and sea-craft, was approached through a high-water marsh flitting with swallows and yellow-headed blackbirds. The whiffy lake lapped the disheveled shoreline and black Antelope Island, barren and rocky, sprawled off shore.

The Great Salt Lake, the largest body of water in the Western Hemisphere, is a remnant of Lake Bonneville, which formed over fifty-thousand years ago and lasted half that time. Evaporation left behind billions of tons of salts and other minerals, six feet deep on the Bonneville Flats.

On our return to town, we breezed by one of Camping's Judgment Day billboards. "The Bible guarantees it." Ha!

Thursday, May 26, 2011

Back in Tucson again. We had lunch Tuesday at the Corner Bakery Café in SLC and set off for the stadium at two-thirty. With a fearsome sun beating down, we were allowed to rest our dogs in an orange-tarped security area. We sat there for the better part of an hour, unaware of a *Credentials Checked* sign that swung over our table. From policemen to security workers to media types, all flashing laminate badges, we nonchalantly advised everyone who asked, of closed gates and redirected entrances.

Three minutes from our self-imposed sound-check deadline, a blacked-out vehicle pulled up, Bono waving out the window. The gathered throng exploded. We kept well out of the way in the meagre shade of some steel girders.

Edge, Bono, and Adam approached the crowd, now eight or nine persons deep. A cameraman and a woman with a microphone captured Bono's attention, and he regaled them with details of his back surgery, relating how tired he was, and then suggesting that a wheelchair-bound girl wear something warmer for what was expected to be a cold night. He posed lengthily with three young blonde girls—perhaps the trio from Phoenix—telling them how beautiful their city was. Edge quizzed fans on the weather and they assured him, rather predictably, that it would be a "beautiful day."

With the crowd clumped up on the left, I'd maneuvered toward the table behind which Bono now stood, when a huge bloke hurled himself through the air, landing on the table-top. Security whisked him away and Bono veered off to glad-hand on the far right. I fought my way out of the thickening crowd then, to watch the chaos from the sidelines. One young woman plowed forward in slow motion, inching toward the front, as relentless and determined as an ice-breaker.

Here's the set-list for Salt Lake City: Better Than the Real Thing; I Will Follow; Get on Your Boots; Magnificent; Mysterious Ways; Elevation; End of the World; All I Want is You/Love Rescue Me; Happy Birthday (to Bob Dylan); Stay; Beautiful Day/Here Comes the Sun; Pride; Miss Sarajevo; Zooropa; City of Blinding Lights; Vertigo/It's Only Rock and Roll; Crazy/Discotheque/Mofo; Sunday Bloody Sunday; Scarlet; Walk On/You'll Never Walk Alone//One/Blowin' in the Wind/The Times They are Achangin'; Streets// Hold me Thrill Me; With or Without You; Moment of Surrender.

In a smaller venue, with a capacity crowd of forty-three-thousand, Salt Lake City bettered Denver in both sound and intensity. The band took the stage at quarter to nine, the screens blinking statistics well before Bowie's Space Oddity kicked in. One crawl noted eighteen shows left to play, though that should have been eighteen venues.

On Adam's side, in row six again, we saw a lot more of Bono this time around. We were thanked for our patience, and the Fray was acknowledged.

"Vorsprung durch technique . . . . rebuilt by better design," Bono said. "What do you make of Robo-Bono?" A lot could happen in one year. "Something about the way this man is walking and moving around the stage," he said of Adam. "A certain manliness." Larry had contributed to an art film with Donald Sutherland, and was due to play Billy Idol—"after (Billy) cleaned himself up." A bio-pic. The Donald Sutherland snippet was true. Larry does play a robber in a flick filmed in Orangeville, near Toronto. [*The Man on the Train* opened with limited release the week of October 31, 2011.] The Billy Idol bit left Larry in stitches.

Some things, however, stayed the same. For example, Edge's hotel room lacked hot water for several days. Did Edge complain to management? Did he storm out of the hotel? Did he throw a fit? No. "He went out and bought a kettle. He bought several kettles and an old radiator and a plastic water container. And he rebuilt the plumbing system."

What did Edge want to play next, Bono asked, and All I Want is You segued into two verses of Love Rescue Me, in tribute to Bob Dylan, who was marking his seventieth birthday. "Happy Birthday Bob Dylan from Salt Lake City" Bono shouted. We offered up a Happy Birthday chorus, and then, accompanying himself on acoustic guitar, Bono sang gorgeous fragments of Blowin' in the Wind and The Times They are Achangin'.

"Where's my three sisters?" he asked again, and three blonde girls, who may have been the same three at sound-check, hopped onstage. Each recited a verse of Minnie Hardy's *Utah**, reading the last verse together with Bono.

*[Utah
by Minnie Hardy (1895-1971)

Utah, I'm glad to be here where the mountains rise
Dazzling white 'neath the clear blue skies
From crimson dawn 'til the dear day dies
Way out west in Utah.

Where the mountain air is pure and sweet
Where fresh, cool water flows down the street

And the climate! Friend it can't be beat;
Delightful, magnificent Utah.

God made Utah and he made it grand,
The beauty spot of his glorious land,
Where plenty supplies with a generous hand
All of our needs and wants in Utah.

Mighty mountains, sylvan vales,
Picturesque canyons and rugged trails,
Joy's your companion, health never fails,
Happiness dwells in Utah.]

This charming slice of 360 is doomed. Where's the hipness. And where's the poem for Moncton, New Brunswick?

Astronaut Mark Kelly displayed a cut-out "Beautiful Day" for the song, and recited Bowie's Space Oddity, telling his wife, Gabby Giffords, he was coming home. He missed her very much. Zooropa still lets me down, but City of Blinding Lights, Vertigo, and Crazy all shone. And for Hold Me Thrill Me, a MacPhisto tune, Mac/Bono pranced around the stage and wheeled about on his oversized radio mike.

"Tonight was really special. Thanks for making it so," Bono said after With or Without You. "Make the light brighter." And as Moment of Surrender closed the show, cell-phones transformed the stadium into a sea of glittering gold. "No need to kick out the darkness . . . . Hold on to this beautiful world . . . . Hold on tight."

Sunday, May 29, 2011

The lads play Winnipeg—Winter Pig—tonight.

Friday, June 24, 2011

It's U2 in Glastonbury tonight.

Monday, July 4, 2011

9:00 p.m. I'm at the Embassy Suites Airport Hotel in Minneapolis, Minnesota. I ought to be an hour from landing in Montreal. I left Tucson at one-twelve this afternoon, arriving in

Minneapolis to discover my Montreal connection had "broken down." I'm booked for six-thirty tomorrow morning, through Detroit. From the bedroom of my sixth floor room, I've been watching Fourth of July fireworks all across the city.

Tuesday, July 5, 2011

In our Rue St. André flat in Montreal, mid-way between Rue Beaubien and Rue Belle Chasse. I caught the five-thirty shuttle to the Minneapolis airport this morning and ended up in the comfy first-class cabin for my hour-long Detroit flight. Free refreshments in real glasses. An hour and fifteen minutes brought me to Montreal.

Our apartment, La Petite Patrie, has polished hardwood floors everywhere, but for a bright yellow-and-white tiled kitchen. A garden, with white plastic furniture and walls covered in lush vines, juts off from the sitting area. Located at the front of the house, my room, pleasant enough, rattles with distant traffic and honking horns. We're in a French neighborhood of two-storied flats, outside staircases to second floors climbing up from shade-tree yards or garden plots—ours blooming in white lilies.

9:00 p.m. We ate supper at Le Plaza, a square, dark restaurant on Rue St.-Hubert, long shutter/doors thrown open to the night air. The heat and humidity this far north has come as something of a shock.

Wednesday, July 6, 2011

6:00 p.m. Off this morning, the Orange Line from Beaubien Metro Station to Peel Station on the Green Line, the underground clean and efficient. From Peel, we walked over to Dorchester Square for a double-decker hop-on/hop-off city tour with Grey Lines. I'm not overly impressed with the city. The tour guide actually pointed out the Red Roses Flour Mill as a harbor attraction.

Our first stop, however, Notre Dame Basilica, came as a welcome respite from the day's rain. With an unremarkable exterior, the cathedral's interior breathes serenity—carved wooden pulpit, mosaic tiled columns, glass votive candles in ranks of red, green, white, blue, and gold, and a deep-blue ceiling of rose-window lights with sculpted gold-leaf stars inbetween.

The next several stops swept us past a shopping area, the Montreal Casino, and the Science Museum in the harbor. Only when we crossed the mighty St. Lawrence to one of the river islands, could I see the dome of Biosphere and the tattered blocks of Habitat for Humanity, both unchanged from my first Montreal visit for the *Canadian Centennial Exposition* [*Expo '67*].

We all declined to trek up the legion of cement steps to the stunning St. Joseph's Oratory. I'd visited with Dan years ago, in searing winter cold, impressed by the stunning interior.

Our final stop, the summit of Mount Royal, comprised a rich expanse of forest paths and small meadows. We stopped for tea and sandwiches at Le Café Smith on Chemin Remembrance. On backtracking down the mountain, our bus idled at an overlook with vistas of the sprawling city, the grey St. Lawrence a thin line on the horizon.

Descriptive commentaries posed a significant challenge throughout the tour. Our second guide, an elderly fellow who remained seated below, lost his voice to a faulty microphone. His narration dwindled to the garbled adult *wah, wah, wah* of a Peanuts cartoon, a muffled "Saint Laurent" or "Québec" thrown in for good measure.

11:00 p.m. Michelle dropped by, having come from a Soundgarden show at the *Ottawa Bluesfest* and Debbi arrived an hour later. We passed the evening with wine and fettuccini in our back garden.

Thursday, July 7, 2011

In from crisp grilled sardines at Casa do Alentejo, a Portuguese restaurant on Rue St.-Hubert.

Friday, July 8, 2011

10:00 a.m. Julie and Debbi have set off to queue for general admission at the Hippodrome de Montréal. A group of fans have been assigning themselves numbers and passwords to avoid waiting in line the endless hours required for good GM pitch positioning. They're off for naps or lunch and expect to come back to their previous places in line. People with the dedication and staying power to wait in line, possibly for days, with only short loo breaks and meals, should not be tossed aside by someone returning from a four-hour nap. In retrospect, that lad in the elevator in Denver must have been a member of this group.

We wandered through a colorful market on Rue St. Hubert yesterday. Old ball-gowns hung about like theatre costumes, as though a '50s warehouse had been upended.

Sunday, July 10, 2011

11:20 a.m. Settled in on our roomy Via Rail Canada coach. We depart for Toronto in twenty minutes, a five-hour ride. I'll write up the Montreal shows while I have the time.

On the first night, Sue and I headed for the venue at five-thirty—Beaubien Metro Station to Namur. The English are well known for a serious tea addiction. They'll "kill" for a cup of tea. Or as Sue would put it, she'd "murder a cuppa." She feels much the same about a cigarette. "I could murder a fag," she told me on the metro, instantly grasping that she was in the wrong country for such an expression!

Julie and Debbi managed the inner circle on Edge's side, and Sue and I found a fine position by the railing, just outside the Red Zone on Adam's side. The layout and the organization of the venue both proved dismal, slap-dash affairs. The worst in all my many years of touring.

After a breezy ten-minute walk from the metro to the venue, things went rapidly downhill, but for the concert. The Claw, too big for Montreal's Olympic Stadium, required that the lads pony up four-million dollars for a temporary stadium at the Hippodrome, the site of the old Blue Bonnets racetrack.

Vendors sold merchandise, food, and drinks on an acreage dotted with white peaked tents like a medieval tournament. The authorities would later claim that the delay in opening the show rested with "late comers," but clearly the root-cause lay with the lack of any orderly entrance system. "Fan Jam" signs sprinkled about the stadium took on a whole new meaning. Eventually though, we made our way to the metal scaffolding steps and benches that made up the grandstands.

Here's the set-list: Even Better Than the Real Thing; The Fly; Mysterious Ways/Arms Around the World; End of the World/Where Have All the Flowers Gone; I Will Follow; Get on Your Boots; Still Haven't Found/Promised Land; Stay; Beautiful Day/Space Oddity; Elevation; Pride; Miss Sarajevo; Zooropa; City of Blinding Lights; Vertigo; Crazy/Discotheque/Psycho Killer/Life During Wartime; Sunday Bloody Sunday; Scarlet; Walk On/Never Walk Alone// One/Will You Still Love Me Tomorrow; Streets//Hold Me Thrill Me; With or Without You; Moment of Surrender; Rain

Interpol, the opening band, played a twenty-five minute set, the spitting image of Dan's internist on drums. Their songs all blended together to me, each finishing with a squeal of feedback.

U2 arrived onstage at twenty minutes after nine, and after the first few tunes, with their attendant exertion, a worn Bono asked for a couple of minutes to catch his breath. By way of band intros, he brought up the royal tour [The UK's Prince William and Lady Kate were then in Canada]. The band was on a royal tour of its own, Bono said. Larry was Bonnie Prince William, Adam, Kate Winslett, Edge, the Prince of Wales. And he, Bono, was the "chien royal . . . corgis, you know." Not many in the predominantly French-Canadian crowd grasped what he was on about.

"Hello Montreal," Mark Kelly called out from the space station for Beautiful Day and ended with Bowie's "tell my wife I love her very much, she knows." End of the World closed with Bono on the bridge on Adam's side, and when he sang Where Have all the Flowers Gone, Bono tossed roses into the audience. Still Haven't Found included Bruce Springsteen's Promised Land, and Miss Sarajevo was stunning. Rejoice, from Scarlet, Walk On with Amnesty volunteers and their lanterns, and Streets, all produced a remarkable finish to the main set.

McPhisto/Mirror Ball Man careened in for an encore, swinging on his oversized red microphone for Hold Me Thrill Me. For With or Without You, The Singer is drawn toward some recognition of normality, and he's one of us again. A crew member bolted onstage to hang up Bono's jacket, and earned himself a big bear hug.

Throughout this show, Bono had taken repeated stabs at a rather hit-and-miss French, on-screen translations always unintentionally amusing. Quite confident in his delivery of "Merci, Montréal," he reiterated that phrase often. And "Viva la difference, viva Québec," ended the night.

Thunderstorms predicted for the afternoon and evening, had thrown down the odd drop of rain for With or Without You. As Moment of Surrender revved up, the skies opened and rods of rain slashed down. "Rain, we don't mind," Bono sang, and I'm sure he didn't, as he retreated to cozy backstage comfort, laughing as he moved down the back staircase.

For the rest of us, high winds blew sheets of rain horizontally. Umbrellas inverted, and Sue and I struggled mightily with the thin blue plastic ponchos we'd scarfed up on our bus tour. Eighty-thousand people, thoroughly soaked, half from the floor, half from the stands, oozed through the storm, inching toward buses and metro stations lit up by recurrent shocks of lightning.

At one point, with neither security nor guiding barriers, we caught a scream of whistles, and a cadre of policemen on bicycles parted the crowd behind us. At last, we thought . . . the crushing masses approaching Namur Station—that glowing glob of light in the rain-blurred distance—would be apportioned for easier entry.

But no. The officers defined a pathway through which an ambulance silently passed—a band runner?—and then they peddled off into the raging night.

A hundred feet ahead, two open doors pinpointed the entrance to Namur, one side blocked by a Metro guard. Two hours later, we seeped into the station and descended to the platform, where our soggy return tickets were duly checked. This may have prevented the seething mob from surging in front of an oncoming train.

By the time we reached Beaubien at 2:00 a.m., the rain had stopped. Pizza, champagne, and a U2 Quiz, and we were to bed by five-thirty, just as the sky lightened to dawn-blue.

12:55 p.m. After whipping through flat farmland alongside the St. Lawrence, we're idled in Cornwall, Ontario. I've a dismal cup of tea from the trolley.

We came in from last night's second Montreal gig at two o'clock this morning, and were off to the train station by ten, after a light breakfast.

2:40 p.m. Kingston. Blue skies. High, thin clouds.

Debbi and Sue joined Michelle at the St. James Hotel early yesterday afternoon. Edge came out to meet and greet and sign autographs. He has a twitter account and has been posting tour photos. One from the hotel is already up, Sue, Debbi, and Michelle front and center.

Close to six-thirty last night, Julie and I headed off for the second U2 show. Beaubien Station to Namur, a half-hour to forty-five minutes. Organization non-existent, we crawled along in the single zigzag entrance queue for well over an hour. We were twenty feet from the next zig. We were fifteen from the next zag. We were ten; we were five. Our seats, on benches in the high metal-scaffolding stands on Adam's side, felt disconcerting at first, swaying and shuddering as they did.

3:15 p.m. Wide green pastures, fields of hay and corn, brushy woods and small farms now, dust-blue chicory and Queen Anne's lace in bloom along the tracks, Lake Ontario silvery-white to the left.

Streamed live by *U2.com*, second Montreal was better than the first. My French being tentative, I welcomed Bono's assertion that he would be "speaking more English." Québécois could avoid hearing him "mangle (their) beautiful language."

Here's the set-list: Better Than the Real Thing; The Fly; Mysterious Ways; End of the World/ Where Have All the Flowers Gone; Out of Control; Boots; All I Want is You; Stuck in a Moment;

Beautiful Day/Space Oddity; Elevation; New Year's Day; Miss Sarajevo; Zooropa; Blinding Lights; Vertigo/Teenage Kicks; Crazy; Discotheque; Please/Life During Wartime/Psycho Killer; Sunday Bloody Sunday; Scarlet; Walk On//One/Hallelujah; Streets// Ultraviolet; With or Without You.

Band intros came with Out of Control, U2's first single. With the tour nearly over, what were they going to do? Bono asked. Joining a band had been like running away with the circus. "Maybe we need to find another circus." Larry could be . . . the sword-swallower? The fire eater? The world's strongest man? Larry chose lion tamer. Adam would be the bearded lady. Edge . . . the trapeze artist? The high-wire act? Edge elected to be the knife-thrower, and directed his aim at Bono, who claimed the role of clown.

One of the high-points of this show came with Boots, when a Sikh man, onstage with Bono, blasted out "let me in the sound." An acoustic Stuck in a Moment for Michael Hutchence, concluded with "Don't lose your faith in a crowd," a phrase with two very distinct meanings, depending on the emphasis. For Elevation, Paco, a little boy of about five, did a lot of expert mimicking of Bono, who hoisted him up on his shoulder.

For the home-town boy, Leonard Cohen, One had a snatch of Hallelujah, and With or Without You finished with 'Stars'. [We'll shine like stars in the summer night. We'll shine like stars in the winter night. One heart, one hope, one love.] Emotional, intimate, celebratory, and so communicative in magical 'best of U2' fashion, this show slipped into a club show in the confines of a huge stadium.

Vacating the venue proved much easier without the rain, though police and security did little more than dally about in little pods. We waited in the stands and then the grass, people watching as the crowd flowed past like a stream of lava. Namur Station in short order, and MacDonald's on Beaubien before bed.

10:10 p.m. Hallelujah! Dan's here!

Monday, July 11, 2011
Sitting at the lake end of Pier 4, off Queen's Quay West, on a

hot and muggy day. We look out on Toronto Island. To our right the Police Basin's eight docking-slots are all occupied, one of them holding *The Yankee Lady*, a ferry to the island. On the left, *The Perfect Alibi* yacht lies at anchor. Sail boats ply the calm waters of the lake, and closer in, private yachts fill Marina Basin—*Blissful, Trophy, Amore, Smitten, Ruffian,* and the *Wayward Sun.*

Quarter to five yesterday, our train pulled into Union Station, and Sue, Debbi, and Julie went off to the Hotel Novotel. Dan and I are staying at the Radisson Admiral Toronto Harbourfront.

5:00 p.m. We all met for lunch at the Radisson's fifth floor Watermark Restaurant—greens with strawberries, candied pecans, and goat cheese—and then we wandered over to the venue [Rogers Centre], a ten minute walk.

The backstage entrance lay far below street level, and the only area possible to await sound-check arrival was lightly peopled with fans harassed by venue security, a pudgy fellow with greasy, spiked hair. Dan and I sauntered over to the Royal York Hotel instead. We've just come back to cool off before tonight's gig.

Tuesday, July 12, 2011

9:00 a.m. No one stopped when the band arrived yesterday, Sue said. "We got a wave," she wrote. "He looked good." Or in text-speak, "gt wav he lukd gud."

Dan and I moseyed over to Rogers Centre at seven-thirty, the band onstage about nine. With the stadium roof retracted, The Claw stood in front of a sort of half-shell, the underbelly all scaffolding and metal stairs. The outer rim of the building remained covered, though forecasted thunderstorms never materialized.

Interpol still hammered away as we took our seats. No lines anywhere, in stark contrast to Montreal. Straight in at Gate 11 and into our seats, two sections from the front, on Edge's side, row five. We overlooked a spread of cramped GA floor space. The entire crowd reached sixty-thousand.

Here's the set-list: Better Than the Real Thing; The Fly; Mysterious Ways/Someone Somewhere in Summer Time; End of the World; Anthem; I Will Follow; Boots; Still Haven't Found; Stay; Beautiful Day; Elevation; Pride; Miss Sarajevo; Zooropa; City of Blinding Lights; Vertigo; Crazy/Discotheque; Sunday Bloody Sunday; Scarlet (Rejoice); Walk On//One/Will You Still Love me Tomorrow; Streets//Hold Me Thrill Me; With or Without You; Moment of Surrender.

Band intros mirrored Salt Lake City's—Adam's fatherhood, Larry's movie, Edge's spider bite. Zooropa still falls flat to me, though the on-screen questions resolve to "the more you see, the less you know," which appropriately introduces City of Blinding Lights.

The CN Tower soared opposite us, wild with a rainbow of color streaming up and down the concrete column, pods lit up in sequence. Moreover, a waxing gibbous moon, poised just out of sight behind the stadium—a moon "smiling down on us," Bono said—flashed up on-screen a time or two.

A crap crowd though. Bono fought hard to get their attention, to keep them involved—and got so little in return. At one point, where he usually stops singing altogether and lets the audience carry on, only a small percentage did.

Streets brought down the house, as did McPhisto's "showtime" Hold Me Thrill Me. On one of the bridges, making his way to the stage, Bono planted a Canadian flag into the back of his trousers. "Canada shining out his backside," he said.

A compelling moment came for me near the very end. I was swaying with the rhythm of Moment of Surrender. Back and forth. Back and forth. Fans in the few rows ahead had already left, the floor streaming out. I zeroed in on the screens, the sets, the lights, the music, always aware that this could be my last ever live U2 show.

Bono stood directly opposite, backlit, looking our way—and we were swaying exactly in unison. Back and forth. Back and forth. A trifling, but deeply personal moment for me. The perfect note on which to end my *360 Tour*. Twenty-four years a fan. Eighty-one concerts.

12:40 p.m. After breakfast this morning, we cruised Toronto

Island on the *Harbour Star*. Fourteen islands comprise the grouping, a welcome retreat for such a metropolis, comparable to Central Park in New York City or the Forest Preserves in Chicago. Ducks and geese, cormorants and swans glided on the deep olive-green water or rested in shoreline grasses under summer trees. Rogers Centre and the CN Tower, the focal point of the city, dominated the skyline.

Back on shore, I waited while Dan had a quick gander at the Power Plant Gallery. I'd stepped in to a rough concrete slab taking up the floor of one room and a handle-less *Freed Door* braced against the wall of another. *Suitcase with Undershirt* was exactly that.

Wednesday, July 13, 2011

Last night, we ate, fittingly, at the 360 Restaurant in the CN Tower. The restaurant revolves 360 degrees every seventy-two minutes. The city darkened below against a vermillion sunset, and lights popped out everywhere, while the Full Buck Moon burnished the lake with silver. We took in the glass-bottomed viewing platform a couple floors down, and did a windblown stint on the outdoor deck.

2:00 p.m. At Gate 164 in Toronto International for a flight to Chicago and on home to Tucson. My *360* ends here!

Wednesday, August 3, 2011

U2 wrapped up their *360 Tour* in Moncton, New Brunswick on Saturday night with 40, a warm, intimate rendition that I watched in black-and-white on *YouTube*. The perfect defense for my long-time love of this remarkable band.

Sue has written this of the *360* experience on her blog:

So U2's *360 Tour* is over. For me it's been a memorable three summers in the UK, Ireland, France, Germany, and Canada. Great times with friends, amazing sights seen, fab food eaten, copious amounts of wine and champagne drunk, lots of laughs had. Shows that were all good, but a few that had that special U2 magic that touched me deep inside and created an intimacy that made a stadium like a small club.

Twenty-eight years of being a fan have seen all kinds of changes in my life, but the band's music has always been there, often in the background, but there. My views on U2 have varied too, and sometimes I've been close to divorcing them! They may or may not be past their glory days of musical creativity, but they are still a damn sight better than most and have been for thirty-four years. Bono has said, "Live is where we live." And there is no doubt in my mind that is true. Live, they are simply brilliant. And I'm not talking about the massive Claw this time round. As lovely as the effects were, the set doesn't really matter to me. I'm talking about them as musicians, performers, and friends. There is something about them playing live that is totally captivating—and very hard to put into words because it's something you feel, a spirituality. I'm not being very articulate here, but other fans will know what I mean, right?

Here's a video of the last song, 40, from the last show of this tour in Moncton, Canada. I'm not ashamed to say it made me cry, and it was the perfect ending to the tour. God willing (well, both the band and long-time fans like me are getting on a bit now!) in a little while we'll be on the road again.

Thursday, September 8, 2011

The lads in town tonight to open the *Toronto International Film Festival* with their *Achtung Baby* documentary *Down from the Sky*. We're at the cottage another week [Conestoga River, Ontario, Canada], so I toyed with the idea of going down. But the chaos and the crowds brought me to my senses.

Monday, October 17, 2011

Saturday night, I watched the *Clinton Foundation's* 10th Anniversary celebration, streamed on *Yahoo* from the Hollywood Bowl. Actually, I sat by the fire and checked for updates on the computer in my office, finding the program long and fairly boring, musically speaking, many acts all spectacle, though Lady Gaga impressed.

After three hours or so, President Clinton and Chelsea came onstage and I thought Bono and Edge would perhaps not perform after all. And then, all at once, there they were. They gave us seven tunes—Desire, Still Haven't Found What I'm Looking For, A Man and a Woman, Sunday Bloody Sunday, Staring at the Sun, One, and Miss Sarajevo.

Skittish at the start, Bono settled down in time. The band was "old school," he said. "Hope you like our new direction." Mostly acoustic, that worked for me, though Bono would be hard-pressed to tolerate such a classic sound long-term. He and Edge were two of a foursome, he said. "The tall skinny guys, the good-looking ones."

I loved the new version of A Man and A Woman, and for Sunday Bloody Sunday, Bono coaxed a little girl to the stage, and then praised Hillary Clinton for all she's done in her capacity as Secretary of State. Staring at the Sun brought brief remarks about Bill Clinton's status in Ireland as the most beloved US president since JFK. Bono spent a good deal of time on a ramp that veered toward the President and his family, extolling the *Clinton Foundation*'s many achievements in making our world a better place.

"This next song wasn't a hit either," Bono said on opening One. Cell-phones glowed all around. He extended the song with "Love and sex and faith and fear, and all the things that keep us here," and finished with "Jessie, that was for you."

Being in a band was like working on an oil rig, he said. No women. And so Edge brought out a women's string section. Having left the stage, Bono and Edge returned with President Clinton, a tall, tall man, striding out as though escorting his two adolescent sons. The Hollywood Bowl would "pull the plug" on the festivities in ten minutes, Clinton announced. And so, after he'd commended Bono for *DATA* and *One*, Edge for *Music Rising*, Bono and Edge performed a breath-taking Miss Sarajevo finale.

Tuesday, October 18, 2011

In *Down from the Sky*, Edge says he recognized "from the word go" that Bono was a big idea man, and that as a band, they could go anywhere "with this guy out front."

In an interview from Toronto, Bono ponders U2's contemporary relevance.

Sunday, November 6, 2011

The Reverend Harold Camping, of 'end of the world' notoriety has retired. Three times he'd divined the end times. And nothing to show for it. Three strikes and you're out.

Friday, November 25, 2011

Loved *Down from the Sky*. *Achtung Baby* was so clearly a reaction to *Rattle and Hum* criticism. The aim of *R and H* was to present the band as fans of American roots music, not in any way to assume a place in its chronology. But the music press chose to interpret this as egotism, and by so doing they warped the band into prima donnas.

For the band, the answer was to back away from the sound and images of *The Joshua Tree*'s expansive Americana and look homeward for something European, something industrial and dance-oriented. Finding that, Bono turned directly to the place from which the criticism had come and stared it down. The perfect foundation for The Fly and MacPhisto. So you think *we're* ego-maniacs? Well check this out. Here's Mirror-Ball-Man. Here's The Fly. Here's MacPhisto. Here's what ego-mania *really* looks like.

Bill Flanagan has explained *Achtung Baby* best, I think. "They escaped the corner in which they had painted themselves in the eighties by blowing up the house."

Monday, December 26, 2011

Bono out busking for charity on Christmas Eve again.

Friday, March 23, 2012

Finally, I have all of my reading caught up, including a *Q Magazine* Sue sent ages ago. In a special on *Achtung Baby*'s re-release, Bono says "I understand all the projectile vomiting aspects to shaking hands with politicians and having an interest in religion."

Monday, April 2, 2012

Twenty-five years of U2 fandom for me, my first concert being Phoenix, April 2, 1987, *The Joshua Tree Tour*, that album having been released March 9, 1987.

Thursday, April 19, 2012

On a visit to Jerusalem, Bono left this touching message in his hotel room:

"In Jerusalem hope springs eternal. Hope is like a faithful dog, sometimes she runs ahead of me to check the future, to sniff it out, and then I call to her: Hope, Hope, come here, and she comes to me. I pet her, she eats out of my hand, and sometimes she stays behind, near some other hope maybe to sniff out whatever was. Then I call her my Despair. I call out to her. Here, my little Despair, come here, and she comes and snuggles up, and again I call her Hope."

The note was signed, "With great thanks for great room in great hotel in great city. Bono. Reading Amichai [Israeli poet] April 2012."

Thursday, May 31, 2012

Bono, with a group of "luminaries" at a reception for Queen Elizabeth's *Diamond Jubilee* in London's Royal Academy of Art, said to Her Majesty, "I want to take this opportunity to acknowledge the extraordinary magic that you made on your trip to Ireland last year. Did you have fun at all or was it all work?"

Tuesday, June 12, 2012

Bono accompanied Aung San Suu Kyi to Norway, where she picked up her 1991 *Nobel Peace Prize*. In Dublin, yesterday, he presented her with Amnesty International's *Ambassador of Conscience Award*. When he finally got to meet her in person after so many years of espousing her cause onstage and off, he was "star struck."

Sunday, September 16, 2012

Just crossed the Ambassador Bridge, Windsor to Detroit. Homeland Security was questioning vehicle occupants at random, and as Dan and I were both wearing U2 t-shirts, an officer asked if we'd been to the closing show in Moncton.

Sadly, no, we confessed.

He'd been there himself, he said. An "awesome show."

Monday, September 24, 2012

The Little Museum at St. Stephen's Green intends to open a

permanent U2 exhibit, the first for Dublin.

Sunday, November 18, 2012

Last week, Bono met with President Obama and Vice-president Biden. Such a relief for Obama to have been re-elected. The Mormatron 2000 [Mitt Romney] would have been detrimental to the country in many ways.

Wednesday, November 28, 2012

The host of an English TV program Sharon watches elicits stories from the audience as part of the show. One fellow and his girlfriend, both U2 fans, had recently been in a Dublin pub where Bono was dining with a friend. Not wanting to disturb his meal, when Bono stepped out to the loo, they asked the friend if he'd signal them if autographs and photos would be permitted.

Bono returned and the friend beckoned them over. Photos and autographs later, Bono and friend departed. On paying their bill, the young couple was chuffed to find that their ticket had been "taken care of." By Bono? they asked. "No," the publican answered. "By Bruce Springsteen."

December 14, 2012

Some berserk young man opened fire with an automatic weapon at Sandy Hook Elementary School in Newtown, Connecticut, killing twenty children and six adults.

What more could it possibly take to unify the country behind expanded gun-control legislation?

Thursday, January 3, 2013

Bono busking for charity on Christmas Eve again. Bless him.

Saturday, January 19, 2013

Jason Bond, a biologist at Auburn University [Alabama,] has discovered thirty-three new species of trapdoor spiders, three of them in Joshua Tree National Monument. Two he named for Native American tribes, the third he christened *A. bonoi*, for Bono.

Previous such spiders had honored Angelina Jolie, President Obama, Stephen Colbert, and Neil Young.

Tuesday, January 22, 2013

Inauguration Day and MLK Day rolled into one. So fitting for Obama's re-election as our first African-American president. His address cited everything we could be as a nation if the forces of regression and intolerance—today's Republican Party—would either step up or step aside.

Saturday, February 9, 2013

My *Down from the Sky* finally arrived, filled with impressive photography. Inside, Larry describes U2's creative process as "If it ain't broke, break it."

Wondering now what they'll see fit to break next.

4.

The iNNOCENCE + eEXPERIENCE Tour
(i/e Tour Part 1)

"The older the fiddle, the sweeter the tune"
– An Old Irish Proverb

February 17, 2013

In a recent *Hot Press* interview with Adam, he says, "We very much want to have a record out by the end of this year. September, October, November, that kind of time . . . . It feels very liberating at the moment—anything goes . . . . To make the best record you can, you have to steer away from the ones you can make easily."

Wednesday, March 27, 2013

Bono delivered an informative talk on combatting extreme poverty at the *TED Conference* on the West Coast. He was—as always—articulate, knowledgeable, and funny. [*TED* is a non-profit started up in 1984 to bring together people in *t*echnology, *e*ntertainment, and *d*esign. It has since expanded to include science, business, and global issues.]

Monday, April 22, 2013

We just listened to *U22* for the run over to the cabin [Chiricahua Mountains, Arizona]. Live is where the band lives, as this compilation proves. I nearly drove off the road when Bad from Rome, October 2010, came up.

Friday, May 10, 2013

In Morrison [Colorado] this afternoon, visiting Dinosaur Ridge.

Just out of town, the sandstone rise of Red Rocks Amphitheatre [the site of U2's *Under a Blood Red Sky*] juts dramatically above the

Rooney Valley floor, from a pastoral setting of rolling short-grass hills and rocky outcrops. Red Rocks has long been sacred to the areas Ute tribes.

Tuesday, May 23, 2013

Charlie Rose interviewed Bono earlier this month. "The problems of the world are the problems of the human spirit," Bono said. "And the problems of the human spirit are the problems of the human heart . . . The songs come out of that . . . those times when joy is an act of defiance."

"It's what you haven't got that makes you Irish . . . it means you go out to discover and explore."

Artists like Bob Dylan, John Lennon, and Bob Marley showed him that "the world outside my window was not fixed."

"I try to put into words what the melody is saying," he said. "Songs are a preoccupation of your spirit . . . . Songs have been arriving lately . . . I've been drilling down into the mine [to find] the difference between gold and coal. What I'm looking for is ten reasons to exist."

Thursday, May 30, 2013

U2 at work on the new album with Danger Mouse [Brian Joseph Burton] at Electric Lady Studio in New York City.

Friday, June 14, 2013

A video shoot on Electric Lady Studio's rooftop earlier this month, an acoustic Sunday Bloody Sunday, was destined for a protest-song collection ahead of the upcoming G8 summit in Northern Ireland.

Saturday, June 22, 2013

In *USA Today*, Bono expresses support for Tony Bennett's *Voices against Violence* campaign, aimed at encouraging "common-sense" gun laws. The campaign marks the six-month anniversary of the Newtown massacre.

Wednesday, July 17, 2013

Just passed the turnoff to Eastland [Texas]. A lush roll to the land here in Texas Hill Country, with Deer Run Ranch, Brack Ranch, Ranger Hill Ranch, 10 Sky Ranch, Wild Hill Ranch, La Loca Range Ranch. And then, forty miles west of Fort Worth, on #20—U2 Ranch.

Monday, July 22, 2013

Off to Northwood on #2. East, ten miles, to Bono [Ohio] on Lake Erie, a neat little village of scattered clapboard houses surrounding the whitewashed Bono Baptist Church.

Declining the Bono Tavern's Monday Special—the Bono Burger—we snacked instead on deep-fried zucchini, mushrooms, cauliflower, and onions, washed down with a Pennsylvania brew called Yuengling. We all purchased new t-shirts too—"Get Roasted!!! at the Bono Tavern."

According to the publican, the village, originally called Shepherdsville, had been rechristened in honor of a Native American named Bunno, a name subsequently misspelled. Rather incredulously, she also claimed never to have heard of either U2 or Bono.

Monday, September 2, 2013

On Irish *Newstalk FM*, Bono spoke about the band's upcoming album. "I think we're nearly there and once we're there we'll know it," he said. "I'd like to think that next year, there'll be a U2 release . . . . It's a very different, very fresh sound, and some beautiful songs . . . big hooks."

Sunday, September 29, 2013

Bono spoke about the new album on Dave Letterman's late night talk show. "You know Quincy Jones said to me 'Bono, you've got to wait for God to walk through the room.' And I said 'Q, why is God so unreliable in the music department?' And he said 'Just to teach you to wait.'

"So we're waiting. . . . We have a deal with our audience. They give us a great life, and they expect us to be great, and that's lucky. As you get better you get very good and very good is kind of the enemy of great. You can mistake it for great. People don't get excited about us being very good . . . .We have to make a great U2 album, and they don't care about waiting, as long as it's great."

Sunday, October 6, 2013

We're in our cozy flat in Smithfield Tower [Smithfield Market, Dublin] on a sunny blue day, the area bustling and well-worn. We hopped the Luas to the Dart, and then went on to Killiney Beach, where inky waves pounded the shingled shore. Over to Dalkey's Finnegan's Pub then, where Bono had recently dined with Michelle Obama.

Tuesday, October 8, 2013

U2's new album will be released in February or March of next year, a tour in May.

Thursday, October 10, 2013

12:40 a.m. Down from the penthouse for dinner in Cleaver East, the Tea Room's replacement at the Clarence Hotel. Tapas all the rage. I rather missed the Tea Room's beef and lamb. "A balanced diet is a glass of wine in each hand," one server's t-shirt read.

Declan crossed paths with Joe O'Herlihy in a Dublin hardware store a short time back. Surprised to hear his name, Joe struggled to recollect exactly how he 'knew' Declan, who, seizing the moment, asked after the band. With "a problem" at HQ, they'd gone on to record outside the city, Joe said.

9:25 p.m. Noonish, we returned to Smithfield from the Clarence, our social station, once again, descending with the penthouse elevator.

Thursday, Octobert 17, 2013

A trailer for the upcoming biopic *Mandela* introduced a compelling U2 tune called Ordinary Love.

Saturday, November 16, 2013

Paul McGuinness, U2 manager since 1978, has sold Principle Management to Live Nation, Guy Oseary taking Paul's place. "As I approach the musically relevant age of 64," McGuinness said in the *New York Times*, "I have resolved to take a less hands-on role as the band embark on the next cycle of their extraordinary career."

Wednesday, November 6, 2013

In the wind-up to Bono's *Rolling Stone* tribute to the late Lou Reed, he writes,

"This is how I will remember him, a still figure in the eye of a metallic hurricane, an artist pulling strange shapes out of the formless void that is pop culture, a songwriter pulling melodies out of the dissonance of what Yeats called 'this filthy modern tide' and, yes, pop's truly great poker face—with so much comedy dancing around those piercing eyes. The universe is not laughing today."

Thursday, December 26, 2013

Bono busking on Christmas Eve for the Simon Community, a Dublin charity for the homeless.

Tuesday, December 31, 2013

10:00 p.m. Awaiting the midnight chiming of the bells of Christchurch Cathedral [Dublin]. "I believe in the bells of Christchurch ringing through this land."

Earlier today, before the New Year's Eve Light Parade on Grafton Street, we wandered over to St. Stephen's Green and The Little Museum of Dublin, which opened in October of 2011.

The collection of items, donated by locals, covers three floors in an old Georgian townhouse. A Christmas tree brightened the second floor, where an eclectic mix of artifacts illustrated Irish history. Among these was a letter to Samuel Beckett written by a twelve-year-old boy as part of a school project which required students to reach out to someone who'd previously lived in their homes.

"You used to live in my bedroom," the boy wrote. "Can you tell me a little about yourself?"

Becket responded with a postcard on which he detailed where he'd gone to school and where his own room had been in the shared home, closing with, "Yours antiquatedly, Sam Becket."

An excellent one-room U2 exhibit—the first and only in Dublin—included a mock Trabant, a rather creepy McPhisto statue, and Paul McGuinness' cut-crystal Joshua tree, the only one to survive intact from the *Freedom of the City* ceremony.

Friday, January 3, 2014

In the Manchester airport, awaiting a flight to Reykjavik [Iceland].

Our bus tour of Dublin yesterday swept us past the Guinness Storehouse, the Kilmainham Gaol, Phoenix Park, the Writers Museum, and the Charles Stewart Parnell Monument on O'Connell Street. The monument's plaque reads, "No man has a right to fix the boundary to the march of a nation. To say to his country thus far shall thou go and no further. We have never attempted to fix the ne plus ultra to the progress of Ireland's nation hood and we never shall."

At Killiney Beach yesterday, we amassed over a dozen 'holey' stones, from which we culled five.

Sunday, January 26, 2014

Jay Leno retires from *The Tonight Show* next month. The first musical guest of his replacement—Jimmy Fallon—will be U2, on February 17.

Saturday, February 1, 2014

In partnership with the Bank of America, Bono's *RED CAMPAIGN* will premiere a new U2 tune—Invisible—at the Super Bowl, making it free on *iTunes* for twenty-four hours beginning at six o'clock tomorrow night. BofA will then donate a dollar per download, up to two-million, to the charity.

Monday, February 3, 2014

I found U2's Invisible uplifting and universal.

Sunday, February 16, 2014

Finally had a look at Invisible's black-and-white video. The band plays straight-ahead rock 'n' roll in a hangar at the Santa Monica Airport. No gimmicks. No razzle-dazzle.

Tuesday, February 18, 2014

Sundown, on a cold night in New York City, on the observation deck of the GE Building, U2 played Invisible and an acoustic version of Ordinary Love on *The Tonight Show* with Jimmy Fallon. Urban lights sparkled all around them, the audience chosen from registered NYC *U2.com* members. Adam had his Ralph Lauren on—the hair, the scarf.

The new album will be released in June.

Saturday, March 1, 2014

Woke up to a gentle rain this morning. Overcast and breezy now. Winter has been brutal back east. Travel agents have been inundated with "get-me-out-of-here" pleas.

U2 will offer up their *Mandela* contribution, Ordinary Love, at the *Academy Awards* tomorrow night. In January, the song won a *Golden Globe* for Best Original Song, the same award it's up for at the Oscars.

Invisible's lyrics grew out of the band's first venture away from home, Bono has said, when, broke and alone, they rolled into London's Euston Station for the first time.

I had something of the same liberating experience when I first left Canada for Arizona—all the promise and possibility of moving beyond other people's expectations. "I'm more than you know, more than you see here, more than you let me be."

Or in Bono's case, "I am not my father's son."

Sunday, March 16, 2014

A soft spring day, the daffodils done, but lantana, primrose, and verbena all in vibrant bloom.

U2 won Best Original Song at the *Golden Globes*, performed on *The Tonight Show* and at the *Academy Awards*. They featured Invisible in a Super Bowl ad and made the cover of *The Hollywood Reporter*. *Billboard Magazine* also posted an article on the upcoming album, still unfinished, as per Danger Mouse.

Ryan Tedder and Paul Epworth, who produced Adele's best-selling *21*, have been roped in as producers for U2's new album. Tedder once opened for U2 with his band, One Republic, whose "spiritually-minded" single, Counting Stars, synced with Bono's thoughts on song-writing.

"I feel a responsibility to actually write and sing about things that have a level of human gravity to them," Bono told Tedder. A "source close to the project," says "that magic that the band always seems to capture . . . . they have yet to capture it."

Way back in 2011, at the *Toronto Film Festival*, Bono said that he felt the band was "really close to the edge of relevance . . . . There's a giant chasm between the very good and the great. And U2 right now is in danger of surrendering to the very good."

They're obviously still struggling. In this February's issue of *The Hollywood Reporter*, he added that "to be relevant is a lot harder than to be successful."

Thursday, May 15, 2014

Had a quick listen to Adam on the *Ray Foley Show* [*Dublin Radio*]. He anticipates an album wrap-up by the end of summer, a tour next year. As a patron of *Walk in My Shoes*, a mental health group that works with young people, he spoke about depression and suicide in the "under-twenty-five crowd," which U2 consider their audience. Much as the band might prefer it, I'm not sure that demographic is terribly accurate anymore.

Wednesday, May 28, 2014

Devastating news from Florida. One of our Zoo Crew—Lyn McCann, a life-long U2 fan—died suddenly yesterday! Lyn struggled all her life with challenging health issues, and yet she stayed focused and positive. Bono always had a soft spot for her.

Tuesday, August 12, 2014

U2 in Nice [France], working on a music video, a single from the new album to be released in September.

Wednesday, August 20, 2014

Shared a shrimp, crayfish, and salmon salad with olive-studded bread at The Edge Restaurant [Oslo, Norway], their audio system playing an instrumental Bad.

Wednesday, September 10, 2014

Yesterday, with all of five minutes' notice, Apple dropped U2's new album, *Songs of Innocence*, free to *iTunes* subscribers. I'll have a proper listen when we're back home from Canada.

Monday, September 15, 2014

Two full days of catch-up.

I had a go at *Songs of Innocence* and I love it! Countless complaints swirling around about the release. But for heaven's sake, if you don't want it, just delete it!

Friday, September 19, 2014

Out of five-hundred-million *iTunes* users, thirty-three-million downloaded the new U2 album. The numbers still growing. In retrospect, Apple should perhaps have emailed subscribers first, with an option to download. But still—it's much ado about nothing.

Monday, September 22, 2014

Edge is in negotiations for a five-mansion compound in Malibu, overlooking the Pacific. Objections from neighbors and environmentalists have blossomed, but I'm guessing it's a done deal.

Saturday, September 27, 2014

A U2 photo-shoot for *Rolling Stone Magazine* swept up a woman out walking her dogs. Bono gathered in the pooches and they became part of the session's 'plot'.

Songs of Experience, a follow-up to *Songs of Innocence* will be released "in twelve to eighteen months," on an "anti-pirating format still in development."

Sunday, September 28, 2014

"When I was five years old, my mother told me that happiness was the key to life. When I went to school, they asked me what I wanted to be when I grew up. I wrote down 'happy'. They told me I didn't understand the assignment, and I told them they didn't understand life." – John Lennon

Tuesday, September 30, 2014

Finished up a *Songs of Innocence* review.

SONGS OF INNOCENCE

Cyberspace moves at the speed of light, so U2's new album

release, *Songs of Innocence*, is already old news. Nevertheless, I thought I'd post a review of this amazing collection.

It would appear that U2 jettisoned their planned *Songs from the Ascent* compilation in favor of *Songs of Innocence*, their thirteenth studio album. In reality, though, they seem to be one and the same. The focus of the ascent has perhaps changed, along with the album's title, which was taken from a book of William Blake poetry. These are not songs inspired by a pilgrim's ascent to Jerusalem. But they're "songs from the ascent" all the same. "We're pilgrims on our way," Bono sings in the opening track.

I loved this album from the start, with its blissfully rocked-out energy and it's deeply personal lyrics—a cohesive collection touching on the early days of one of rock music's most iconic bands as it rose from obscurity to fame and fortune. Everything I've always loved about U2 is here—the power, the passion, the voice, the vision, the words, the music. These are the ideas, the events, the people, and the places that inspired, influenced, and gave shape to the formative years of U2's extraordinary career; an intimate story-telling of their innocent past as seen through the eyes of an experienced present. *Songs from the Ascent.*

THE MIRACLE (OF JOEY RAMONE) will be fabulous live, with its catchy lyrics and Edge's aggressive fuzz guitar. The chorus makes it a natural for a concert opening and it sets the stage for the band's ascent to a place where their "voices will be heard." They're pilgrims on their way.

In a literal sense, punk rock—personified by the Ramones—saved Bono's life after the devastating loss of his mother at an early age. Discovering punk rock was a miracle that woke him up to the possibility of making sense of the world through music. (Joey Ramone also showed him that it was ok to "sing like a girl"!)

EVERY BREAKING WAVE – A gorgeous, classic U2 song somewhat reminiscent of *The Joshua Tree*'s With or Without You, everything about this song, my album favorite, is beautiful, especially Edge's minimalist, lyrical guitar. Every Breaking Wave seems to address a decisive moment in Bono and Ali's relationship—the struggle engendered by committing yourself to a career path that might end in defeat.

Somewhere in our lives, all of us have probably played it safe, ending something before we began, out of fear of failure. But sometimes you just have to jump in and let yourself be swept off your feet. After all "drowning is no sin." Sometimes you have to take a chance. Just give it a try. Fittingly, **Every Breaking Wave** segues into **California (There is No End to Love),** which opens with breaking waves.

CALIFORNIA (THERE IS NO END TO LOVE) – **California** tells the story of the band's almost magical first trip to California, home of The Beach Boys, another of their musical influences. Beyond admiration of Brian Wilson's song-writing chops and the shared experience of unsupportive fathers, Bono seems to have used The Beach Boys' California to represent that moment when the lads allowed themselves to be swept off their feet and took a chance. ("Then we fell into the shining sea.")

I love the opening sound of waves and mission bells, but the Beach Boys vibe clicks in best for me only after the music kicks in. Jumping in seems to have taken the lads where they needed to be (though Zuma Beach—actually in Malibu—is about sixty-five miles south of Santa Barbara.) Leaving home often gives you the opportunity to find your own name. "I'm more than you know; more than you see here; more than you let me be." (**Invisible**)

SONG FOR SOMEONE – Once again, the chorus is something special in this one, along with Edge's acoustic guitar opening. It should be a 'small-stage' quiet-moment acoustic duet in concert. Bono has always addressed Divinity and faith in his song-writing and the subject continues to inspire.

Some great lyrics again. "If there is a light, you can't always see and there is a world, we can't always be. If there is a dark, that we shouldn't doubt, and there is a light, don't let it go out." And there's a lovely connection here to **Iris**, the song that follows, with that song's "I've got your light inside of me."

IRIS – A moving tribute to Bono's mother, Iris, who died when he was fourteen, Iris opens with angelic voices and Edge's haunting, shimmering guitar. It comes and goes as if from another world, like a visitation. Mothers may routinely tell their children, with a laugh, "You'll be the death of me." Death rarely follows and of course a sensitive child would naturally take that to heart, however mistaken.

Iris obviously had a profound effect on Bono's life with her encouragement, her gentle spirit, and her support. "She tells me I can do it all . . . . Free yourself to be yourself. If only you could see yourself." Iris' death was an equally powerful influence. "The ache in my heart is so much a part of who I am."

VOLCANO is yet another song that will really rock the house in concert. It's explosive, wild, and energetic, with some 'primitive' tribal chanting and some great bass guitar from Adam. Volcanic could certainly describe Bono's state of mind after the death of his mother. He's explosive, out in the wild, and something in him "wants to blow." Yet he still seems to be aware of his mother's light inside of him, the light that tells him he can do it all. "You were alone; but now you're not alone; you and I are rock and roll." He already seems to know where he needs to be and what he needs to do.

Musically, **Volcano** is connected to **Raised by Wolves**, which follows, by the similarity of the three notes of both choruses title words.

RAISED BY WOLVES – The immediate focus of **Raised by Wolves** is a car bomb in Dublin on May 17, 1974 in which thirty-three people were murdered.

The Troubles, the under-stated euphemism given to a broad period of sectarian violence in Ireland, has been an undercurrent and influence on the band for decades, beginning with **Sunday Bloody Sunday**, where they made their first political statement.

I'm a bit ambivalent about those sniffing sounds and, of course, equating the human penchant for cruelty and evil, uncivilized tribal vengeance and such to wolves is a definite slur against the latter.

But sectarian violence of the Troubles sort has to shake your faith. "I don't believe anymore," Bono sings here. "The worst things in the world are justified by belief." How true! And where is God in the real world, anyway? "If I open my eyes, you disappear." At any given time, large portions of our world seem to have been "raised by wolves." Daesch [ISIS] comes to mind.

Great lyrics and Larry's pounding drums build tension and emphasize how 'primitive' we humans often still are at our core.

CEDARWOOD ROAD – With Edge's driving guitar and Larry and Adam's pounding rhythms, along the lines of **I Will Follow** and **Electric Co.**, **Cedarwood Road** has an early U2 punk sound with a gutsier more aggressive fuzz guitar from Edge. Dedicated to Bono's lifelong friend, Guggi, it gives credit to friendship and how, after Iris' death, those Lypton Village connections of Bono's warzone teen years helped him handle living in a city where bombs went off on a fairly regular basis. Friendship "once it's won, is won."

It may be a long way from north-side Cedarwood Road to south-side Killiney Beach, but in his heart, Bono never left. "I'm still standing on that street."

SLEEP LIKE A BABY TONIGHT – My current least favorite tune from *Songs of Innocence*, **Sleep Like a Baby Tonight**, is saved for me by Edge's crackling, grungy fuzz guitar, which says just enough. I can't quite make this song out and Bono's falsetto, as usual, does nothing for me. Perhaps it's a comment on the influence of politics and power on the band's social conscience. People in the purple robes of power, whether political or ecclesiastical, often appear to go through their days as easily as a knife through butter, with only an outward show of caring, when in reality they're so sheltered from reality they only *dress* in the colors of forgiveness, never feeling anyone else's pain. (MacPhisto must have lived like this.)

THIS IS WHERE YOU CAN REACH ME NOW – The liner notes of *Songs of Innocence* describe Joe Strummer, lead singer and co-founder of the Clash, and to whom this song is dedicated, as a soldier who's weapon was his guitar, as a man who signed up for the cause, which would appear to be taking on political and world matters in his music. U2 followed suit and signed themselves up to music and all you can say with it, just as the Clash did.

The seagulls hark back to **California**; "You don't lose if you don't play," echoes **Every Breaking Waves**' "We end before we begin;" and **Iris**'s "Don't fear the world, it isn't there," becomes "If you won't let us in your world, your world just isn't there."

As supportive as Iris was, Bono's father seems to have been rather the opposite. Is Bob Hewson "the old man (who) knows that I never listen, so how could I have something to say?" Is he the "old man (who) knows how to cheat ambition?" You don't lose if you don't play.

THE TROUBLES, with another excellent chorus, some soft strings, and more great guitar work from Edge, comes as a fitting end to Part One of U2's story. Lykke Li's voice is the very sound of innocence. These are not the Troubles of Irish history, but the troubles in the trajectory of the band's career. There's a sudden realization that little by little they've lost control of the plot. Expectations are high, but they aren't U2's. Somehow they allowed someone else too much power. A friend made enemy. "Somebody stepped inside your soul . . . someone else was in control."

You obviously can't end U2's story with someone else in control. They learned a great deal from the myriad experiences and influences of their formative years. But I remember something that was written about post-*Joshua Tree* U2. When they'd painted themselves into a corner, the band's master-stroke was to blow the house up.

So there's so much more to come. I'm already looking forward to *Songs from the Ascent*, Part Two—*Songs of Experience.*

Wednesday, October 1, 2014

U2 will tour arenas next year, just as we'd speculated. A stadium tour in 2016.

Thursday, October 23, 2014

"Dublin in 1978 was a very primitive, grey, dull, miserable

place," Gavin Friday says in the *U2.com* subscriber gift, *U2 in Dublin 1978-1983* [Niall Stokes, Ed., Hot Press for *U2.com*; 2014]. Such a vivid impression of what it must have been like growing up then and there. Those dates mesh well with *Songs of Innocence*. You can appreciate the profound personal connection among those who struggled through such harsh times together. The Troubles must have furnished a unique and intense layer of time and place.

Bono and Edge performed acoustic renditions of The Miracle of Joey Ramone and Every Breaking wave on *The Late Late Show*. Bono confessed to waking up one morning questioning whether he'd done right by writing and releasing Iris. He remembered then that his mother had died in September, and uncertain of the exact date, he shot off a text to his brother Norman, who contacted an uncle in the know. The date was the very one on which Bono had experienced his ambivalence. He spoke of it as a 'visitation,' though he never used that word, rather he invoked the possibility that his mother's spirit was looking out for him.

Friday, December 5, 2014

Back on November 16, Bono suffered a "high energy" biking accident in Central Park [New York City.] Going downhill, he swerved to avoid a bicyclist who'd entered the path right in front of him. He flew over the handlebars, fracturing his left pinky, the orbital bone of his left eye, his left shoulder blade in four places, and his left elbow in eight. A shattered bone that had punched through his skin required a five-hour operation, the elbow, three metal plates and eighteen screws. He's returned to Dublin, and for a full recovery, has been instructed to remain immobile for at least two months, with therapy twice a day to keep the joints limber.

The *i-NNOCENCE + e-XPERIENCE Tour* (*i/e Tour*) schedule came out last Wednesday. Pre-sale tickets for *U2.com's* e-XPERIENCE group—us old fans—went on sale yesterday morning. I snagged two for the first Phoenix show in May. Hoping for Glasgow and London in the fall, as well.

U2 Minus 1—Edge, Larry, and Adam—played a surprise

concert in Times Square [NYC] for the *RED CAMPAIGN*. Chris Martin and Bruce Springsteen shared lead vocals. The band had never played live without Bono before, and Edge said it felt like they were cheating on him.

Saturday, December 13, 2014

Two London shows in October, with Declan, Sharon, and Jane. Glasgow with Sue and Debbi, and two Phoenix with Danielle.

Thursday, January 1, 2015

Just finished Bono's on-line *Little Book of a Big Year*, an A to Z of 2014, written as he recovers from his biking accident. He speaks eloquently of family, friends, fans, band members, capitalism, the internet, *One*, *Red*, Christianity, glaucoma, and more.

"The biggest breakthroughs are always in the way we see the world," was a favorite line.

Saturday, January 10, 2015

An Irish fellow arranged to propose to his girlfriend on Killiney Hill, last summer. Testing out a new camera, he filmed the entire event, including a chance run-in with Bono and Ali.

Marriage was "a grand madness," Bono told them. You jump off Killiney Hill and discover you can fly.

Thursday, April 16, 2015

U2 have set up in Vancouver for a month of rehearsals.

Wednesday, May 6, 2015

Dressed as aging hippies, U2 busked at the 42nd Street subway station in New York City.

Sunday, May 10, 2015

Four days to the *i/e Tour* opener in Vancouver, British Columbia. Friday night the band performed Beautiful Day and Song for Someone on *The Tonight Show*. They also put together a clever skit with Jimmy Fallon, touching on Bono's first post-accident bike ride.

Rumors of tour staging specifics indicate a fixed first half, a varied second, one short intermission, and no opening band. One walkway joins a large rectangular 'I' stage to a smaller round 'e' stage, a second walkway, between LED screens, suspended above the first.

Wednesday, May 13, 2015

Sad to say, Larry's dad died last Sunday.

Thursday, May 14, 2015

U2's *i/e Tour* opened at Rogers Arena in Vancouver.

Friday, May 15, 2015

BB King passed away yesterday, at the age of eighty-nine. "The Thrill is Gone."

Saturday, May 16, 2015

i/e in Vancouver went well, but for one small glitch. Edge, strolling the walkway between the two stages, stepped right off the ramp!

The second show featured When Love Comes to Town for BB King, and Bono joined in on the Internet antics about Edge's misstep. "Somebody said that The Edge had downloaded himself into the audience without asking permission," he said.

And in the encore—Bad!

Wednesday, May 20, 2015

U2 play San Jose tonight.

Thursday, May 21, 2015

In an eye-opening interview in *Rolling Stone* about *i/e* staging, Bono says that "The core behind the *iNNOCENCE + eXPERIENCE Tour* is this movement from 'them and us' to 'there is no them, only us.'"

Edge adds, "What we're doing with this show is following the contour of the circumference of the building and putting the speakers above the people. So you sit no further than maybe fifty feet from a set of speakers. Everything is delivering sound at the same time, so you don't have any of the time alignment issues of other speakers."

Sounds good, all the way around.

Off to Phoenix tomorrow for my first *i/e* show!

Friday, May 22, 2015

5:15 p.m. Here we are, Dan and I, at the Paloma Hotel on Jefferson and Central Avenue in Phoenix. US Airways Arena is almost across the street, a ten minute walk. The drive up from Tucson passed smoothly until we reached the city at four o'clock. Lots of jockeying for position and lane-hopping after that.

Saturday, May 23, 2015

Outside Starbucks at the Paloma on a gorgeous spring day. Danielle arrived at six-fifty last night and we were in our seats well before U2 opened at eight o'clock.

Here's the set-list: The Miracle of Joey Ramone (snippets of Send in the Clowns; I Can See for Miles; Anyway Anyhow); Vertigo (a Sex Pistols God Save the Queen snippet); I Will Follow; Iris; Cedarwood Road; Song for Someone; Sunday Bloody Sunday; Raised by Wolves (Psalm 23); End of the World// The Wanderer (Intermission); Invisible; Better than the Real Thing; Mysterious Ways (Young Americans snippet); Desire; In God's Country; The Sweetest Thing; Every Breaking Wave; Bullet the Blue Sky; Pride (The Hands that Built America snippet); Beautiful Day (Sargent Pepper's Lonely Heart Club Band snippet); Bad (snippet of Moment of Surrender); With or Without You// City of Blinding Lights; Where the Streets Have no Name (snippet of Mother and Child Reunion); Still Haven't Found What I'm Looking For (snippet of California)

So much to say about this show. With End of the World, scraps of paper from the rafters fluttered down on the audience. I snapped up a fragment of Dante's *Divine Comedy* and Danielle picked up *Psalm* 100 and *Psalm* 101.

"Why are we still here?" Bono asked at the end. "I don't mean in the existential sense. I think you answered the question tonight. There's still so much for us to do."

Monday, May 25, 2015

I've whipped up a review of the first Phoenix show to post to my blog.

THE iNNOCENCE + eXPERIENCE TOUR

As an avid U2 fan for decades, I've had the pleasure of seeing the band in concert dozens of times. This past Memorial Day weekend, I had the privilege of attending both of their *Innocence/Experience Tour* concerts at US Airways Arena in Phoenix.

U2 is the consummate live band. Live is where they live, and while both concerts were extraordinary, as most U2 shows are, Friday night's, only the fifth from the tour opener in Vancouver on May 14, was one of the best U2 concerts I've ever seen. My daughter, a lapsed fan, found the show just as compelling.

The band's finest shows—and there have been many—are intimate, celebratory, energetic, passionate, and powerful affairs. Carlos Santana once told interviewer Charlie Rose, in studied Santana prose, that "music changes the molecular structure of the room, man." U2 do that quite regularly and with seeming ease. But there are times when they raise the roof even higher, seamlessly establishing a communal and rarefied atmosphere even in a stadium. Friday night was such an occasion.

With the literal center of their last outing—the massive *360 Tour*—being a monstrosity dubbed The Crab, the band had hoped to break down barriers and connect more fully with their audience. Their hearts were in the right place, but The Crab only seemed to layer a few more bricks on a wall of separation, and style and spectacle threatened to overshadow substance.

With *i/e*'s set-up, they've found what they were looking for. (Sorry!) Two stages—one rectangular for the 'i' of innocence, the other circular for the 'e' of experience—are linked by a walkway with a cage/screen suspended above. The audience, closer than ever, is pulled right into both the story and the performance.

For Friday's show, we had a couple of the best seats in the house—three rows up on the left side of the arena, mid-way down the walkway, with straight-on views of both stages, as well as all of the connecting apparatus.

Structurally, *i/e* concerts are divided into two distinct sections.

Act I, Innocence, and Act II, Experience, a story-line that follows Bono's personal journey from childhood to adulthood.

Under a single bare light-bulb, Act I opens with The Miracle of Joey Ramone, the Ramones being one of the band's primary musical influences. Punk is then represented by U2's own Electric Co and I Will Follow. Vertigo is here too. The '70s punk scene was, after all, pretty dizzying stuff.

If art is an attempt to identify yourself, then with his mother's death and his reaction to it, Bono, at age fourteen, first became an artist. Iris, Cedarwood Road, and Song for Someone lay out further influences on Bono's creative expression. "She said free yourself to be yourself. If only you could see yourself," he sings in Iris, while footage of his parents' wedding unfolds on-screen. And then he takes us right into his childhood home on Cedarwood Road, where, room by room, visuals become a reflection of enigmatic memory, of family and friends.

Song for Someone has always had a sense of Bono's personal faith about it to me—"In you I found a rhyme . . . . I'm a long way from your hill of Calvary."—thoughts on finding inspiration on a higher plane, about feeling protected and guided through difficult times. "If there is a light you can't always see and there is a world we can't always be . . . if there is a dark that we shouldn't doubt and there is a light, don't let it go out."

When the Irish Troubles of Sunday Bloody Sunday boil over into Bono's life, made personal by a friend's witnessing of a 1974 Dublin car bomb that killed thirty-three innocent people, his faith is challenged. "I don't believe anymore . . . . When I open my eyes, you disappear," he sings in Raised by Wolves, while the relative normality and color of his life on Cedarwood Road warps into the black war-like remnants of sectarian violence. He closes out the tune on his knees, with a recitation of The Lord's Prayer.

Act I ends, fittingly, with Until the End of the World. Life as Bono has known it is gone, and images of Cedarwood Road, its cars, its trees, its homes, are up-rooted, wave by wave, and swept away.

Johnny Cash lopes in then with U2's own The Wanderer for a short, lights-off intermission lasting only as long as the song. An innocent childhood has come to an end and Bono is off on that age-old adolescent journey to discover his true self—that person capable of molding a turbulent past into a singular future.

"I passed by a thousand signs looking for my own name," The Wanderer sings. As a child, Bono could have just as easily collapsed under the weight of despair and loss. Instead, he joined a band, and music—literally—saved his life.

With U2's experience, achievement, and longevity, there's a lot that could go into Act II, and content is evolving as the tour continues. But Invisible makes the perfect opening. Anyone who's ever left home—a neighborhood, a town, a country—has some measure of the process expressed in this song. Other people's expectations frequently come into play when you stay where you are. Or you may find yourself accepting and internalizing how others have defined you. Leaving changes that dynamic.

"I finally found my real name. I won't be me when you see me again. No, I won't be my father's son. I'm more than you know, more than you see here, more than you let me be." Sometimes you can only be all the people that you are with a fresh start.

For Invisible, band members materialize by degrees inside the suspended cage, making their way toward a glowing future.

In Act II, matured and experienced, Bono gets to comment on contemporary events, to acknowledge special tour memories attached to specific places. For that first night in Phoenix, we had a fun and deeply appreciated In God's Country. Act II also gives the band—especially Bono—a chance to meld a bit with the audience on a physical level, inviting fans to the stage, as he's done so often on previous tours. Three lovely young sisters [from New York City, Salt Lake City, and Phoenix] are brought up for Desire and Mysterious Ways, filming on their cell-phones. An enthusiastic guitarist plays rhythm for In God's Country, passing out hugs on arrival. And eight-year-old "Adam, the first boy" walks the ramp with Bono for

I Will Follow.

From their lengthy and impressive back-catalog, U2 offer up passionate anthems and poignant and fresh renditions of old staples, along with a prized handful of their most recent work, ending with With or Without You. But the high-point for me was Bad! After all the years and all the inspired genius of their work, Bad remains my all-time favorite U2 song.

A single encore that begins with City of Blinding Lights and closes with I Still Haven't Found What I'm Looking For, is capped by the explosive celebration of Where the Streets Have No Name. House lights are up and walls are down everywhere. "There is no them. There is only us."

As Bono has said, U2 in full flight is something to behold. For me, the band's natural live energy, intimacy, and passion coalesced with the perfect set-list, the inclusion of Bad, an incomparable sense of inclusiveness born of an innovative stage set-up, and gorgeous and gifted song-writing, to produce an experience of monumental proportions. What fan could ask for more?

Tuesday, May 26, 2015

Though Friday's concert remains my favorite i/e, second Phoenix Saturday night was definitely a winner. Guy Oseary was in the GA audience that night too.

Here's the set-list: The Miracle of Joey Ramone; Vertigo (snippet); Out of Control (snippet of Do You Remember Rock and Roll); Vertigo/I Will Follow; Iris; Cedarwood Road; Song for Someone; Sunday Bloody Sunday; Raised by Wolves (Psalm 23); End of the World (MacBeth snippet); Wanderer (Intermission); Invisible; Even Better Than the Real Thing; Mysterious Ways (snippet of Young Americans); Angel of Harlem; Love Comes to Town; Every Breaking Wave; Bullet the Blue Sky (snippets of Whole Lotta Love and 19); Pride (snippet of Hands that Built America; Beautiful Day (snippet of One); With or Without You//Miracle Drug; Where the Streets Have no Name (snippet of Mother and Child Reunion); One (snippet of California)

"On this very day," Bono said around Pride. "We have true equality in Ireland, because millions turned up to vote yesterday to say love is the highest law in the land. Love! The biggest turnout in the history of the State . . . . Because if God loves us, whoever we love, wherever we come from, then why can't the State?"

Ireland said 'yes' to marriage equality! "Free at last, they took your life, they could not take your gay pride." Beautiful Day was introduced with "putting the gay into Gaelic."

"Lately we've been asking ourselves, why we are still a band?" Bono said on approaching band intros. "Why did Adam Clayton become a bass player. He's not answering that, but it's something we are very, very grateful for. What made Larry Mullen a drummer? When I ask him that he says I should keep philosophical questions to myself. This man gave us our first job and we are still in it.

"The Edge is a special case. He's a Welshman, comes to Ireland. What are the odds of that? What are the odds that I would meet these three men? I met someone the other day and they said 'You know, my mother met your mother and at the time you weren't getting on too well at your school. And it was my mother that told your mother to send you to Mount Temple.' That's where I met these three men. What a wild ride of a coincidence.

"So do what your mother tells you. For me, it was when my mother left me, age fourteen. That's when I became an artist and I sing—we sing—this for her. For Iris, beautiful Iris."

"Put your hands up into your gigantic Arizona sky," Bono said at I Will Follow. "You don't always have to do what your dad says. Your Mom, yeah. Always listen to your mother." Right on!

Americans had ruined the word 'awesome,' Bono alleged. But it did apply to "the miracle of a landscape that is Arizona." In a recording, Stephen Hawking spoke of "one planet, one human race. We are not the same. But we are one. We must become global citizens and live together with tolerance and respect."

Saturday, May 30, 2015

Dennis Sheehan suffered a fatal heart attack just hours after the end of the first LA show! Only in his late sixties, he'd been U2's stage-manager for thirty-three years.

Saturday, May 31, 2015

In another LA show, Bono dedicated "this song", "this concert", in fact "this whole tour" to Dennis, and ended with 40, especially meaningful under the circumstances. Many years ago, at Red Rocks in June of 1983, Dennis' lone voice had rescued and brought back to life 40's stalled "how long" refrain.

The band performed for five-hundred fans at LA's Roxy Theatre.

Thursday, June 4, 2015

The Doors John Densmore chatted drums with Larry at Densmore's very first U2 show.

Wednesday, June 18 2015

Thirty or forty fans scrambled onstage for Where the Streets Have No Name and Still Haven't Found at U2's final Montreal show.

Friday, August 28, 2015

Illustrator/photographer Matt Mahurin's compelling black-and-white video for Song for Someone has a strong sense of a spiritual dimension.

Friday, September 4, 2015

The European *i/e Tour* revved up in Turin [Italy] today. Yesterday, Bono brought out pizza to fans waiting in the GA line.

Tuesday, September 8, 2015

U2 in Amsterdam. Dublin scheduled for the end of November.

Saturday, September 19, 2015

Journalist Brian Boyd interviewed Bono after the second Turin show. Remarking on various facets of the music, Bono played a few tunes for him from the upcoming *Songs of Experience* album.

"At a late hour, I leave him there in the dark," Boyd writes in his poignant description of the encounter. "In a lay-by somewhere between Turin and Milan, lost in his music. The scene is like a visual representation of Hank Williams' *Lost Highway* song. Before closing the door, I hear him sing 'I can take the growing old' and then plaintively asking how he can turn off the songs playing on his phone. 'I can't turn off the music. I don't know how to turn off the music.'

'Just press the stop button.'

'I don't know where the stop button is.'"

Monday, October 26, 2015

5:50 p.m. In Dallas/Ft. Worth awaiting a Newark, New Jersey flight. Age is telling on me these days. The Dallas change of terminals completely wore me out.

Tuesday, October 27, 2015

8:00 a.m. At gate C90 for a London Heathrow connection, departing at nine-thirty. After three-hours sleep last night, I hopped the seven a.m. hotel shuttle back to Newark airport. The NYC skyline materialized by degrees as we rolled in.

Wednesday, October 28, 2015

10:00 a.m. Eight hours of sleep here in the Ibis Hotel at London Heathrow. I so coveted those Global First-class beds on the six-hour UK flight, even the spacious cubicles and footrests of Business First-class. Miles and miles and miles of hiking in Heathrow, and an eternity to track down my hotel shuttle. I had to ratchet around in my bag for the requisite five-pound fee as the driver pulled away. I think he relished flinging me about the bus.

12:35 p.m. Heathrow. Terminal 2. The London Underground entrance. Awaiting Sharon's arrival from York.

5:10 p.m. In our room, #714, at the Holiday Inn Express, North Greenwich. When Sharon pulled in on the Underground about one-thirty, we set off for Green Park, changing to the Jubilee Line and so on to Greenwich North, where the tube station stands opposite the O2 [U2's venue]. The amble over to the hotel took about twenty minutes.

8:00 p.m. Chicken and leek pie in the Great Room downstairs, glutted with U2 fans.

Friday, October 30, 2015

11:35 a.m. Home alone on a cool and rainy day. The others have gone into town on a Thames ferry.

Off-loaded Declan's luggage at the hotel yesterday and took the #188 bus to the Cutty Sark in central Greenwich. A regal three-masted China tea clipper, built in 1869, the Cutty Sark later carried wool from Australia. Suspended above the river just below the Greenwich Observatory, she has eleven miles of rigging in her masts and exceptional museum exhibits on all decks. Her copper hull forms the ceiling of the Even Keel Café.

Back to Greenwich then to collect Jane, who was due in from Leeds on the Underground. Quite by accident, we bumped into Debbi, who was returning from the Claridge Hotel. She'd just given Bono a copy of *Spectacular Sky*, a book of her writing and Sue's artwork the two of them had put together. (A short time later, at the O2 pier, they each got a hug and a kiss from him!)

At five o'clock, we headed for the O2. An amazing place, rather like a Las Vegas casino, with bustling city streets and eateries all under one roof. Pronounced a boondoggle at its inception, the O2 has well paid its way since.

We found our seats, half-way up the stands, on Adam's side of the main stage, in line with Larry's drums.

Here's the set-list: The Miracle of Joey Ramone; Gloria (Them's Gloria snippet); Vertigo; I Will Follow; Iris; Cedarwood Road; Song for Someone; Sunday Bloody Sunday; Raised by Wolves (Psalm 23); End of the World (Love and Peace or Else snippet)// The Fly (Intermission); Invisible; Even Better than the Real Thing; Mysterious Ways (Burning Down the House snippet); Elevation; New Year's Day; Every Breaking Wave; October; Bullet the Blue Sky (Ode to Joy and 19 snippets); Zooropa; Where the Streets Have no Name (California snippet); Pride; With or Without You//City of Blinding Lights; Beautiful Day; (Mother/Child Reunion snippet); Bad (Gloria snippet); People Have the Power with Patti Smith.

A delivery of The Fly, accompanied by images of the Berlin Wall, took the place of Johnny Cash's Wanderer, and there was emphasis on Syrian refugees instead of the Aids epidemic of American shows. Bono recognized the Sarajevo woman brought up for Mysterious Ways as someone who'd been up there before. He should perhaps have sent her back then in favor of a new face. She imposed herself quite intrusively on both the song and the set.

A high-point of this show, for me, came at the very end, when Patti Smith, in person, reprised People Have the Power.

3:00 p.m. The others returned a half-hour ago, Jane and Declan having stomached a queasy ride on a Greenwich gondola, in a high wind.

Saturday, October 31, 2015

1:35 p.m. On the 13:30 Edinburgh train, calling at York, a two-hour ride on a blue-sky, sunshine day. Declan headed home after breakfast.

9:00 p.m. At Sharon's in York. Crawling around London with luggage proved quite an ordeal. This line to that line. This station to that station. Stairs and escalators. Hallways and lifts. Dragging ourselves into King's Cross/St. Pancras at quarter to one, we collected a sandwich for lunch and sat in the sunshine until Jane set off for Leeds. Sharon and I arrived in York about three-thirty.

Must finish up my second London, U2's fourth London gig.

Here's the set-list: Miracle; Electric Co.; Vertigo; I Will Follow; Iris; Cedarwood Road; Song for Someone; Sunday Bloody Sunday; Raised by Wolves; End of the World; The Fly; Invisible; Better Than the Real Thing; Mysterious Ways; Desire; All I Want is You; Breaking Wave; October; Bullet; Zooropa; Streets; Pride; With or Without You; Blinding Lights; Beautiful Day; Mother Child Reunion; One

Our seats, on Adam's side, were behind the main stage. A small screen threw up live shots of the band in place of the main screen graphics. All I Want is You was dedicated to Ali. Matt Damon, a Red supporter, was among the VIPs, and Clare, Bono's Mysterious Ways pick, embodied the song, poised and self-confident.

Though both London shows proved powerful and emotional,

first Phoenix remains my favorite *i/e* thus far.

Monday, November 2, 2015

7:30 p.m. Spent the afternoon at the Yorkshire Sculpture Park, a five-hundred acre spread near Wakefield. Heavy fog created a haunting atmosphere. We'd come for The Wave, part of the *Bloodswept Lands and Seas of Red* installation at the Tower of London in the fall of 2014 [by artist Paul Cummins, designer Tom Piper]. Two segments constructed of ceramic poppies—The Wave and The Weeping Window—commemorated the start of World War I. Eight-hundred-thousand other poppies, each 'planted' to represent a fatality of The Great War, had flowed into the Tower's moat like spilled blood. Such an eloquent representation of loss and sacrifice. The poppies from London had then been sold, ten-percent of the proceeds going to charity.

At the sculpture park, The Wave had been placed on the Cascade Bridge. I was reminded of the Twin Towers' 911 installation in New York City. Art at its best. Brilliant creativity addressing a profound tragedy, without words.

Wednesday, November 4, 2015

11:40 a.m. A gloomy day. Workmen installing gutters at Sharon's this morning spoke with posh English accents and asked for a cup of tea before setting to work.

10:15 p.m. At Sue's in Carlisle. An hour first-class on the train from York brought me to Newcastle, where I caught the Whitehaven train to Carlisle. For one brief and ecstatic moment, the sun came out!

Arrived in Carlisle at six-o-three, Sue at the station exit. She'd prepared an outstanding Cumbrian Tattie Pot for supper—lamb with potatoes, onions, and carrots. The meat was a little sparse, she confessed. One large chunk had slipped off the plate and Ellie—one of Sue's three sweet dachshunds—had snatched it up mid-air.

Thursday, November 5, 2015

8:40 p.m. A fabulous meal at the Lowther Arms pub in Cumwhinton, with Sue and her cousin, Glenn. Steak and ale pie with carrots, cabbage, and chips. On a cold, wet night, the Lowther Arms, all dark wood and lamp-light, just oozed coziness.

9:20 p.m. An overabundance of fireworks tonight for Guy Fawkes Day sounded much like a war zone, a sound and fury that terrified the dogs.

Friday, November 6, 2015

12:40 p.m. On the 12:02 Carlisle to Glasgow Central on a dull, grey day. We'll reach Glasgow by two-thirty. All the mountains on our route, topped with fog, are blackened with bracken and winter trees. A ravens-and-black-rain country, all lonely fells and silver becks.

3:00 p.m. In our flat at the Glasgow Clydeside Apartments on Lancefield Quay, overlooking the River Clyde. We arrived by taxi in a downpour. Our cab driver had inquired as to our respective origins.

"Arizona," I said.

"Came here for the weather then, did you?" he asked.

3:45 p.m. Hallelujah! The sun is out!

Saturday, November 7, 2015

The SSE Hydro is a pretty venue, a space-ship in blue and green. Clyde Built our U2 tickets say. The architecture imitates the hull of a ship, Glasgow being a centuries-old ship builder.

Our seats, half-way up on Adam's side by the e-stage, were spacious and comfortable, backed by the end of a tier. With great views all around, this Glasgow show excelled. I slipped into the first song, Miracle, and just never came out.

Here's the set-list: Miracle Drug; Electric Co; Vertigo; I Will Follow; Iris; Cedarwood Road; Song for Someone; Sunday Bloody Sunday; Raised by Wolves; End of the World/The Fly; Invisible; Better that the Real Thing; Mysterious Ways (Burning Down the House); Elevation; Sweetest Thing; Every Breaking Wave; October; Bullet; Zooropa; Streets; Pride; With or Without You/ City of Blinding Lights; Beautiful Day (I Remember You); One (Mother and Child)

The woman brought up for Mysterious Ways, one of those svelte, sexy young things, hailed from Fife. She dispensed kisses all around, a lip lock for Adam.

Sunday, November 8, 2015

On-board flight 162, Glasgow to Newark, due to depart at 9:00 a.m. on a cold and soggy, muddy, windy day. I left the flat by taxi this morning at six-thirty. Sue and Debbi threw their coats over their jammies and came down to see me off. Good-bye hugs all around, including the driver. A clinch for Sue. A clinch for Debbi. An "ok, get in" for me.

Over the years, I've become ever more adept at Scottish accents. However, at one point in the airport, rather like slalom skiing, I lost the rhythm altogether. The flow of broad Glaswegian suddenly morphed into a completely foreign language. I just nodded, and that seemed to satisfy.

I surprised myself yesterday and joined Sue and Deb for sound-check arrivals, entertained by a contingent from a Spanish fan-club. One young fellow would fluff his hair in his cell-phone camera. Hat on? Hat off? The approach of any vehicle with even a miniscule whiff of celebrity would set him sprucing anew.

After untold ages, despite the rain and the cold, Adam—bless him—came out to fans. Afterwards, we retreated for dinner to the warmth of Yen, a nearby fan-jammed Oriental restaurant.

This second Glasgow show was simply the best. Here's the set-list: Miracle; Gloria; Vertigo; I Will Follow; Iris; Cedarwood Road; Song for Someone; Sunday Bloody Sunday; Raised by Wolves; End of the World//The Fly; Invisible; Better Than the Real Thing; Mysterious Ways (Burning Down the House); Desire; Angel of Harlem; Breaking Wave; October; Bullet; Zooropa; Streets; Pride; With or Without You (Love Will Tear us Apart); City of Blinding Lights; Beautiful Day; Bad (Mother/ChildReunion); 40.

Perfection, but for Angel of Harlem in place of The Sweetest Thing, this concert's exuberant, enthusiastic Scottish audience put it right over the top.

At City of Blinding Lights, Bono hauled up a Scottish lad who very much resembled his son, Eli, as he appears on-screen for Song for Someone. They exchanged jackets and Bono gave him his shades. The young man came from Annan, very near to Dawn's home town. Later on, Bono groped for something in his coat pocket, and, of course, it wasn't there.

Both Love Will Tear us Apart, and 'Stars'—added to With or Without You—made for a magical, incomparable evening. Such a spirited, emotional, intimate, communal performance. Everything a U2 show should be and more. The Bad/40 ending was just transcendent!

"We'll never forget this," Bono said.

Neither will we. My eighty-seventh U2 show, going way back to 1987.

Monday, November 9, 2015

4:30 p.m. Not much to see out the window of my flight home. Northern New York, with colored trees wrapped around lakes or climbing low hillsides, gave way by degrees to villages, then towns and cities until, finally, there, once again, flashed the sky-line of New York City.

When we touched down in Newark forty-five minutes early, the pilot advised that a fuel spill had closed the alley to our gate. So we sat off the runway until our original gate opened at eleven o'clock.

At Terminal C, the serious young immigration officer I landed plied me with questions. How long had I been gone? Where did I go? What was the purpose of my trip? Where did I work? What did I do? I was a writer. What did I write? I answered all and sundry.

And then suddenly he said something to me that had 'green' in it. I was so worn by then that I thought he'd remarked on some published book or other. Had I read it?

"No," I said.

He eyed me with deep dismay and then instructed me, a second time, to put three fingers of my right hand on the *green* light!

I beat my way to my Denver connection and was home by nine.

Tuesday, November 10, 2015

U2 play Paris tonight. A concert to be broadcast on *HBO* this Saturday.

Friday, November 13, 2015

Seven coordinated terrorist attacks in Paris today! At least one-hundred people dead, eighty-nine at the Bataclan Theatre during an Eagles of Death Metal concert. The city is in lock-down. Paris! The birthplace of freedom! The birthplace of the Enlightenment!

Saturday, November 14, 2015

The Paris death toll stands at one-hundred twenty-nine, with three-hundred fifty-three injuries, ninety-nine of them critical. Raids have been launched on terrorist cells in Belgium, in the same neighborhood as that of the Charlie Hebdo terrorists earlier this year.

Sunday, November 15, 2015

U2 have cancelled their last Paris shows and left flowers outside Bataclan.

Saturday, November 28, 2015

Michelle just posted a photo from her visit to The Little Museum in Dublin. On a low table sit three or four U2 books, among them *A Grand Madness, Ten Years on the Road with U2.* I was chuffed.

Friday, December 11, 2015

U2 reinstated their Paris shows Sunday and Monday nights, the last, recorded by *HBO*, featured California's Eagles of Death Metal.

Monday January 11, 2016

David Bowie has died of cancer after releasing his last album as "a parting gift to the world." He'd turned sixty-nine two days earlier. An extraordinary man, so multi-talented and innovative. The Rialto Theatre downtown installed the Major Tom portion of

Space Oddity on their marquee.

The Thin White Duke is gone.

Friday March 25, 2016

Bono is on the cover of *Fortune Magazine* as one of the world's fifty most influential people.

Monday April 4, 2016

On Sunday, Bono and Edge accepted the 2016 *iHeart Radio Innovation Award* in Los Angeles. They dedicated the award to all those imprisoned for making music around the world.

"That could never happen here," Bono added to a remark about being "punched in the face for not agreeing with some politician." And, of course, it had—at a Trump rally.

They're at work on the new album in LA, culling twenty songs from fifty musical possibilities.

Friday, April 15, 2016

Jerry Mele, head of U2 security from 1989 to 1997, passed away Tuesday in Phoenix. Julian Lennon posted a notice to *Facebook*, Jerry being his first body guard. From my very limited experience, Jerry was always a top-notch professional and a very caring individual.

Friday, May 20, 2016

U2 Paris *i/e* has been released in a three CD set. The deluxe edition—with book and postcards—can be yours for $140!

Monday, July 18, 2016

Last Friday, Islamic terrorists slammed a truck into a street crowd in Nice, France, killing eighty-four people. Bono, co-owner with Edge of a villa in a nearby village, was dining with friends at an upscale Nice restaurant and had to be 'rescued.'

"Love is bigger than anything in its way," *U2.com* posted on *Facebook*.

Wednesday, August 3, 2016

Edge, Bono, and Adam, attended a wedding in Valencia, where they were quizzed about the new album. Still working on it, they said. A tour in 2017.

Thursday, September 15, 2016

From the Mississippi, we headed west, stopping at the rustic Dalton Hideout in Meade, Kansas. Eva Dalton Whipple's tiny restored two-story house and barn comprised a museum on Pearlette Avenue. A tunnel leading from the house, discovered after the Whipples had moved out, is assumed to have been use by the Dalton gang. Several Dalton brothers died in 1892, when they attempted the robbery of two Coffeyville, Kansas banks simultaneously.

Not quite the gentle, homey stuff of U2's Dalton Brothers.

Wednesday, September 21, 2016

Bono's mind whirls with all he wants to say and all that needs to be said. So passionate about both his music and his activism. In a recent Charlie Rose Interview, he calls *Songs of Experience*, which the band hope to tour next year, "internal . . . in the sense of navel gazing."

Sunday, September 25, 2016

Forty years ago today, fourteen-year-old Larry Mullen, Jr. tacked up a handwritten note on the bulletin board of Mount Temple School in Dublin, auditions for the Larry Mullen Band to be held in his kitchen in Artane. Edge (David Evans) arrived first. Adam, in a full-length Afghan coat, proclaimed himself both the band's manager and its bass player. Bono (Paul Hewson) came last. He couldn't play guitar, so Larry suggested he sing.

This same lineup is still making outstanding music forty years and twenty-two Grammys later. A profound achievement.

Thursday, September 28, 2016

The band posted a video on *Facebook* marking a special *U240* celebration September 24 and 25 at the Rock and Roll Hall of Fame in Cleveland. Looking totally disinterested, they're lazing around a long empty table. Birthday music erupts and Bono pops a balloon, startling himself.

Thursday, October 6, 2016

Yesterday, in conjunction with Dreamfest, U2 played a *Concert for Kids* to benefit Benioff Children's Hospital in San Francisco. The set included a brilliant anti-Trump Bullet.

Friday, October 7, 2016

The *i/e Tour*'s December 7, 2015 concert in Paris is just stunning. Bad put tears in my eyes and when the concert finished, I felt hopeful again—despite the state of American politics.

Wednesday, November 2, 2016

The *Q Awards*. U2—Best Live Act!

Thursday, November 3, 2016

Bono has been fingered for *Glamour Magazine*'s Women of the Year issue in honor of his work to empower women and girls. Their first Man of the Year

Wednesday, November 9, 2016

Donald J. Trump has won the presidential election!! A devastating blow for the country and the world. Because of America's antiquated Electoral College, which over-rides any popular vote, the country has empowered an arrogant, thin-skinned, rude, ignorant, incompetent, obnoxious, lying, tax-dodging, racist/misogynist as the next president. [My journals are filled with the countless excruciating ways Trump has systematically dismantled American democracy and made a mockery of the Presidency. For obvious reasons, I've limited my observations.]

Monday, December 26, 2016

U2 will tour stadiums next year, in celebration of the thirtieth anniversary of the release of *The Joshua Tree*. April 2 marks the thirtieth anniversary of my first U2 show—*The Joshua Tree* opener at ASU [Arizona State University] in Phoenix. Thirty years a U2 fan.

5.

The Joshua Tree Tour 2017

"America is an idea that belongs to people who need it most."
—Bono

Wednesday, January 4, 2017

U2 will announce the dates for their thirtieth anniversary tour of *The Joshua Tree* on Monday.

Friday, January 6, 2017

On re-reading *A Grand Madness, Ten Years on the Road with U2*, I came across this quote from the April 2, 1992 ASU [Arizona State University, Tempe] *Zoo TV* concert: "There's an election," Bono says. "I hope you find the president you're looking for. Because, let's face it, if you don't get the right president, we're all fucked."

And look what we have twenty-five years on!

Tuesday, January 10, 2017

The U2 tour schedule came out yesterday. Sharon, Jane, Declan, and I will try for Dublin. Pasadena with Dan, Danielle, and Chris. Pre-sale tickets for the Red Hill Group—us oldies—opens 9:00 a.m. tomorrow. "We always like to cater to our uber-fans," Edge says in *Rolling Stone*.

Obama delivered a powerful farewell address from the McCormick Center in Chicago. Stirring words, especially his closing remarks. I miss him already. The best president in my life-time. He walked onstage to U2's Beautiful Day.

Wednesday, January 11, 2017

Declan scored tickets to Dublin's July 20 *JT2017* show and the silent riot of on-line tickets for Pasadena went smoothly.

Thursday, January 12, 2017

"Thirty years ago, *The Joshua Tree* found common ground by reaching for higher ground," Bono says on *U2.com*. "This is a tour for red and blue, the coast and the heartland . . . because music can pull people together as surely as politics can pull people apart."

In *Q Magazine*, he says that he enjoys "the test of trying to keep hold of what's sacred and still (be) wide awake."

Saturday, January 21, 2017

Dan and I were inspired to join Tucson's Women's March this morning, Armory Park to the Roy Laos Transit Center on Broadway. Despite the cold wind and a spit of rain, over fifteen-thousand people participated!

"Hey hey, ho ho, Donald Trump has got to go."

"No Trump, no KKK. No fascist USA."

Tuesday, March 14, 2017

U2.com posted a couple U2 Spinal Tap moments. On leaving his hotel on the original *Joshua Tree Tour*, Edge waved to a nearby klatch of fans, who were actually commuters waiting for a bus. Bono walked out of the studio one evening and got into the back of his own car.

Wednesday, March 13, 2017

Dublin hotel and flight all settled.

Wednesday, March 22, 2017

A snippet on *NPR* [*National Public Radio*] about 1987's *Joshua Tree Tour* reflecting a divided America. And here we are—déjà vu all over again.

Sunday, April 2, 2017

We're sitting under a froth of apple blossoms at the cabin [Chiricahua Mountains, southeastern Arizona] on a crisp but sunny day. Thirty years ago today, *The Joshua Tree Tour* opened at ASU.

Tuesday, April 25, 2017

Thirty years ago today, *The Joshua Tree* reached #1 on the Billboard Charts.

Friday, May 12, 2017

The Joshua Tree Tour 2017 fires up in Vancouver tonight, Bono in meet and greet with fans on Wednesday, for his birthday.

Saturday, May 13, 2017

U2's staging at BC Place featured the back-drop of a Joshua Tree, with the red light/black silhouettes of the original tour. Early songs were performed on a small space jutting out from the main stage. The whole of *The Joshua Tree* album unfolded then, on the larger stage, the band returning to the second for more recent tunes.

Friday, May 19, 2017

6:25 p.m. On-board our one hour, eight minute flight—#3015—to Los Angeles. Just flew over Palm Springs, cruising alongside the Coast Range now, the desert unfurling below in the hazy pinkish-grey of sunset.

10:30 p.m. At the Marriott Courtyard Pasadena Old Town on Four Oaks Avenue. A forty-five minute taxi ride brought us through an outskirts of pleasantly rolling hills to the city center, and we checked in about 7:00 p.m. We'll hop a shuttle to the Rose Bowl tomorrow, fivish.

Saturday, May 20, 2017

On a hot, hot day awash in the perfumes of blooming gingko, myrtle, and jacaranda trees, we've just finished breakfast croissants in the hotel's outdoor patio.

12:50 p.m. After a late lunch at the Tibetan Nepal House— "Once you go yak, you never go back."—we're dozing under a eucalyptus tree at the Pasadena Museum of History on Walnut Street. The rush of traffic encircles us, vying with bird-song and the drone of air-conditioners. To our right rises one of the museum's mansion tour draws—a palatial white colonnaded three-story pile at the top of a sweeping staircase.

The museum hosted two commendable exhibits. One, the street art of the *Pasadena Chalk Art Festival*, the other a train-travel presentation titled *The Art of Getting There.*

Sunday, May 21, 2017

Seated at LAX Gate 52E, for our return flight to Tucson.

Tuesday, May 23, 2017

Here's the set-list for the Pasadena show: Sunday Bloody Sunday; New Year's Day; A Sort of Homecoming; Pride; Where the Streets Have no Name; Still Haven't Found What I'm Looking For; With or Without You; Bullet the Blue Sky; Running to Stand Still; Red Hill Mining Town; In God's Country; Trip Through Your Wires; One Tree Hill; Exit; Mothers of the Disappeared// Beautiful Day; Elevation; Ultraviolet; One; Miss Sarajevo; BAD; I Will Follow.

I've just posted a review on-line:

THE JOSHUA TREE TOUR 2017
Pasadena, California

It's tempting to credit *The Joshua Tree 2017 Tour* with bringing *The Joshua Tree* album full circle. The first Pasadena Rose Bowl concert, May 20, was one of U2's best ever, a direct conduit to my first live U2 experience, *The Joshua Tree* in Tempe, Arizona, April 2, 1987. The same hopefulness, warmth, and communal celebration. The same power, passion, sound, words, vision, voice—to the nth degree.

But the strength of *JT2017* is not simply nostalgia. It's the upshot of expansion and growth, a path spiraling upward through time. Circular movement to the fourth dimension. A t-shirt popular at *JT* merchandise stalls says, succinctly, *I want to run 1987*—on the front; *I want to hide 2017*—on the back. The idealism and energy of a young band balanced against the mature, conflicted realism, and updated relevance of its present.

The simplicity of *JT2017*'s staging captures *The Joshua Tree*'s intensely American vibe. The centerpiece, a giant Joshua tree, rises to the right, above a lofty LED screen brimming with stunning visuals. A smaller stage, impressed with a mirror image of the tree, projects into the audience from a slanted walkway.

In liner notes to the 2007 *Joshua Tree* re-issue, Bono wrote that inspiration for the album came from "two Americas, the mythic and the real America—harsh reality alongside the dream. It was prosperous and it was parched and I began to see this era as a spiritual drought. I started thinking about the desert and what came together was quite a clear picture of where I was at, personally—a little off-kilter in my emotional life but very much waking up as a writer and as a commentator on what I saw around me, my love of America and my fear of what America could become." (Prophetic words given the negativity, fear-mongering, and incompetence of America's current administration.)

Prior to both U2 and The Lumineers—a winning opener—poetry scrolls up the tan-colored, two-hundred by forty-five foot screen, the largest high-resolution LED video equipment ever used on a tour. If you're paying attention, the intimacy and sense of place this streaming poetry builds is both novel and unprecedented, even for a U2 show.

I recognized Carl Sandburg's *Prairie* and Walt Whitman's *Leaves of Grass* right off. Other pieces were less well known—Lawrence Ferlinghetti's *The World is a Beautiful Place*; Robert Pinsky's *An Explanation of America: A Love of Death*; Arizona's inaugural Poet Laureate Alberto Rio's *The Border: A Double Sonnet*; Elizabeth Alexander's *Preliminary Sketches: Philadelphia* and *Praise Song for the Dead*; William Matthew's *Why We are Truly a Nation*; Pedro Pietri's *Puerto Rican Obituary*; James Dickey's *The Strength of Fields*; Juan Higuera Creek's *Jefferson*; Shirley Geok-Lin-Lim's *Learning to Love America*; Naomi Shahib Nye's *Kindness*; and Yusef Komunyakaa's *Facing It*.

The Rose Bowl hunkers below some dusty Southern California foothills, and is quite spacious in its interior. Our seats, in line with the smaller stage, on the west side—Adam's—were at the foot of the second tier, next to an exit.

At one point, the wide aisle in front of us, bordered opposite by seating for the disabled, collected a security huddle that suddenly swept past. Neighborly opinion put Edge in its midst. He "turned to wave" before heading back down to the pitch. (An Edge clone, in reality. We learned subsequently that a faux Bono had posed for selfies elsewhere in the stadium.)

Genuine celebs in attendance included Katie Holmes with her daughter Suri, Gwyneth Paltrow, and Alicia Keys with her son, Egypt.

The opening set, comprised of Sunday Bloody Sunday, New Year's Day, A Sort of Homecoming, and Pride—which included a snatch of Simon and Garfunkel's America ("All come to look for America")—was performed on the small stage, band members all in black, but for Larry's brilliantly white t-shirt. These popular favorites suitably covered the band's positon on the eve of *The Joshua Tree*'s original release—their early activist-oriented work, together with a deja-vu homecoming to America.

Dr. King's *I Have a Dream* speech crawled across the screens for Pride. "Sing for those holding on to the American dream," Bono said. "The party of Lincoln, the party of Kennedy, and those in-between. You're welcome here tonight. We're reaching for higher ground. Some people think that dream is dead, so sing out. Maybe the dream is just telling us to wake up. . . . The spirit of Dr. King wants to awaken the America of compassion, of community, the America of justice, of joy. Awaken. Awaken." (Personally, I question every day the survival—and even the existence—of the party of Lincoln.)

Proper staging for a full top-to-bottom presentation of *The Joshua Tree* was imperative. Where the Streets Have No Name has become such an emotionally anthemic portion of U2 concerts, that its power and celebration would evaporate if delivered too soon. That four-song intro resolved this sticky issue, allowing band members to be silhouetted against the familiar wash of red light that announced Streets original tour opening, a staccato of flashing lights erupting in the limbs of the Joshua tree. The crimson then melts to a rich saffron—"I want to feel sunlight on my face"—and an empty desert highway, scratched in the vastness of the Mojave Desert, stretches out under dramatic storm clouds. The audience rejoices, seventy-thousand strong.

I Still Haven't Found What I'm Looking For extends this desert imagery to sunset-fired hills, With or Without You incorporates a small bit of Breathe, and a blistering Bullet the Blue Sky features helmeted 'citizens' on-screen.

Pre-U2 music had included the Clash, Fleetwood Mac's The Chain, and Future Islands, which slipped into a revved up Black Hole Sun, in tribute to Soundgarden's Chris Cornell, who had tragically committed suicide three days earlier. An especially moving Running to Stand Still is performed "for the lion that was Chris Cornell. We send a prayer to his lioness, Vicky" and their children. "A beautiful sweet soul."

The brass band on-screen for Red Hill Mining Town appears to play opposite U2 at times. Never before played live, this song had a depth of feeling in the original video that seemed muted to me in this incarnation "We've been blowing a little fluff off the needle these past few days," Bono said at the end. "And wondering why we never played that last tune, Red Hill Mining Town. Never played it on the original tour. One of those songs that just feels right for the times. Not just in England but here in America."

"The next song is for the landscape of this country," Bono says, on introducing a spine-tingling In God's Country, so apropos for our wide western deserts. "Not just physical but psychological and spiritual." A Joshua tree, mid-screen, changes color against low rolling hills behind. "These desert songs mean a lot to us and it seems they mean so much to you too." A gorgeous One Tree Hill for Maori roadie Greg Carroll follows, with images of native people and a reddish eclipsed blood-moon.

Exit is preceded by a snippet from a 1958 episode of Trackdown. The western TV series, starring Robert Culp as bounty hunter Hoby Gilman, aired from 1957 to 1959. Gilman calls out a grifter named Trump, another con-artist promising another wall.

"You're a liar, Trump," Gilman asserts to raucous cheers,

before Exit kicks in. An extraordinarily expressive Mothers of the Disappeared follows. Women wrapped in deep blue light hold candles that flicker out one by one.

El Pueblo Vencera wraps up the glories of *The Joshua Tree* with gratitude and deep emotion, and after thanks all around, Bono dedicates the show to Guus Van Hove (manager of the pop venue 013 in Tilburg, the Netherlands) and his girlfriend, Helena Nuellett. Both U2 fans succumbed to 104ºF heat in August of 2011, searching California's Joshua Tree National Monument for the site of *The Joshua Tree* album cover shoot, which, in reality, lay hours to the north, closer to Death Valley.

Beautiful Day opens the single encore, with Bono back on the smaller stage. He incorporates a portion of *LaLa Land's* City of Stars, closing with "it's a beautiful day when we respect human rights. When sisters around the world can sit in schools like their brothers, that's a beautiful day. It's a beautiful day when people call home the place they want to live. It's a beautiful day when women of the world unite to re-write history as Herstory."

Spoken lyrics usher in Elevation. "I believe in you," Bono sings to the band. "Who doesn't believe in Larry Mullen Jr?" he asks, as Larry gives a thumbs-up to the camera behind him.

Ultraviolet is unparalleled in every way. "Would it be indulgent for the band to give thanks to the women in our lives?" Bono asks. "To Ali, to Morleigh, to Ann, to Mariana. To the women on our crew. To the women in the audience that we feel we know. To the women in faraway places who we can never know the shit they have to deal with. And the women who stand up or sit down for their rights, who insist, persist, who resist—these women light our way. This goes out to my two daughters Jordon and Eve, who are here tonight. Thank you for lighting my way."

During this rousing track, portraits of pioneering women of all sorts flash up on the screen—Ellen Degeneres, Virginia Wolfe, Lena Dunham, Michelle Obama, Hillary Clinton, Rosa Parks, Angela Davis, Melinda Gates, Ruth Ellis, Rosetta Tharpe, Saffujah

Khan, Pussy Riot, Oprah Winfrey, Grace Jones, Bell Hooks, Angela Merkel, Wasp Women Airforce Pilots, Ellen Sirleaf, Patti Smith, Eunice Kennedy Shriver, Sandra Day O'Connor, the Women's Land Army, Suffragettes, Women of Iceland.

"Poverty is Sexist" and "Women of the World Unite," close out the visuals.

"Nothing scares the shit out of politicians more than people organized," Bono says. "Government should fear its people not the other way around. Organize don't agonize. Sometimes it's luminous figures that light the way. But most times its social movements that actually change history."

Prior to a compelling One, Bono addresses his *ONE* organization. "We're very proud that *One* now has eight-million members," he says. "Eighteen-million Aids sufferers saved with one pill a day thanks largely to the USA. If you're a tax-payer you're an Aids activist." Adam returns to the smaller stage and *One* is dedicated to David Wojnarowicz and Mark Pellington, both involved with One video visuals, the former for the buffalo shots now on-screen.

Footage from a Jordanian refugee camp accompanies a powerful Miss Sarajevo, all four band members together again on the small stage.

"Is it a time for saving your neighbor, whether an enemy or a friend?" Bono asks and recites the inspirational words on the plaque of the Statue of Liberty. A young Syrian girl on-screen speaks about the stark realities of her world, about the strength and resilience of her dreams, while a large silken square of fabric printed with her face passes hand to hand around the lower tier.

Miss Sarajevo finishes with thanks to the French artist who made the film "and to Anton Corbjn, who made the earlier films and made a lot of our artwork over the years and, of course, thanks to the great A-Team that put together this show. Willie Williams, Joe O, Smasher, the U2 crew. The A-team. They tell me I'm the only B on the A-Team." Bono laughs. "Any way, thanks for giving us a great life. Let's do this again in 2047". (Not a chance!)

As a stunning surprise, Bad, in blue light, reprises the same snippet of Simon and Garfunkel's America. I'd mourned Bad's absence a tad at the beginning of the concert. Bad had shown up in two prior shows, as part of the opening set, and I had resigned myself to being deprived. The Little Things that Give You Away, from the band's upcoming *Songs of Expe*rience, had apparently even appeared on the night's printed set-list. What a blessing then to hear those spine-tingling opening notes! Bad! My all-time favorite U2 track.

A group huddle afterwards resulted in the bonus track I Will Follow, which brought the house down all over again. "Biggest thrill ever, LA, turning on the radio and they're playing a song that sounds a little like this," Bono said beforehand. "We surrender, surrender to your love. . . ."

Thunderous audience participation and a pogoing Edge.

And then my *Joshua Tree Tour 2017* came to a close. Uber fans and other fans could not have asked for a more magical, hopeful, inspirational, and joyful Saturday night. Musically spot on, Bad in the last set, with U2's heart and social conscience at full throttle.

What a band! What a night!

Friday, May 26, 2017

Ali, with daughters Jordon and Eve, accompanied Bono to *Glamour's Women of the Year Awards.* She and Bono were also celebrating the fortieth anniversary of their first date. Bono had asked Ali what she thought he should say at the *Glamour* festivities. She told him then what she's been telling him since they were teenagers. "Don't look down on me, but don't look up at me either. Look across to me. I'm here."

Such a powerful message.

U2 performed I Still Haven't Found What I'm Looking For on *Jimmy Kimmel Live* Wednesday night. A gospel choir, scattered in the audience, gathered onstage for the finale. The band also offered up a tease from their forthcoming *Songs of Experience*—The Little Things That Give You Away, which they've occasionally played on the *JT2017* tour.

Wednesday, June 14, 2017

North on #89 from Jackson Hole [Wyoming], we stumbled on The National Museum of Wildlife Art, on a low rise opposite the vast grassland and forested foothills of the National Elk Sanctuary. The museum presented some outstanding pieces, mostly in oil. A narrow corridor displayed hummingbird watercolors, and a separate room held posters from the U.S. Department of the Interior, Joshua Tree National Monument among them.

Monday, June 19, 2017

7:05 p.m. In our room—#110—at the Kenora Travelodge [Kenora, Ontario]. Just discovered that the band will present *The Joshua Tree* at the University of Phoenix Stadium in Glendale, September 19. Red Hill ticket pre-sale starts tomorrow at 10:00 a.m., Phoenix time. I've no internet access at present, but I'll give it a shot tomorrow night.

Tuesday, June 20, 2017

Here we are in Thunder Bay [Ontario]. Ages to get here, with four or five one-lane construction zones on-route. But the landscape, Kenora to Thunder Bay, unfolds with magnificence, a vast, remote, primordial wilderness of conifer forest and crystalline lakes.

Worked all evening with Ticketmaster. Dan's code finally pulled up a package deal with extraordinary seats. So we're in!

Thursday, July 20, 2017

Chagrined to discover, yesterday, that I'd booked myself into Dublin for *JT 2017* shows through Chicago, departing from Waterloo—*Iowa*!

Months ago, on Travelocity, I'd entered Waterloo Regional Airport, and up it came, with neither code nor city. I sprang for it. As it happens, Waterloo, *Iowa* claims Waterloo Regional Airport. Southern Ontario's, the airport I was after, is the Region of Waterloo Airport. Travelocity now offers both options.

I wrestled hours with all and sundry, in a futile attempt to amend my flight any way possible.

Saturday, July 22, 2017

Filed a complaint and cancellation claim with Travelocity, citing their initial lack of choice in airports. Claim denied! No "illness," no "death," no "traffic accident," no "kidnapping," no "quarantine"!

Friday, July 28, 2017

A "good show," Dublin, Sharon said, and Declan spoke of "an extraordinary performance" on "a very special evening."

Sunday, September 3, 2017

U2 have released a video for an upcoming *Songs of Experience* track called The Blackout. A good solid rock song, timely lyrics, and a fresh sound.

Monday, September 11, 2017

The band debuted another *Songs of Experience* tune—You're the Best Thing About Me—on *The Tonight Show,* calling it "funk-Motown." (Perhaps in some other incarnation.) A pop-tune at heart, I thought, though the sing-along chorus is pretty. "Joy as an act of defiance," Bono says. Writing joy is harder than writing any other emotion, such as anger or sorrow. That has a certain legitimacy, especially in hard times, I suppose, and I can understand the impetus. But still—this is a boy-band pop-tune at heart.

The theme of *Songs of Innocence* figures in the lyrics to Rejoice from the band's second album, *Gloria,* Bono explains. "I can't change the world. But I can change the world in me." For *Songs of Experience,* the notion is "I can't change the world in me. But I can change the world . . . . The most wily and fearsome of enemies is yourself. And that's experience."

Sunday, September 17, 2017

Off tomorrow for U2 in Glendale.

Grave unrest in Missouri after the acquittal of yet another white police office in the fatal shooting of a black man. The band cancelled their St. Louis concert, citing inadequate security.

Tuesday, September 19, 2017

In my room at the Holiday Inn Express, at the Tucson airport.

I flew in last night about 7:00 p.m.

After breakfast in Alma [Ontario, Canada] about 9:00 a.m., Dan and I set out for my shuttle pick-up at the Inn of Waterloo. A smooth run to Toronto followed, and, thanks to my driver, I am now well-versed in the intricacies of Slowball.

A lengthy scavenger-hunt slog to Gate A9 in Toronto International—self-check-in at a kiosk, boarding-pass scan at A Gates security, boarding-pass scan at customs, hand-sweep for my green-card, and a photo print-out to be turned in at customs/immigration. One final boarding-pass scan and I was spit out into duty-free.

Off to Chicago, on a spanking new EMB140, assembled in Brazil. My modest carry-on, which would fit neither under the seat, nor in an overhead bin, had to be stashed in a closet with the crew's luggage.

Wednesday, September 20, 2017

10:30 a.m. In the Tucson airport, awaiting a return flight to Chicago.

Danielle cruised by the Holiday Inn on Tuesday, close to three-thirty, and we headed off to Glendale. The Arizona Department of Transportation had programmed their I-10 overhead notice-boards to reflect U2's Arizona presence. One sign flashed "Drive Safely. It's a Beautiful Day," another read "Don't Change Lanes in Mysterious Ways. Use Your Blinker."

Traffic snarled as we neared the venue, with rush-hour and concert-goers reducing movement to a crawl through Phoenix—I-10 to L101 to Bethany Home Road. Six-thirty, as we inched our way toward the stadium, two lanes to our left, in the car-share lane, a pair of motorcycle cops materialized. Others appeared between black vans and SUVs. Riding shot-gun in the only sedan, Bono sat, held up in traffic like the rest of us.

We found VIP parking at Gate 1, and after collecting tickets and laminates at a VIP Party tent, we stepped inside to a long over-slung backstage area decorated with U2 photos. A wide

Red Zone banner was tacked up on the back wall. Below us, the band's eighteen-wheeler transport trucks stood in the midst of an assemblage of backstage equipment. The party food—beef brisket, chicken breast, salad, corn on the cob, baked beans, and pie—more than satisfied, but I wouldn't opt for any such package again.

Desperate times called for desperate measures.

Our seats excelled—in the first tier on Adam's side, Section 107, row 6, seats 9 and 10. The opener, Beck, a stick of a man, pumped up the crowd handily and U2 came on close to nine-thirty.

Here's the set-list: (The Whole of the Moon); Sunday Bloody Sunday, New Year's Day; Bad (America); Pride//the whole of *The Joshua Tree*//Miss Sarajevo; Beautiful Day; Elevation; Vertigo; You're the Best Thing About Me; Ultraviolet; One

With the incomparable sound of this concert, I immersed myself in each song, soaring into that fifth dimension so prevalent with the very best of U2 shows. Bad, Exit, and Elevation were especially intense, as was Edge's expansive Bullet solo. A "very, very special night," Bono pronounced at the close.

The *JT Tour 2017* will wrap up late October with four shows in Sao Paulo, Brazil. The band anticipates performing for upwards of three-hundred-thousand people.

For the rest of us, it's *i/e* Part 2, the *eXPERIENCE TOUR*, next year.

Red Rocks Amphitheater, Rooney Valley, Morrison, Colorado – May 10, 2013

Bono Tavern, Bono, Ohio – July 22, 2013

The Little Museum of Dublin – December 31, 2013

Killiney Beach, Dublin – January 1, 2013

The Edge Restaurant, Oslo, Norway – August 20, 2014

The *iNNOCENCE + eXPERIENCE TOUR*, US Airways Center,
Phoenix, Arizona – May 22, 2015

The Sweetest Thing, US Airways Center – May 22, 2015

Adam, Sunday Bloody Sunday, US Airways Center – May 22, 2015

Larry, Sunday Bloody Sunday, US Airways Center – May 22, 2015

Mysterious Ways, US Airways Center – May 22, 2015

One, US Airways Center – May 23, 2015

The O2, Greenwich, London, UK – October 29, 2015

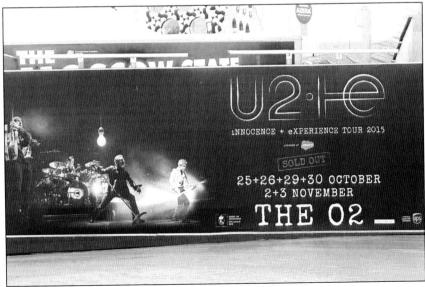

U2 *i/e* billboard, Greenwich – October 29, 2015

Interior of the O2, Greenwich – October 29, 2015

The Fly at the O2 – October 29, 2015

Sue and Debbi meet Bono at the
O2 – October 28, 2015 (Sue Fell)

A portion of The
Wave (from *Bloodswept
Lands and Seas of Red*),
installation at The
Yorkshire Sculpture
Park, Wakefield, York,
UK –November 2,
2015

The O2 – October 30, 2015

The SSE Hydro, Glasgow, Scotland – November 6, 2015

The Fly at the SSE Hydro – November 6, 2015

Mysterious Ways at the SSE Hydro – November 6, 2015

Adam at sound check at the SSE Hydro – November 7, 2015

A Grand Madness, Ten Years on the Road with U2 at the Little Museum of Dublin – posted on Facebook on November 28, 2015 (Michelle Perez)

The Dalton Gang Hideout, Meade, Kansas – September 15, 2016

The Women's March, Tucson, Arizona – January 21, 2017 (Dan Beeaff)

Joshua Tree Tour 2017 – Where the Streets have no Name, The Rose Bowl, Pasadena, California – May 20, 2017

I Still Haven't Found What I'm Looking For, The Rose Bowl, Pasadena, CA – May 20, 2017

Elevation, The Rose Bowl, Pasadena, CA – May 20, 2017

Joshua Tree
National
Monument Poster,
National Wildlife
Museum, Jackson
Hole, Wyoming –
June 14, 2017

"Drive Safely It's a Beautiful Day," Interstate 10 to Phoenix – September 20, 2017

Ultraviolet, University of Phoenix Stadium, Glendale, Arizona – September 20, 2017

Bono, Bullet the Blue Sky, University of Phoenix Stadium, Glendale, Arizona – September 20, 2017

Edge, Vertigo, University of Phoenix Stadium, Glendale, Arizona – September 20, 2017

In God's Country, University of Phoenix Stadium, Glendale, Arizona – September 20, 2017

6.

The eXPERIENCE + iNNOCENCE Tour
(i/e Tour Part 2)

"When you think you're done, you've just begun."
— Bono

Tuesday, September 26, 2017

U2's new album—*Songs of Experience*—will be released December 1. The UK's *Daily Mail* posted an article about the album, with the Bono headline, "There's a Bully in the Pulpit. Silence is not an Option." Bono says "For the first time in many years, maybe in our lifetime, the moral arc of the universe, as Dr. King used to call it, (is) not bending in the direction of fairness, equality, and justice for all . . . . Democracy is a blip in history and it requires a lot of focus and concentration to keep it intact."

Tuesday, October 10, 2018

The video for You're the Best Thing About Me, from U2's *Songs of Experience*, has the band knocking about New York City. Lots of bright lights, live performances, and big-city action. The clip closes with a line from Emma Lazarus' *The New Colossus* [the poem engraved on the Statue of Liberty]. "I lift my lamp beside the golden door."

Thursday, November 2, 2017

Yesterday, U2 announced the dates for their *eXPERIENCE + iNNOCENCE TOUR* (*i/e Tour*, Part 2), which opens in Tulsa, Oklahoma, early May of next year. To thwart scalpers, *U2.com* requires registration as a "Verified Fan," with a link to Ticketmaster. Two to four hours before the November 14 pre-sale, ticket codes will arrive by text message.

Friday, November 3, 2017

I've booked New York New York Hotel and Casino for next year's Las Vegas U2 concert.

Sunday, November 12, 2017

Bob Geldof surrendered his Dublin *Freedom of the City* award. In no way did he want to be associated with Aung San Suu Kyi after her failure to speak out against the current genocide in Myanmar.

Another track from U2's *Songs of Experience*—Get Out of Your Own Way, recorded in London's Trafalgar Square for *MTV's Europe Music Awards*—features Edge's signature watery-bells guitar. As in all the best of U2, hope softens realism.

Tuesday, November 14, 2017

Two tickets for U2 in Las Vegas, at a hefty price. But we're in!

Saturday, November 18, 2017

Watched Pasadena's first *Joshua Tree 2017* concert on *YouTube*. As magnificent as I remembered. Where the Streets Have No Name was especially powerful.

U2 has embodied artistic originality for over forty years. They can't always churn out a block-buster like Streets. Still, I'm holding out for something more from this new album than You're the Best Thing About Me.

Wednesday, November 22, 2017

In a collection of short U2-related films, available on-line from *U2.com*, Sammy [Larry's drum tech, Sam O'Sullivan] takes us backstage. Dallas Schoo [Edges's guitar tech] navigates the guitars and amps of Edgeworld. There's a clip of U2 fans at the Rosebowl, and production director Jake Berry, show-cases the riggers—"We are the riggers. We hang everything in the air." Lastly, Lumineers' lead singer, Wesley Schultz, says of U2's music—"It cleanses you."

Wednesday, November 29, 2017

Four o'clock this afternoon, *Amazon Music* opened a twenty-four hour *U2 Experience* broadcast, stellar music sprinkled with brief interviews.

Thursday, November 30, 2017

A cool and overcast day, with a chance of rain—next Wednesday.

Ahead of tomorrow's World Aids Day, Jimmy Kimmel presented a live *Red Special* to raise funds and awareness for Aids. Sean Penn tended a red lit bar where Bono crooned Frank Sinatra's One For My Baby, accompanied on piano by Coldplay's Chris Martin.

Friday, December 1, 2017

U2's new album was released today.

Monday, December 4, 2017

Last weekend, on *Saturday Night Live*, U2 performed Get Out of Your Own Way and American Soul, the latter with an animated Lamar Kendel intro.

Tuesday, December 5, 2017

With no ordered album arriving from *U2.com*, I had to spring for one at Target.

Friday, December 8, 2017

Edge has explained that *Songs of Experience* had been delayed in order to "adjust to changes in the world order."

Bono had also experienced a "very serious health-related episode" that sharply influenced his writing. "We had to stop and take account of what was going on in the world," he says in *Q Magazine*. "I don't want to get too into the details of (what was going on in *my* world) for fear of the melodramatic reality TV kerfuffle. A lot of people have these moments. I've had a few. Not quite at this level."

"Where that brought him to as a writer was an amazing place," Edge adds.

Monday, December 11, 2017

Posted a *Songs of Experience* review today. Fellow *Wordpress* blogger, Neil, responded, saying that in the early 1980s he'd gone to a U2 concert in Philly where the price of admission was one dollar!

U2's SONGS OF EXPERIENCE – A REVIEW

U2'S SONGS OF EXPERIENCE, arduous in the making—three years, nine producers, fifteen engineers—is outstanding both musically and lyrically, a classic in sound and vision, but for the occasional overreach for updated uber 'relevance'. To me the production focus falls squarely on Bono's rich voice and Edge's lyrical guitar, along with musings on Light and Love, in all their manifestations—some of which are purely poetic. Like the best of U2, optimism is tempered by realism, with neither Pollyanna blindness nor a wallow in cynicism and despair.

U2 albums tend to come in pairs—*Rattle and Hum* as commentary to *The Joshua Tree*, *Zooropa* as an adjunct to *Achtung Baby*, even *How to Dismantle an Atomic Bomb* as the flip side to *All That You Can't Leave Behind*. Of course *Songs of Experience* was fully intended as an extension of *Songs of Innocence*, the stories of Bono's Irish youth blossoming into precepts of the present. To that end, the same lyrics are used in different contexts.

The Irish poet Brendan Kennelly suggested to Bono that "if you really want to get to where the writing lives, write as if you're dead." And so Bono did, a strategy which has produced an album that is deeply spiritual, reaching for higher ground.

The collection divides itself into two distinct portions. The actual *Songs of Experience* album is book-ended by two ethereal tunes, Love is All We Have Left and 13 (There is a Light), appended by a small grouping of bonus tracks. Here's the blow by blow:

LOVE IS ALL WE HAVE LEFT – The perfect opening for both the album and the concert—played off-stage before Lights of Home kicks in, akin to the introduction of *The Joshua Tree* by Clannad's Harry's Game—Love is All We have Left, despite a hint of sadness, still gives me goosebumps with its otherworldly sound, its gorgeous vocals, and its outstanding lyrics. This tune says we can rise above everything and live fully in the present. With "nothing to stop this being the best day ever," there's "joy as defiance" here, along the lines of Beautiful Day's "Sky falls, you feel like it's a beautiful day."

When everything's gone, including your earthly presence, only the joy of love will remain. Happiness is a fleeting, momentary ease. Joy endures. I especially love the line, "This is no time not to be alive."

LIGHTS OF HOME – The acoustic opening of this one—seemingly about the recovery of Bono's faith ("I can see the lights in front of me . . . one more push and I'll be born again")—is augmented by Edge's melodious guitar and the stability of Larry's percussion. Nothing like a near-death experience to open your eyes to your own mortality or renew your appreciation of the miracle of life, to demonstrate that you're not as invincible as you once thought, that your head is not harder than ground. ("I shouldn't be here 'cause I should be dead.")

Is the light of home Iris? Ali? God? Whoever or whatever, it's easy to see how saints are made. "Free yourself to be yourself" connects directly back to *Songs of Innocence*'s Iris.

YOU'RE THE BEST THING ABOUT ME – I found this single disappointing and I still haven't warmed to it much. The band is capable of so much more, in my view, as the bulk of *Songs of Experience* proves. You're the Best Thing About Me is a bit too generic, a bit too pop for me, something many a boy-band might offer up. It's a toe-tapping singalong and there's nothing wrong with that. And the rousing communal chorus will have everyone on their feet. But there's still too much of a "don't worry, be happy" vibe about it. I do love the line "there's no risky thing for a man who's determined to fall."

GET OUT OF YOUR OWN WAY – Wow! Get Out of Your Own Way is everything I hope for in a rock song from U2—moving lyrics, a stunning chorus, great aggressive guitar from Edge, Larry's driving drums over Adam's steady bass foundation. Get Out of Your Own Way is a song for anyone—including Bono's children—who is facing adversity or just wading through the vagaries of life. Given current world affairs, especially those here in the U.S., this one is wildly inspirational and hopeful. As a letter to America—with "the promised land is there for those who need it," Lincoln's ghost, and a smack to the face of Liberty—it's outstanding. "I can help you, but it's your fight."

The only thing necessary for evil to triumph is for good people to do nothing. Resist!

AMERICAN SOUL – I love this one. It's yet another favorite, punctuated by Edge's superb guitar work, Larry's fierce drumming, and inspired lyrics. The chanting, explosive quality of the bridge is also a plus. Rapper Kendrick Lamar segues from Get Out of Your Own Way into American Soul, an open letter to America, the birthplace of rock 'n' roll. This powerful tune calls up America's best attributes, inspiring revolt against the rising power of the Alt-right, which Edge has so aptly described as the "mental illness of racism" unmasked. "It's not a place. This country is to me a sound . . . . a thought . . . . a dream the whole world owns." The chant of "You are Rock and Roll. You and I are Rock and Roll," pulls us right back into *Songs of Innocence*. (Volcano)

SUMMER OF LOVE – A pretty song, accented by the minor quality of Edge's guitar, Summer of Love didn't click on my first listen, but has grown on me since. Just as The Troubles on *SOI* did not refer to "the one that everyone knows," so too Summer of Love speaks to neither the West Coast of California in 1969, nor its earlier U2 innocence in California (There is No End to Love). This summer is refugees washing up on European beaches—"Flowers growing in a bomb crater."

"When all is lost we find out what remains." Love.

RED FLAG DAY – This love song equally conjures up *SOI*'s California (There is No End to Love), as well as the stunning Every Breaking Wave, crashing waves now morphed into wilder storm-tossed seas—at least until those bodies wash up. I love the lines "Today we can't afford to be afraid of what we fear," and "Paradise is a place you can't see when it's yours." (I've been incredibly lucky to have Paradise and know it!)

"Let's get into the water . . . taken out by the waves to where we've never been before," is very much like Electrical Storm's seeing colors we've never seen and going places we've never been.

THE SHOWMAN (A LITTLE MORE BETTER) – I especially appreciate the sentiment of The Showman and its winsome opening, fun atmosphere, and carnival-like ending. This is, of course, a letter to the band's audience, to their listeners, and to their fans. U2 write the songs, their audience gives them meaning. This has always been the power of music from its earliest days, Bad and the Hallelujah Chorus to Sprach Zarathustra.

In another lifetime, in high-school, I studied *Tuscan Villa* by the Canadian poet, Douglas Le Pan. Wrestling with the themes of the piece, I contacted Le Pan for his input. In response, I received a letter stating that it was "dangerous for a poet to interpret his own work." This hardly satisfied me then. Or now.

Writers can choose to speak to what was in their hearts or minds when they created a specific work. When they've finished, they might find they've birthed something totally opposite to what they intended. But they can still choose to speak. They have a right to speak. Listeners will uncover other interpretations, other perspectives, depending on their own experiences, where they find themselves in life—physically, mentally, emotionally, spiritually, even chronologically, in terms of age.

"So many ways of seeing."

"Reality is an agreed upon fiction," writer Diane Ackerman says in her best-selling memoir, *A Natural History of the Senses* [Vintage Books, Knopf Doubleday, NY, 1990]. "We may leave it to the seers, the shamans, the ascetics, the religious teachers, the artists among us to reach a higher state of awareness."

"The showman gives you front row to his heart. . . . prays his heartache will chart. . . . I lie for a living, I love to let on, but you make it true when you sing along."

THE LITTLE THINGS THAT GIVE YOU AWAY – A "dialogue between innocence and experience," The Little Things that Give You Away is yet another pop sound that still hasn't grabbed me, though I do love the ending. It just takes a little long to get there. "At the far end of experience, through wisdom, you receive your innocence." This is in essence the Wise Fool of spiritual circles.

LANDLADY – Landlady, with fab lyrics layered on a very contemporary sound, is a song for Ali on the order of Wild Honey. I remember reading this story in some Bono interview or other, so there's no lie here! For me, I feel something of a Raised by Wolves vibe in the intro, the possible reflection of a shared childhood. My favorite bits are the marching drums and the 'every-this-and-that' ending. Incredibly moving lyrics once again, with "When I'm losing ground, you know she gives it back to me."

"Don't do. Just be"—the power of living in the present, returning to the "love and only love" of Electrical Storm.

THE BLACKOUT – A hopeful letter to the present moment, The Blackout is yet another favorite—powerful chorus, great music, and some winning interim electronics that present drums like treading water. I love the way the last line—"when the lights go out"—fades away with the words.

Fabulous, poetic lyrics like "In the darkness where you learn to see," "It takes darkness to see what's lost," and "When the lights go out, don't you ever doubt the light that we can really be."

LOVE IS BIGGER THAN ANYTHING IN ITS WAY – Love this one. A genuine feel-good song with mechanical overtones, there's the smidgen of an underlying sense of trying too hard to be cutting edge/contemporary here, to be (self-consciously) anthemic. But none of that distracts from a musically and lyrically uplifting, passionate, inspirational tune, filled with hope and beauty. I can hear this as a powerful audience singalong closing out the concert or an encore.

"When you think you're done, you've just begun."

13 (THERE IS A LIGHT) – This tune, with emphasis again on Bono's lush voice and Edge's atmospheric guitar, finishes the album for me, a bookmark balanced by the equally ethereal opening

Love is all We Have Left. The rest is bonus material.

This is an adult perspective of Song for Someone and includes that song's signature lyrics. There's the sense again of becoming a Wise Fool, of regaining a lost innocence. "Guard your innocence from hallucination and know that the darkness always gathers around the light. Hold on." A perfect example of a song written about one subject evolving into something else.

ORDINARY LOVE – Are you tough enough for ordinary love. An old tune, but I love it as much as ever. Pleased to see it included on *Songs of Experience*.

THE BOOK OF YOUR HEART – The Book of Your Heart, with a Spanish musical vibe, once again highlights Bono's voice, and displays some of *Songs of Experience*'s best and most poetic lyrics, including the very writerly "the long descriptive passage where you don't know what to say."

LIGHTS OF HOME (ST. PETER"S STRING VERSION – Nothing much to add.

YOU'RE THE BEST THING ABOUT ME (U2vKYGO) – The pop electronic dance beat does not help.

AS A FAN, I couldn't have asked for more from a band I've admired and enjoyed throughout much of my life. All in all, *Songs of Experience* presents us with an album that reflects the very best of U2's talent, with classic songs that resonate on so many levels, with brilliant writing, incomparable music, and spiritual depth. An album that, in fact, reveals a man who has regained his faith, a man who has perhaps found what he's been looking for.

Tuesday, December 12, 2017

U2 topped the Billboard 200 Chart for the eighth time with *Songs of Experience*, the only band to have done so in each decade from the 1980s on.

In an upcoming *BBC* U2 special that airs December 19, the band performs in the Abbey Road Studios. In the midst of a moving rendition of All I Want is You, with choir and orchestra, Bono recites lyrics from Walk to the Water. What a treat. They also played the *Howard Stern Show.*

Friday, December 29, 2017

In a December 27 *Rolling Stone* interview by Jann Werner, Bono references his health issue as an "extinction event," and calls *Songs of Experience* meditations on the power of love. But a remark about new music being "girly," lacking boldness or anger, avoiding big issues, brought me back to You're the Best Thing About Me. Where's the boldness? What big issue?

But I did appreciate a comment about our so-called President. "Big primates have been around a lot longer than democracy. This dude who shall not be named, he's just a new manifestation of that big primate."

Saturday, January 6, 2018

A gorgeous day. Much of the rest of the country gearing up for raw winter, with snow predicted south to Georgia and Florida. In essence, a Category 1 hurricane will dump a foot of snow on Long Island. With the wind-chill factor, one spot in New Hampshire's White Mountains threatens to reach -100°F.

U2.com put up a black-and-white video by film-maker and photographer Matt Mahurin, with a Bono voice-over reciting the liner notes from *Songs of Experience.* "You start with emptiness, you start with nothing, you start with the void . . ."

Sunday, January 21, 2018

An animated video for Get Out of Your Own Way has KKK creatures in pointy-headed bed-sheets, frothing and fuming outside the White House, before retreating to their homes armed only with briefcases.

Sunday, January 28, 2018

No U2 nominations for the *Grammy Awards* tonight, but they'll play "live on tape" from a barge Friday night on the Hudson River.

Saturday, February 3, 2018

Hope to close out *A Grand Madness, U2 Twenty Years After*, the follow-up to *A Grand Madness, Ten Years on the Road with U2*, with two November *eXperience Tour* shows in Dublin, with Sharon, Jane, and Declan.

Wednesday, February 13, 2018

A couple of Pairs Short Program participants in *Winter Olympics* figure-skating performed to Jeff Beck and the Beatles in Pyeongchang, China last night. Where was U2? I thought. And up popped Canadians Meagan Duhamel and Eric Radford, skating to Provo, Utah native April Meservy's sultry rendition of With or Without you.

Sunday, February 18, 2018

In the true spirit of the Olympics, a forty-three-year-old skier from Mexico came in dead last in Cross-country Skiing. As he approached the finish-line, someone handed him a huge Mexican flag. Four fellow skiers had waited behind to congratulate him.

Thursday, February 22, 2018

On Valentine's Day, a mentally ill nineteen-year-old shot up a high-school in Parkland, Florida, killing three adults and fourteen young people between the ages of fourteen and seventeen! At a *CNN Town Hall*, the school's theatre troupe delivered Shine, a powerful song written by students Sawyer Garrity and Andrea Pena, about getting back up when you've been knocked down. Such inspiration from articulate, courageous survivors.

Thursday, April 12, 2018

U2 rehearsing in Laval, Quèbec.

Saturday, April 28, 2018

A lustrous blue day here at the cabin [Chiricahua Mountains, Arizona], with a cloud of yellow irises glowing out front and the north-side apple trees a froth of creamy pink petals.

GA fans are already in line for U2 in Tulsa next week.

Wednesday, May 2, 2018

Bougainvillea, paloverde, bird of paradise, and oleander are all in vibrant bloom in the back yard, with limey new leaves layered against the dusty mauve of the mountains.

The sound-check crowd for U2's *eXPERIENCE + iNNOCENCE TOUR* opener in Tulsa showcased just how many older fans are now bringing their children.

Thursday, May 3, 2018

The lads fired up the *xPERIENCE TOUR* at 8:00 p.m. last night. Twenty-seven songs, Wild Horses and Hold Me Thrill Me among them. No opening act. And no one fell off the stage!

Sunday, May 6, 2018

1:40 p.m. On our flight to San Jose [California]. Half an hour to Phoenix, a short sprint Concourse B to Concourse A, a forty-five minute wait, and we were off.

5:00 p.m. In our room—#416—at the Hotel de Anza on Santa Clara Avenue. We skirted the foothills of the city on landing and hopped a taxi into town. Room service has just delivered a salmon fillet with risotto, steak with mashed potatoes and mushroom cream sauce, crispy onions, and roasted Brussels sprouts.

Outside our fourth floor window, San Jose Shark hockey fans came and went from the nearby U2 venue, SAP Arena, glum on their return, having lost to the Las Vegas Golden Knights in *Stanley Cup* playoffs.

Monday, May 7, 2018

Sitting in flowery San Pedro Market. The two-room Peralta Adobe here, part of the Fallon House Historic Site, commemorates the founding of El Pueblo de San Jose de Guadalupe. Manuel Gonzalez—first resident and second mayor—an Apache member of Juan Bautista de Anza's expedition from Tubac, Arizona to San Francisco, erected the small, white-washed adobe with shingled roof and heavy wooden door, in 1797. (Luis Maria Peralta was the adobe's second occupant.) An ox-yoke dangles from the rafters of the front porch, and a beehive oven—a horno—rises to the right, in a bank of prickly-pear.

2:00 p.m. Riding the Downtown-Mountain View trolley back to San Jose. We wandered Market Street, popping into St. Joseph's Basilica, and then had a seafood lunch outdoors at McCormick and Schmidt's—sour dough bread, lobster bisque, tuna tartare, and coconut shrimp.

The impressive sculpture next door, *Ursa Mater*—mama bear—had been raised by Alameda artists Mr. and Mrs. Ferguson, using two-hundred-fifty-thousand Canadian pennies. Some copper-based coins had already turned green, reflecting sunlight like ruffled fur.

The light-rail to Mountain View afforded an occasional glimpse of smoke-blue hills as we chugged through Silicon Valley, all upscale housing estates, retail strips, and lushly landscaped commercial enclaves—Yahoo, Google, Lockheed, PayPal, NBC, Canon, Samsung, Kawasaki. At the terminus, Mountain View spread out in a California ambience of rose gardens, boutiques, hedge-rows, and towering eucalyptus, magnolia, and ironwood trees.

2:30 p.m. Rolling back through Santa Clara, under bright blue skies.

2:50 p.m. Bumper to bumper multi-lane California traffic on US101 (LA/San Francisco).

Wednesday, May 9, 2018

Arrived in Tucson yesterday at 4:05 p.m.

Before Las Vegas is upon me, here's the San Jose set-list: Love is All we Have Left; The Blackout; The Lights of Home (St. Peter's String Version); Beautiful Day (Many Rivers to Cross); I Will Follow (Mother); Gloria (with a bit of Van Morrison's); All Because of You; The Ocean; Iris; Cedarwood Road; Sunday Bloody Sunday; Raised by Wolves (Psalm 23); End of the World (Amsterdam)//Hold Me Thrill Me Kiss Me Kill Me//Elevation; Vertigo; Desire; Acrobat (Sympathy for the Devil); Best Thing About Me (Landlady); Staring at the Sun; Pride (This is not America); Get Out of Your Own Way; American Soul; City of Blinding Lights//One; Love is Bigger Than

Anything in its Way; 13 (There is a Light)

The opening screens, eight to eight-thirty, threw up a variety of slogans—Empowered Women Empower Women, Nowhere on earth do women have as many opportunities as men, Vote, Equal=Rights, Herstory, Refugees We Welcome, Educate a girl, empower a woman—and pre-show music included De Peche Mode's All I Ever Wanted and John Lydon's Anger is our Energy.

The set-up mirrored the *iNNOCENCE TOUR*, two stages and a cat-walk, with suspended screen and detachable elements above. *Songs of Innocence* tunes comprised a rather large portion of the first hour and I had trouble with mushy sound, which one reviewer described as "over-amplification." Moreover, the e-stage presented an excess of rear views, the band playing predominantly to the right side of the arena.

Love is All We Have Left opened in darkness, Bono concealed at first inside a blue/black screen. The Blackout kicked in then with band member silhouettes. Beautiful Day, in crimson, included a snippet of Jimmy Cliff's Many Rivers to Cross. "Jerry Harrison right in front of you," Bono sang, the Talking Heads guitar/keyboardist presumably in the audience.

This present-moment snapshot segued into the *Innocence* portion of the show. Songs from I Will Follow, Gloria, and The Ocean, to Cedarwood Road, an acoustic Sunday Bloody Sunday, Raised by Wolves (ending with Psalm 23,) and End of the World, marked the childhood events and experiences that had propelled Bono into music. An animated Hold Me Thrill Me with "Our Heroes" making their way to the big time, marked a short intermission.

On the e-stage then, the band delivered Elevation, Vertigo, and Desire, a trio of potent *Experience* tunes. "Haven't seen you in quite a while," Bono declared as he morphed into MacPhisto, whose creepy, filed-tooth face flits over Bono's for Acrobat. "Desire, greed, lust, deceit, vanity, all essentials to the showman in all his forms."

You're the Best Thing About Me opened with a snippet of Landlady, a full moon reflected on the stage floor. An acoustic

Staring at the Sun came next, with Edge and Bono, an eclipsed sun projected on the floor, the digital screen overflowing with Charlottesville KKK images.

A red-lit Stars-and-Stripes flag backed American Soul—my favorite portion of *Experience* shows—and the main set closed with City of Blinding Lights, drone shots of San Jose on-screen.

The single encore presented One, along with the positivism of Love is Bigger Than Anything in its Way and then Bono retreated to the e-stage for 13 (There is a Light). Here he pulled up the giant light-bulb of the *iNNOCENCE TOUR* from inside a miniature Cedarwood Road house, sent it swinging toward the main stage, and then disappeared by a roped off side-aisle.

Thursday, May 10, 2018

7:00 p.m. In our room—#3914—in the Empire (State Building) Tower of New York New York Hotel and Casino in Las Vegas. Dan and I set off for the airport at ten-thirty this morning, only fifty-seven minutes in the air, take-off and landing both turbulent affairs from rising desert heat. We ate supper at the cozy Nine Fine Irishmen Pub here in the hotel—seafood chowder and a rather soupy Irish stew. The hockey game on-screen in the bar advanced the *Stanley Cup* playoffs, with Washington, DC up against Winnipeg, Manitoba, the winner to face the Las Vegas Golden Knights for the trophy.

Outside of the casino portion of the hotel, which is all noise and light and color, the hotel's interior periphery reconstructs the quieter back streets of New York City—the tenements, shop fronts, and eateries. Our high-rise room looks down on The Strip, where Bono is likely to be out celebrating his fifty-eighth birthday later tonight. To our left, the MGM Grand's walkway crosses over to the Tropicana. A second bridge takes pedestrians to the Excalibur, behind which rise the Luxor and Mandalay Bay. Further out, beyond the hotels and casinos, the airport runs at right angles to The Strip.

T-Mobile Arena stands just next door, reached through NYNY's parking garage. An outdoor escalator descends to the U2 venue's front door on Toshiba Plaza.

Friday, May 11, 2018

4:10 p.m. We drifted through the shops on the casino floor and then had supper at Fulton's fish and chips shop—deep-fried cod, fried clams, and clam chowder. We ate at an 'outdoor' table on a faux cobblestone street, under a faux fire-escape balcony, beside a faux apple tree. Hagen Daz and people-watching then, on the second floor.

Monday, May 14, 2018

Lazed about Saturday morning until nine. Then up, packed, and to the airport by eleven. A Mother's Day dinner Sunday at Tucson's Outback.

We headed for the venue Friday night about seven-thirty. A twenty minute wait in the Will Call line, fifteen more at security, and we were in. We sat with a fine young couple from Las Vegas, married only three years. Originally from Palatine, Illinois, the woman, in her forties—though looking much younger—had grown up with U2. She seemed a tad hesitant to admit to having seen the band in concert six times. (Las Vegas was my ninety-first show!)

Here's the set-list: Love is all We Have Left; The Blackout; The Lights of Home; Beautiful Day; I Will Follow (Mother); Gloria (Van Morrison); Red Flag Day; The Ocean; Iris; Cedarwood Road; Sunday Bloody Sunday (When Johnny Comes Marching Home); Raised by Wolves; End of the World (Amsterdam); Elevation; Vertigo (It's Only Rock and Roll but I Like it); Desire (Hunka Burning Love); Acrobat (Landlady); Best Thing; Staring at the Sun; Pride (This is Not America); Get Out of Your Own Way; American Soul; City of Blinding Lights; One (Invisible); Love is Bigger Than Anything in its Way; 13 (There is a Light)

I've already worked up a blog-post review.

U2's eXPERIENCE + iNNOCENCE Tour in Las Vegas

Recently, Dan and I headed up to Sin City for the fifth installment of U2's *eXPERIENCE + iNNOCENCE Tour.* 2016's *iNNOCENCE + eXPERIENCE* outing (Part 1 of their on-gong *i/e Tour*) had been followed by the 30th Anniversary tour of U2's classic album, *The Joshua Tree*, and with Phoenix uncharacteristically absent from their current schedule, Las Vegas—and San Jose earlier in the week—were the closest to home U2 would come.

At this stage in my life, a little Las Vegas goes a long way. The city has changed only superficially from earlier visits going back thirty, even forty years. Statuesque call-girls on the arms of suited-up business men, and plumped out housewives pumping one-armed bandits, have been largely replaced by more 'ordinary' sorts—families with young children, even infants, show-goers in spandex, short-shorts, and flowing summer dresses, and clusters of girls'-and-boys'-night-outers—all of them wrapped up, as ever, in perpetual casino twilight, and the incessant electronic hums and bleeps of gaming pods themed with cable TV shows, *Game of Thrones* to *The Walking Dead*.

I've never been a gambler myself—at least not of the Las Vegas variety—but the steadfast glitz and glare of the city was a small price to pay for a U2 show. We stayed in New York New York, whose second floor meeting rooms connect to a parking garage, where an outside escalator drops down to Toshiba Plaza and the entrance to the U2 venue, T-Mobile Arena.

With no opening act, U2 were at work by eight-thirty, on a set-up that mirrored the *Innocence Tour*—two stages (*I* and *e*), and a catwalk with detachable elements running between them, walled in by two giant video screens. The musical structure of the show broke fittingly into three distinct sections bookended by Love is All we Have Left and 13 (There is a Light). The first several songs—Love is All we Have Left, The Blackout, Lights of Home, and Beautiful Day—make up a sort of intro, a contemporary snapshot that places the show in its context in the present moment. (Significantly, no tunes were drawn from *No Line on the Horizon*, *Zooropa* or, of course, *The Joshua Tree*, that album having been played in its entirety over the last year. Rumors have *Achtung Baby* slated for a 2021 30th

Anniversary tour, with a likely European opener, so *Zooropa* should have its day.)

Out of twenty-six tunes, nine—I Will Follow to Until the End of the World—frame the *Innocence* portion of the concert, comprised of the band's early influences, childhood experiences, memories, and events, not the least of these being Bono's loss of his mother at the age of fourteen. The trio of Red Flag Day, *October*'s The Ocean, and Iris was a highpoint for me. The staging and optics of Iris through Until the End of the World replicate the *iNNOCENCE Tour* and I particularly enjoyed hearing Gloria in the mix, Bono introducing his band mates as of old.

An animated band *Heroes Journey* intermission, accompanied by Gavin Friday's rendition of Hold Me Thrill Me Kiss Me Kill Me, introduces the *Experience* portion of the show, Elevation through City of Blinding Lights. Aspects of present-day politics, past U2 incarnations, and song-writing commentary were featured here. The Elevation, Vertigo, Desire sequence was one of the strongest moments of the entire show for me, as was a stunning and most welcomed performance of *Achtung Baby*'s Acrobat, one of my all-time U2 favorites—never before played live on tour, and so apropos for our times. "And you can dream so dream out loud . . . . And know that your time is coming 'round. So don't let the bastards grind you down!"

MacPhisto, creepier than ever, with sharp pointy teeth and stunted devil horns, made a brief appearance with Acrobat. His eerie face flashed repeatedly over Bono's as he primped in a mirror, reciting bits of Landlady. MacPhisto, who would certainly be preening at this stage in his life—old rock stars never die, they just play Las Vegas—asked rather pointedly (for this city), "Is there a dermatologist in the house?" (And, of course, there was!)

A large portion of *Experience* takes place on the small round *e* stage at the far end of the venue. As Dan and I had superb seats in the arena's back bend on Edge's side, this was quite a boon, though the band—Adam excluded, bless him—appeared to be working on the assumption that no fans whatever were seated in that back corner. We were left with an over-abundance of, literal, rear shots.

A second intermission featured Edge's daughter, Sian, accompanied by Jim O'Rourke's Women of the World. Various placards popped up on-screen—Fight Back, Vote, Don't Shoot, Give Peace a Chance, Sisters and Brothers Stand up for each Other, No one is equal until all of us are equal, and Refugees Welcome. This pulled the audience squarely back to the present and was echoed in the three songs of the encore—One, dedicated to all those affected by the massacre in Las Vegas in October of last year ("Thoughts and prayers are not enough."), Love is Bigger Than Anything in its Way, and 13 (There is a Light), which ends the show with a quiet hopefulness ("Darkness gathers around the light. Hold on."). Yahweh had done the same, following All Because of You on the *Vertigo Tour*, Moment of Surrender on *360*. (There always has to be hope. A full moon on a dark night.) With wisdom, at the far end of Experience, Innocence can be recovered.

As with *The Joshua Tree*, so obviously steeped in American thought and imagery, this leg of *eXPERIENCE + iNNOCENCE* similarly reflected on America, the highpoint, for me, on so many levels, being American Soul, delivered with all the power and passion of Bullet the Blue Sky.

U2 has always had an uncanny ability to seize, interpret, comment on, or expand a moment, and this extraordinary show in Las Vegas was no exception, a never to be forgotten brief moment of magic.

Wednesday, May 16, 2018

The lads, in LA tonight, released a cheeky skit in which Bono and Edge, 'working' as assistants to Ellen DeGeneres, are tasked with procuring refreshments for Ellen's writers. Edge contacts the Commissary to ascertain the soup of the day, while Bono plants his feet on a desk-top and does absolutely nothing.

At the Commissary then, Edge struggles with slats of drinks stacked in a shopping cart and balances them on his lap for the golf-cart ride back to the studio. And again, Bono doesn't lift a finger.

Thursday, May 17, 2018

The second U2 LA Forum show last night.

Booked the final bits of November's Dublin/Halifax trip. These Irish concerts will be the perfect closure for *A Grand Madness,* Part 2.

Thursday, May 24, 2018

Sirius radio will offer a U2 channel—#30—for a month, beginning the first of June. On the eleventh, the band will play the Apollo Theatre in Harlem, an event to be streamed on Sirius two days later.

Saturday, May 26, 2018

No hockey fan by any means, but it seems fair to note that it's the Las Vegas Golden Knights versus the Washington Capitals, vying for the *Stanley Cup* in early June.

Friday, June 1, 2018

Sirius channel #30 fired up today.

Saturday, June 2, 2018

Bono toppled off the stage at one of U2's Chicago shows. Ever The Showman, he carried on as if nothing had happened.

Friday, June 8, 2018

(Last night, the Las Vegas Golden Knights lost the *Stanley Cup* to the Washington Capitals.)

During one of U2's Montreal shows, Bono commended Canada as "a light in dark times."

Sunday, June 10, 2018

Justify won the *Triple Crown.* Invited to the White House, he declined, saying if he wanted to see a horse's ass, he'd have come in second.

In Uniondale, New York last night, U2 sound-checked Red Flag Day, Stuck in a Moment, Who's Gonna Ride Your Wild Horses, and When Love Comes to Town, the latter possibly for the Apollo.

The Peralta Adobe, San Jose, California – May 7, 2018

Ursa Mater, San Jose – May 7, 2018

Ursa Mater, San Jose – May 7, 2018

SAP Center, San Jose – May 7, 2018

Sunday Bloody Sunday in San Jose – May 7, 2018

Desire in San Jose – May 7, 2018

New York New York Hotel and Casino, Las Vegas, Nevada – May 10, 2018

New York New York Registration Desk – May 10, 2018

Las Vegas, Nevada – May 10, 2018

Nine Fine Irishmen Pub, New York New York, Las Vegas – May 10, 2018

New York New York – May 10, 2018

New York New York – May 10, 2018

T-Mobile Arena, Las Vegas – May 11, 2018

Elevation, Las Vegas – May 11, 2018

MacPhisto, Acrobat, Las Vegas – May 11, 2018

Staring at the Sun, Las Vegas – May 11, 2018

Get Out of Your Own Way, Las Vegas – May 11, 2018

Love is Bigger Than Anything in its Way, Las Vegas – May 11, 2018

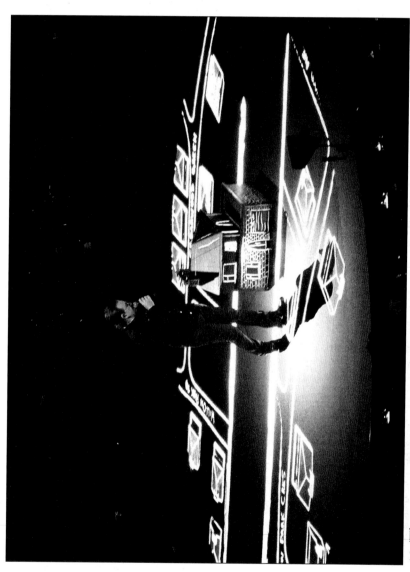

13 (There is a Light), Las Vegas – May 11, 2018

Bono, the New Guinea Singing Dog, Wild Spirit Wolf Sanctuary,
Ramah, New Mexico – June 19, 2018

Danielle, with Elaine Woodhall, displays Elaine's U2 quilt – December
2018

The water meadow and the Conestoga River, The Cottage, Southern Ontario, Canada – August 19, 2018

Wednesday, June 13, 2018

Sirius XM streamed Monday night's U2 performance at the Apollo Theatre in Harlem at 2:00 p.m. this afternoon. The fifteen minutes of Bill Flanagan-emceed pre-show rambling I caught, included an arty Gavin Friday, who duets with Arcade Fire's Régine Chassagne for *eli*'s Hold Me Thrill Me intermission.

A segregated Harlem theater, launched in 1914 as Hurtig and Seamon's New Burlesque Theater, re-opened in 1934 as the Apollo, an ornate venue seating fifteen-hundred. The U2 crowd numbered a thousand.

The evening opened with I Will Follow—"You looked through the window of my soul. I'm lost, now I'm found"—Electric Co, with "I can see for miles and miles and miles" and a bit of Send in the Clowns, and Out of Control, the band's first single, written on Bono's eighteenth birthday. This trio summed up the band's frenetic early days.

"That's enough of the old songs," Bono announced then, slipping into All Because of You. With Vertigo and Elevation, he talked up Adam—"a genuinely funky guy for an Irish guy in Harlem"—and Larry, in his "stylish spectacles."

For Pride, geared toward immigrants with its "boy washed up on an empty beach," Bono confessed to "thinking of the great American poets that turned the Apollo into the great cathedral that it is." And a different kind of poet from Atlanta, Georgia, who had "a dream big enough to fit the whole world, a dream big enough for each and every one of us." Dreamers like "James Brown, Aretha, Billy Holliday, and Harry Belafonte," who was "in the house." Dreamers from Addis Ababa, from Caracao, from Guatemala City, and Dublin. "They're all still waiting to wake up in that dream."

A rousing Get Out of Your Own Way and American Soul followed. How could they come back to the Apollo without "bending the knee" in a "sacred place?" Bono asked.

Several tunes from Desire onward featured New York City brass bands the Sun Ra Arkestra and the Sex Mob Orchestra. When Love

Comes to Town—not usually a favorite—excelled, with spotlighted soloists.

In the recent past, we'd "lost some great people," Bono said. "And gained a few useless ones." (I'm thinking DJT here.) Some by their own hand. Here Bono named Anthony Bourdain, who'd committed suicide just a week or so earlier. Bourdain, a great storyteller, probably "had a lot of stories he couldn't tell us." Stuck in a Moment, inspired by "a great friend of ours—Michael Hutchence," came next.

An achingly beautiful Every Breaking Wave, with solo piano, excelled and Wild Horses' "Don't you look back" set the tone for a band now focused on the future. Love is Bigger than Anything in its Way wrapped up a stellar performance, which like all the best of U2, emphasized the duality of realism and hope. "Be safe. Be brave."

"What a night! Really, what a night!"

Tuesday, June 19, 2018

12:50 p.m. Leaving Wild Spirit Wolf Sanctuary out of Ramah, New Mexico. The refuge grew from the vision of local artist Jacque Evans, whose subject matter evolved from horses to wolves in the early 1990s. Friends and acquaintances began bringing her the wild pets they could no longer handle. Arctic and timber wolves live alongside coyotes, wild-dogs, dingoes, one beautiful red fox named Romeo, and a handful of harmonizing New Guinea Singing Dogs, descended from dingoes separated from the Australian mainland by continental drift. One of the youngest Singing Dogs was Bono, named after the singer himself.

Thursday, June 21, 2018

9:15 a.m. Off on I-70 across Kansas, Sirius U2 Channel 30 operational as we close in on the cottage—City of Blinding Lights, Fool (Demo), The Fly, Kite, Everlasting Love, One, Pride . . . . Bad.

Friday, June 22, 2018

9:30 a.m. The misted hills and bottomlands of western Iowa. Cool and overcast. A gorgeous Oh, Berlin, and Bad from Dublin 1989.

11:45 a.m. Just passed the turn-off to Waterloo . . . *Iowa*. Boo!

3:00 p.m. The wide, coffee-brown Mississippi River, rolling south between brushy banks as we slip into Wisconsin. "I am the black jeep of the family."

Sunday, June 24, 2018

. . . . Bad (Paris, 1987)

6:45 p.m. Here we are at the Holiday Inn, Windsor, Ontario. When Canadian Customs inquired as to the purpose of our trip, Dan explained that we had a cottage on the Conestoga River, near Drayton. But we also wanted to get as far away as possible from our President.

Sirius U2 has been extended through July.

From a review of Madison Square Garden U2 by Ryan Leas, a *Stereogum* journalist: "He pulled something out from inside himself, magnified it and gave it to everyone else." Well put.

Saturday, June 30, 2018

9:30 p.m. From a beach-house veranda on Cape Cod, Bono and Edge serenaded two hundred radio contest winners with Vertigo, Stuck in a Moment, Every Breaking Wave, Summer of Love, Love is Bigger Than Anything in its Way, and One.

U2 have applied for planning permission to build a four-story U2 Exhibition Centre in Dublin, on the site of their old studio at 15-18 Hanover Quay. Hanover will be demolished.

Tuesday, July 3, 2018

The New World leg of *e/i* closes in Connecticut tonight.

Awesome news out of Africa. At least three rhino poachers, who broke into Sibuya Game Reserve in South Africa, were killed and eaten by a pride of lions.

Wednesday, July 11, 2018

Vox posted a *Zooropa* review by writer Dylan Scott, first published July 8, for *Zooropa*'s 25th Anniversary. [*Zooropa* was first released July 5, 1993.] "These guys saw it (the new digital age) and they recognized it, even if they were as perplexed as anyone about what you were supposed to do about it. Their only real conclusion is to do the same thing you did before: You miss your mom, you get mad at your dad, you fall in love, you get high, sometimes you wonder what the point of all this really is. But you don't give up. You keep living. It just sounds a little bit different."

Tuesday, July 31, 2018

A gorgeous late summer day, with high clouds and sunshine. As I listen in on the last of Sirius U2, I'm overlooking the water-meadow at the cottage [Conestoga River, Ontario], reduced in size through the years by advancing tree lines from east and west, and by the broad umbrella of a gigantic white willow on the river bank below. Today the meadow shimmers in green, stem and leaf—apple, beryl, olive, sap, and jade. Dips and hollows and hillocks shelter red-winged blackbird nests, garden-spider webs, and rodent byways. At night fireflies stand in for the cabbage butterflies, monarchs, painted ladies, and white admirals of summer afternoons, and the buzz of cicadas gives way to crickets and the odd gruff mournfulness of a bull frog.

The glowing apricot trumpets of orange day lilies lean south from the lip of the hill, nodding over three-foot-high grasses. The soft radiance of spotted joe-pye weed in dusty mauve and amethyst has opened up all across the meadow and will stay until late fall. By summer's end, the deep purple of New England aster, a half-dozen varieties of goldenrod, and the white froth of Canada fleabane and swamp aster will dominate.

Monday, August 6, 2018

Sirius stats put Bad at the top of their rotation list, played ten times.

Saturday, August 25, 2018

John McCain died today, diagnosed fourteen months ago with the same virulent brain tumor Ted Kennedy succumbed to. He was one of the last decent Republicans standing.

Tuesday, August 28, 2018

Bono, quoted in a German journal, speaks of Europe as

standing together to face down extreme nationalism. Their Old World *Experience Tour* braces to pump up the ideals of a united Europe, even flying an EU flag in defense of diversity, a plea to strengthen and protect democracy.

Thursday, August 30, 2018

European *e/i* opens in Berlin tomorrow night. The band played an entire rehearsal set yesterday. Even Better replaces Desire, Summer of Love stands in for Staring at the Sun, New Year's Day for American Soul. Perfect for a European audience, though I'm so grateful to have heard American Soul live, a highlight of our New World shows.

Friday, August 31, 2018

Aretha Franklin's funeral took place in Detroit today, 8:00 a.m. to 1:00 p.m. Her open-casket viewing had her lying serenely in a flaming red dress and crimson spiked heels.

After a service in Phoenix, John McCain too lies in state at the U.S. capital. Neither DJT nor Sarah Palin have been invited to the funeral, which is as it should be.

Saturday, September 1, 2018

John McCain's memorial honored both the man and the country. A sort of protest. People at all levels sticking a thumb in the so-called President's eye. "You are not what this country is about and we will not let you change us."

Declan took in the opening European U2 *eXPERIENCE* concert in Berlin last night. Fantastic, he said, adding that he was speechless after the show. Five songs into second Berlin, Bono lost his voice and the show was cancelled. Hand to his throat, he'd turned his back to the audience, asked for the smoke machines to be turned off, and the crowd picked up the balance of Red Flag Day. Declan had noticed that the arena seemed smokier than the first night. "You could almost taste it," he said.

Sunday, September 2, 2018

Nothing serious for Bono, we hear. The Berlin concert moved

to mid-November.

Tuesday, September 4, 2018

"McCain staged his death like the final act of *Richard III*, every legitimate force in the state, living and dead, combined against the wicked king." David Frum [Republican speech writer for George W. Bush.]

Thursday, September 13, 2018

In Paris on Sunday, Bono invited a child in a top-hat to the stage for Beautiful Day, a gesture I've missed in *e/i* shows.

From all I've seen or heard of the Continental *Experience* shows, the opening visuals are powerful. Devastating snapshots of European cities that were bombed during World War II—Berlin, Koln, Paris, Dublin—backed by the final speech from Charlie Chaplin's *The Great Dictator*, key words magnified on-screen. Reminiscent of *Zooropa*'s Nazi drummer-boy, I thought. EU flags flying as well, those of individual countries replacing an EU star.

Wednesday, September 19, 2018

Had breakfast in the A La Mode Café [Drayton, Ontario] this morning. A sign on the wall quotes Johnny Cash's response to how he would describe paradise. "This morning, with her, having coffee."

Friday, September 21, 2018

U2 played Spanish Eyes in Madrid tonight.

Monday, September 24, 2018

11:00 a.m. Presently idled in a long, long queue for the crossing of the Ambassador Bridge [Windsor, Ontario to Detroit, Michigan]. With the border tunnel temporarily closed, lines have swelled.

2:40 p.m. Finally reached I-75 south, heading for Ohio. Our customs agent asked if we weren't going on to Tacoma. "Isn't that how the song goes?" he said, and sang us a verse of The Eagles Take it Easy. ["I went from Phoenix, Arizona all the way to Tacoma" is actually from the Steve Miller Band's Rock'n Me. But we did appreciate the agent's spirit.]

Friday, September 28, 2018

The Kavanagh hearings have wrapped up, his accusers dismissed in every sense of the word. An ultra-conservative Supreme Court could stymie U.S. social progress for decades. Moreover, Kavanagh believes a sitting President can't be criminally charged while in office. Is this how democracy dies?

A friend of Bono's, with published pieces in both Irish and English newspapers, has highlighted Bono's "fragility"—Ali helping him off the stage and into a car, grasping hands for steadiness. Larry too must be feeling the strain of touring, with hand-therapy before and after each performance.

Monday, October 8, 2018

The dean of Yale Law School has called the confirmation of Kavanagh to the U.S. Supreme Court "an American tragedy."

Wednesday, October 10, 2018

Rattle and Hum released thirty years ago today.

What a "romantic" idea Europe is, Bono has mused. Countries speaking different languages but being One. The dream of America as the Promised Land is fading.

Saturday, October 13, 2018

U2's first Milan concert opened up the set for more *Songs of Experience*.

Tuesday, October 23, 2018

Everything in order for Ireland/Halifax, but for the Clayton Hotel at Dublin airport.

So flummoxed at a recent London sound-check, Sue had trouble with an Edge selfie. And so Edge, bless him, took the photo himself.

Saturday, October 27, 2018

Edge and Adam both stopped by the Savoy Cinema for Dublin's 30th Anniversary screening of *Rattle and Hum* on Friday night. They spoke briefly to an audience of less than a hundred invitees.

Saturday, November 3, 2018

We ought to be settling into the Maldron Hotel [Tallaight, Dublin] tonight. Instead, serious personal circumstances have kept us in Tucson and we've had to cancel our trip! Sue, Jane, Declan, and Sharon will fill in for me in time with their concert impressions.

Wednesday, November 7, 2018

A *60 Minutes* segment on Sunday introduced the Devil Worm, found twenty-two miles below the surface of the earth in a South African gold mine. The nematode—*Halicephalobus mephisto*—*H. mephisto*, for short—was named for the demon of Faustian legend. Macphisto would love that.

Monday, November 12, 2018

Amnesty International has rescinded Aung San Suu Kyi's *Ambassador of Conscience Award*.

Wednesday, November 14, 2018

"Do not be daunted by the enormity of the world's grief. Do justly, now. Love mercy, now. Walk humbly, now. You are not obligated to complete the work, but neither are you free to abandon it." (The Talmud)

The *eXPERIENCE + iNNOCENCE TOUR* closed in Berlin last night. Bono so emotional, even tearful. "We're going away for a long while," he said.

Declan had a brilliant time in the city, visiting Hansa Ton Studio, among other U2 sites. The hairs on the back of his neck stood up when the tour guide played One over the PA system. Berlin, the final concert of the tour, videoed for eventual DVD release, was another fantastic performance, he said. Some long-time U2 crew members, all exceptionally pleasant, 'accompanied' Declan on his flight back to Dublin.

Sunday, November 26, 2018

Bono and Pharrel Williams crooned a pleasing Beegees' Stayin' Alive on Jimmy Kimmel's *Red Special* last week.

The U2 crew has been asked to set aside dates for next year. Oz must be a go.

Wednesday, November 28, 2018

God wants spiritual fruits from us, not religious nuts.

Wednesday, December 19, 2018

And now for those lost Dublin shows, grateful for friends' input.

Sue writes that "the show on Tuesday, 6 November was one of those magical ones. I had a seat and my friend Debbi was on the floor (I didn't want to do the floor in Dublin), and we both felt that it was one of those 'special' gigs that happen with U2 every now and then. Luckily, I was in a block that stood up, but lots of others sat. (How can you sit at a rock concert?!) The show was amazing right from the beginning, loud audience and the band a hundred percent. We fed off each other and it was powerful. I've a lot of fave parts of the show, but I must admit the *Achtung Baby/Zooropa* segment blew me away. It brought back many memories and the 2018 version was done so well. Bono going into the well-known pose at the mention of Berlin sealed it! I was transported back to those amazing *Zoo* days when we went to lots of shows and when friendships were forged that are still strong today.

"Bono's MacPhisto speech was touching (and different from usual). He spoke of seeing his dad in himself when he looked in the mirror that morning, and that he missed him and hoped he would have been proud of him and his brother. Then he went into a tirade against Trump, the first and only time he did that during the shows I saw. When Love is Bigger finished, the whole crowd sang the 'oh oh's for ages, and Bono was very emotional, just standing on the main stage almost crying. A very moving moment. These are the shows that make me realize why I've stuck with this band for thirty-five years! All U2 shows are good. Some, like this one, are magical. They take you to another almost spiritual level. They've also brought me special friendships with people I met because of a mutual love of U2, but who I've a lot more in common with. And that's pretty amazing as well."

Jane spoke of "excellent visuals, performance, and vocals. An outstanding MacPhisto, and an intimate B-stage.”

Sharon has written: “Such emotional shows, the highlights—for me Acrobat and Wild Horses—wonderfully high! I did feel that their age showed—Bono so stiff doing the small jumps on and off the platforms. Edge totally ‘dad dancing,’ just having fun.

“MacPhisto, when looking in the mirror on the second night, and comparing himself to his dad, seemed so sad it brought tears to my eyes. And if they were not saying ‘goodbye,’ then it was at least ‘au revoir.’ A friend at the last Berlin gig mentioned Bono’s closing remark about going away for a long time. At times, though, I felt they were not all that relaxed or were trying too hard, as they so often do when playing Dublin. Of course, this could all be chalked up to my own mood. I’m often quite sad at a last show, thinking this might well be the last time I’ll see them live.

“As they were leaving, Bono said ‘we are only here cos Larry loves it so much!’ Larry just waved an arm while walking away. (There’s a song in there somewhere!)

“For all I sound a little negative, I still wouldn’t have wanted to be anywhere else. The only thing missing was you, Dianne!”

Bless you, Sharon.

Declan writes: “Four awesome shows at the 3Arena, or Point Depot as I prefer to call it. The venue being relatively small, its B-stage sat in the middle of the runway. Monday, Tuesday, and Saturday I was seated, standing on Friday night when Dirty Day debuted and MacPhisto was in exceptional form. Saturday, the best of my *Experience* shows, saw Acrobat more intense than ever.

“What a week! What a tour! This is no time not to be alive.”

Friday, December 21, 2018

Winter Solstice and the Full Long Nights Moon, hazy with ice crystals, riding high over the Tanque Verde Mountains.

Picked up two quilts Elaine and Larry created from a dozen or so of my old U2 t-shirts. Incredible work! Dazzling and intense. Elaine handles the design, Larry the quilting.

"For Dianne," they'd stitched on one of the labels. "Remember you are the music."

Exercised today to Foo Fighters' Everlong, Fine Young Cannibals' She Drives me Crazy, and the Moody Blues' In Your Wildest Dreams. "When the music plays, I hear the sound I had to follow . . . ."

For me, that sound would be U2's Bad in 1985, when "I heard a song that made some sense out of the world." (The Miracle of Joey Ramone)

Monday, December 31, 2018

. . . . and then, of course, there's U2. One more year of brilliant live performances, filled with passion and power, intimacy and warmth. Not as many as I'd hoped for perhaps, but surely enough. After all, the only thing to follow one experience is another experience. And that one will pass too.

Remarkable that these four old school-mates have made glorious music together for over forty years. Should their touring days be over—and they will be, one day—their musical legacy will continue to be the sound-track of my life, the rhythm of all my days.

Should they find themselves on the road again, I'll be there—for as much grand madness as I can manage.

Afterword

Over thirty years have passed since I first encountered U2's music; nearly twenty since the publication of my first U2 memoir, *A Grand Madness, Ten Years on the Road with U2.*

To many of us, great music is some kind of sacrament. If music can heal, level barriers, and educate, then by its power, timelessness, and inspiration, U2's music will continue to play a distinctive role in contemporary culture, helping us to share our hopes and sorrows, our dignity and joy.

And if art is an attempt to identify yourself, then U2's art shows an honesty, integrity, and depth of commitment that for me has been impossible to resist.

What fan could ask for more?

Appendix – U2 On-line Sites

The following is a brief list of current on-line U2 sites. I did not think it feasible to include the many sites specific to particular countries. I apologize in advance for those and any other omissions.

AtU2.com: News, Lyrics, Tours, Photos, Calendar, Band, Forum.

onlineonthehorizon.com: Joe's U2 Fansite: "This site provides the latest news stories, recordings, and information about U2's music and concerts. The site also hosts the photos I have taken from all the U2 shows I attended in the past."

Team Adam Clayton: "All proceeds from the sale of Team Adam products will be donated to the MusiCares MAP Fun in honor of Adam Clayton, the incomparable bassist of U2."

The Happiest Place in the World is Being at a U2 Concert: U2 Facebook page.

threecordsandthetruth.net: U2 albums, Bios, U2 Quotes, Links, Lyrics, U2 Pics, U2 mp3s.

U2allovertheworld.com: U2 Tours 1979-2015 "Interactive data visualization shows you exactly how U2 became one of the greatest bands of all time."

U2.com: "The official U2 website with all the latest news, video, audio, lyrics, photos, tour dates, and ticket information."

U2europe.com: Closed U2 Facebook page with 6000 + members.

U2exit.com: U2 audio/video.

U2fansites.com: Links to U2 related sites on Art, Associates, Band Members, Bootleg Trading, Charities/Causes, Community, Concerts and Tours, Friends and Family, General, Lyrics and Tabs, Literature, Multi-Media, News, Official U2 Sites, Photos, Sites by Language, Social Media, Tribute Bands.

U2gigs.com: All Tours History, Pictures, Videos, News, Personal Charts.

U2interference.com: U2 News, Featured Articles, Features, Reviews, Commentary and Analysis.

U2 is my Life: "This group is dedicated to all the U2 fans who cannot live without this GREAT band. Feel free to share your stories, photos, experiences etc."

U2radio.com: Zoo Station, Live U2 Radio

U2setlists.com: U2 Unofficial Set-list Archive.

U2songs.com: "U2Songs has . . . expanded to cover the latest band news, tour updates and trivia, in-depth reporting, interviews, information on collectibles, and enhanced U2 Discography and Lyric listings covering physical, digital, and archival releases, as well as a Videography section on Demos."

U2start.com: U2 shows, news, audio recordings, photos, forums, shop.

U2station.com: News, Tours, Forum, Videos, U2ography, Tablature, Fans.

U2 Vision over Visibility: Closed U2 Facebook page with 300+ members.

DIANNE EBERTT BEEAFF has been a free-lance writer for many years, beginning in the area of magazine journalism. She is a member of The Women's Fiction Association, Arizona Professional Writers, The National Federation of Press Women, The Author's Guild, The National Writers Union, Pen America, and the Society of Southwestern Authors. As an artist, Dianne works primarily in graphite and watercolor, and her work has been shown in a variety of local, national, and international galleries.

Dianne's work may be seen at www.debeeaff.wordpress.com.